ssemblée ou les diuers plaisirs   Si l'Amour quelque part bastit son Paradis,
bre, la vûe, et les oreilles.   C'est ou l'on fact Balet, on y void faces d'Anges
rretient, ou les bouches vermeilles   Au lieu d'Astres la joye y est dans les meslanges
s amans librement leur desirs.   D'Ebats et passetemps plus grands qui ne font dats.

Polonaise
Drawing
based on
a 17th-century
engraving by
Abraham Bosse

by Esther B. Aresty

The Best Behavior
The Delectable Past

The
Best Behavior

THE COURSE OF GOOD MANNERS—FROM
ANTIQUITY TO THE PRESENT—AS SEEN
THROUGH COURTESY AND ETIQUETTE BOOKS.

BY

ESTHER B. ARESTY

SIMON AND SCHUSTER
NEW YORK

SBN 671-20336-3
LIBRARY OF CONGRESS CATALOG CARD NUMBER: 71-116500
DESIGNED BY EVE METZ
MANUFACTURED IN THE UNITED STATES OF AMERICA
PRINTED BY THE MURRAY PRINTING CO., FORGE VILLAGE, MASS.
BOUND BY AMERICAN BOOK-STRATFORD PRESS, INC., NEW YORK

"What is a gentleman?" It is to be
honest, to be gentle, to be generous,
to be brave, to be wise; and possessed
of all these qualities to exercise them
in the most graceful manner.
    —William Makepeace Thackeray

TO JULES

WHO FITS THE DESCRIPTION

CONTENTS

INTRODUCTION

It's a funny thing how a random question can set a whole project in motion—for example, this book. It started when I was casually asked why Americans cross the fork from the left hand to the right each time they cut food with a knife. Why don't they retain the fork in the left hand in the European way?

Why indeed? True, more and more Americans are turning to the European style and no longer zigzag their forks. But a glance around any public dining place proves this is not yet the popular way in America.

That casual question about the fork became provocative, and other dissimilarities in the conduct of Americans and Europeans presented themselves. Basically, good manners are universal. But conventions differ greatly. What is correct in France may be unusual in England and utterly strange in America. Kissing a lady's hand in greeting, for example.

I felt sure there was a clue to some of these dissimilarities in the old books on etiquette and table conduct I've collected for years, along with old cookbooks. As I read through some of the earliest American books, starting with the 1830's, it was plain to see that many American conventions, including the fork shift, were the result of a young nation's determination to be free of any vestiges of the old world, and particularly of its determination to honor the spirit of democracy right down to the dinner table—eating like Americans, not "putting on airs" by taking up customs and fads that drifted in from Europe.

By this time I had also dug into some 19th-century English and French etiquette books and found them just as nationalistic. Furthermore, the tantalizing glimpses of past life that they offered made me want to go even further back—to the courtesy books that had guided conduct in earlier centuries.

It proved to be a fascinating trail, and the way led through all the behavior words we use. "Courtesy" which obviously descends from court behavior; "civility," rooted in the Latin word for city and thus representing the reverse of crude country behavior; "politeness," from the Latin verb for polish; and "etiquette," "chivalry" and "gentility."

In the English language these words have become nearly synonymous, but subtle differences remain. I could see what a long road they had traveled before they settled down as behavior words in our vocabulary. And as in an aerial view of a winding road, I could see some of the manners of today—those that separate the couth from the uncouth—threading back to remote and often unsuspected origins.

Take breaking bread, for example. Today, no well-bred person would dream of biting into a slice of bread or into a whole roll, but breaks off a small piece to eat, as every modern etiquette book directs. The well-mannered observed this custom quite as strictly in ancient and medieval times—it was called for in the Talmud—and apparently it was the custom to collect the table leavings for the poor. *The Boke of Curtasye* (c. 1460) explains this to the medieval diner:

> Bite not thy bread and lay it down,
> This is not curtesy to use in town;
> But break as much as you will eat
> The remnant to the poor you shall lete [leave].

What was good manners in medieval times and even earlier still prevails in polite behavior today if it is based on a moral premise. However, many polite customs that developed more recently are now forgotten or discarded.

The rules of etiquette develop slowly and their shifting patterns may reflect their historical times or the personality of a monarch. Very often a good reason has summoned a rule of etiquette into being, and when the reason no longer exists the rule dies out. Take the calling-card etiquette that at one time enveloped the well-bred

Il faut avoir pitié des Pauvres & leur donner l'Aumône.

Beggar receiving food.
Woodcut in *Roti-Cochon,* French conduct book for children, 1696. From the 1840 facsimile edition.

in a pasteboard blizzard. For most people it is now as remote as the bustle, but in the days before telephones and efficient mail service, calling cards served a specific purpose, indicating that a ceremonious visit had been made and a social obligation discharged. Leaving them at important homes also served as a means of social advancement. When the real need for leaving cards ceased, the social custom lingered on as an identification of the upper class.

For years diners hesitated to slash at their lettuce with a knife, obeying a long outmoded rule of etiquette based on a need that no longer existed. Before knife blades of stainless steel or silver came into general use, the acid in salad dressing would discolor the knives. Therefore it was bad manners to use them for this purpose. The lemon used on fish had a similar effect; therefore knives were out for fish as well. Today all etiquette authorities approve of cutting salad with a knife.

As with many social usages that start originally for a good reason, custom dies hard because the reason is forgotten. Unless one understands *why* a rule of etiquette began, it may be difficult to judge when the time has come to set it aside.

However, some rules of etiquette remain constant and unchanging: to rise to one's feet as a mark of respect for an older person or a dignitary is still good manners. To show respect for age has its roots in ethics and goes back to most ancient times; and while respect for dignitaries is not so much ethics as attention to the rules of precedence, these, too, have an ancient history, and rigidly governed all medieval behavior. Precedence is still inflexibly accorded to titles in England and is carefully observed in Washington protocol.

Other vestiges of precedence remain in daily life. The most honored position is still to the right of the host or hostess (whichever is deemed the head of the table), a custom that dates back to ancient times. The right side is mentioned in many medieval records as the position of honor and deference: Froissart describes Black Prince Edward, "Like a courteous knight giving Peter of Spain the Right, or Side of honor, as they rode together." A practical reason for this deference when walking or riding together was the advantage it gave a man to unsheath his sword quickly with his right hand. The wall side was similarly a mark of deference when it provided greater protection. Many reasons are given for the custom of a gentleman walking on the "outside" of a lady— protection from slops being hurled out of windows or protection from open sewers or runaway horses—but the custom clearly traces back to giving the "wall" side as the deferential position. Equally remote, and still with us today, is the custom that led to tipping the hat. In the days when men wore armor they opened the visor to greet a friend or lady.

There has always been a difference between the mechanics of good manners and true courtesy. Elegant bearing and polished diction cannot camouflage the lack of real courtesy in those who make others feel left out or inferior. "Do not talk down to those who know less than you," said the earliest of all behavior books, *The Instructions of Ptahhotep* (c. 2500 B.C.) More than four millennia later, using much the same language, an American etiquette book of 1890, *Decorum*, instructed, "If you are with people who know less than you, do not lead the conversation where they cannot follow."

To bite the hand that feeds you is equally rude. The mechanics of etiquette are gracefully performed when an eloquent thank-you note is sent to a host or hostess after a dinner party. But to speak ill of the dinner to others makes the thank-you false and is a display of atrocious manners by modern or medieval standards. In 1290 Bonvicino wrote: "Blame not the dishes when thou art at entertainment, but say that all are good. I have detected many ere while in this vile habit, saying 'this is ill-cooked' or 'this is ill salted.' " In her 1937 edition Emily Post advised the discomfited guest never to gossip about the quality of the hospitality tendered, once "having broken bread in the house."

The rules and regulations of etiquette have merely been piled on top of ethics and moral conduct. *Etiquette* is a fairly new word in the English language and still retains its original meaning of ticket, label or sticker in French. Derived from the old French verb *estiquer,* to attach, it first became *l'estiquette,* probably describing the list of rules and regulations attached to a post in the courtyards of feudal castles and palaces. *L'estiquette* could be torn down and changed daily if necessary. Etiquette is just as alterable—a rule today, outmoded tomorrow. Yesterday's rules could even become today's bad manners. In 1836, *Etiquette: or a Guide to the Usages of Society* ruled that thin-cut bread was plebeian; thick trencher slices were served at upper-class English tables. By the end of the century the reverse was true and the thick slice had become plebeian. The 1901 *Standard Book of Etiquette* declared that "Bread should be cut in thin slices, and laid on a napkin at the left of each plate." But the rule of breaking bread into morsels before eating has never wavered.

Millions of words have been written over thousands of years in an effort to instill in man the true spirit of good manners. It is a difficult task, since man is not by nature considerate. He learns to be. Even a monkey or a bear can be taught to bow, tip a hat, and pick up the right fork. The task of making manners spring from within, from that superior consciousness that separates man from the lower order of teachables, has been the reason for millions of words of advice and instruction, by turns imploring, cajoling and threatening. They are fascinating even in the repetitiousness that underscores how strongly we are still bound to all the centuries that have preceded us.

Chromolithographic print by F. Kellerhoven in *Manners, Customs and Dress during the Middle Ages* by Paul Lacroix, 1874.

PART ONE

From Antiquity

to the Renaissance

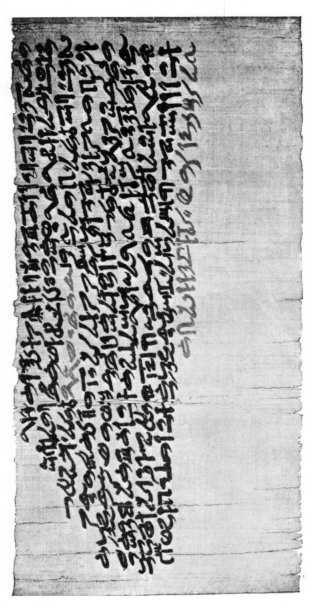

19th-century facsimile drawing. A portion of *The Instructions of Ptahhotep.*

16

1 · AN ANCIENT PAPYRUS

IN A WAY it could be said that the ancient Egyptians invented manners. Along with the plow and the twelve-month calendar they produced the first known book, and since this book, *The Instructions of Ptahhotep,* was a behavior manual containing the seeds of much of Western ethics and conduct, the statement does not seem farfetched.

It was about 2000 B.C. that many of the moral precepts and common-sense rules that still govern good conduct were set down on papyrus sheets by an Egyptian hand. The book, written in the hieratic script of priests, is still preserved in the Bibliothèque Nationale in Paris and is known as the Prisse papyrus (after the name of its donor to the library).

Old as it is, the book was copied from an earlier work, attested to by the later scribe, who said that he had copied it from writings of the fifth dynasty (c. 2560–2420). This would establish that these moral precepts preceded the assembling of the Bible by about two thousand years.

Like all facts that have to do with ancient Egyptology, identities and dates are debatable. Though no one questions the antiquity of the Prisse papyrus, the identity of Ptahhotep is apparently arguable. *Ptah* could mean ruler or god, but the eminent historian and Egyptologist James H. Breasted believes that Ptahhotep was the grand vizier under the Pharaoh Isesi.

The book reads as if it had been prepared as advice for the writer's son, a policy followed by many illustrious parents including King Solomon. However, *The Instructions* had something to say to everybody, and the wise words had probably been going the rounds orally for generations before they were set down on papyrus.

"Heed!" was a key idea. "How worthy it is when a son hearkens to his father!" wrote the old sage, whoever he was. "How many misfortunes befall him who hearkens not! A son who hearkens reaches old age and attains reverence. He speaks likewise to his own children, renewing the instructions of his father . . . his children then speak to their children. . . ." The unbroken chain is here for all to see—how we become what we are—attitudes, values, manners, passed from parent to child. No wonder *The Instructions* have such a familiar ring after five thousand years of unbroken continuity. It is the oldest wisdom in the world, and man has yet to improve on it.

Ptahhotep named character and fortitude the most valuable and durable legacy a parent could leave a child, pointing out that example was more important than words in establishing these qualities. "Attain character," urged the old vizier. "Make righteousness to flourish and thy children shall live. . . . Although misfortune may carry away wealth . . . the power of righteousness is that it endures."

The Instructions were not all abstract ideals but dealt also with social behavior and the practical side of life, particularly where it had to do with pleasing one's superiors. Even at that time men rose from the bottom to the top, and some remained sensitive about their humble origins. Avoid offending such a self-made man, Ptahhotep advised: "Have no knowledge of his former low estate."

To flatter a superior by laughing at his jokes could pay off as readily in 2700 B.C. as today. "Laugh when he laughs," said Ptahhotep; "so shalt thou be very agreeable to his heart and what thou doest will be very pleasant to his heart."

Ptahhotep also had advice for the superior. If he had risen in the world, others might pretend not to remember, but *he* had better not forget it: "If thou hast become great after thou wert little, and hast gained possessions after thou wert in want . . . be not unmindful of how it was with thee before."

To be "boastful of thy wealth" was a prideful error that could often precede a fall. "There is none who knows his fortune when he thinks of tomorrow," warned the sage.

Perhaps his most priceless advice for social success was the wisdom of holding one's tongue, and it has been unceasingly repeated ever since. "Be silent for it is better than teftef flowers," said Ptahhotep. "Let thy mind be deep and thy speech scanty . . . for speech is more difficult than any craft." Those who followed his advice and spoke only after careful reflection and with something to say could count on hearing, "How seemly is that which comes out of his mouth."

Personal and family relationships were reviewed, and Ptahhotep recommended marriage as a blessed state provided a wife were chosen prudently. With a wise choice made and a good wife won, she deserved affection and tender care. The same careful selection, tending, and ultimate reward pertained to friends. Whether in marriage, friendship, or dealing with one's superiors, life would proceed more smoothly if lubricated by a gracious manner and a happy disposition. To this end Ptahhotep urged his reader, "Let thy face be cheerful as long as thou livest."

By the time the Bible began to be assembled, around 700 B.C., Ptahhotep's wisdom was nearly two thousand years old, and one can only guess how long it had been going the rounds in the neighborhood of the Euphrates. Echoes of *The Instructions* can be heard in the vast symphony of the Bible, especially in Proverbs and Ecclesiastes.

What is probably the first explicit discussion of table manners occurs in Ecclesiasticus, c. 135 B.C., the wisdom book of the Apocrypha compiled by Jesus, son of Sirach, often called Ben Sira.

> Eat as it becometh a man, those things which are set before thee; and devour not, lest thou be hated. Leave off first for manner's sake; and be not insatiable, lest thou offend. When thou sittest among many, reach not thine hand out first of all. . . . Be not insatiable in any dainty thing, nor too greedy upon meats.

Such greediness would certainly be inexcusable if the host had followed Ben Sira's advice to set an ample table for his guests: "Whoso is liberal of his meat, men shall speak well of him and the report of his good housekeeping shall be believed."

The role of host was a serious one, even if only honorary, such as toastmaster at a public feast. The raised dais displeased Ben Sira:

> If thou be made the master, lift not thyself up, but be among them as one of the rest; take diligent care for them, and so sit down. . . . And when thou hast done all thy office, take thy place that thou mayest be merry with them, and receive a crown for thy well ordering of the feast.

Judge a man by his appearance, said Ben Sira. "A man's attire, and excessive laughter, and gait, shew what he is." But final judgment should be reserved until a man spoke: "Praise no man before thou hearest him speak, for this is the trial of men."

Like Ptahhotep, Ben Sira spoke of the wisdom of silence, but invariably in the form of a harsh reprimand. "The tongue of man is his fall," about summed up his attitude. Scoldings and warnings to babblers appear throughout the chapters of Ecclesiasticus: "There is one that keepeth silence and is found wise: and another, by much babbling becometh hateful"; "The heart of fools is in their mouth"; "Many have fallen by the edge of the sword, but not as many as have fallen by the tongue"; "To slip upon a pavement is better than to slip with the tongue," to quote a few. Later, variations of his censorious comments appeared regularly in courtesy and etiquette books.

Where superiors were concerned, Ben Sira took a different tack from the deference that Ptahhotep advised. Avoid them entirely, said he.

> Burden not thyself above thy power while thou livest; and have no fellowship with one that is mightier and richer than thyself; for how agree the kettle and the earthen pot together? for if one be smitten against the other, it shall be broken.

On the subject of women Ben Sira got off some particularly sour and picturesque phrases. "A drunken woman . . . a gadder about . . ." were obvious types to avoid in seeking a mate, but he warned against one type in particular:

> Watch over an impudent eye: and marvel not if she trespass

against thee. She will open her mouth as a thirsty traveler when he hath found a fountain, and drink of every water near her: by every hedge she will sit down and open her quiver against every arrow.

Nearly as bad as a promiscuous wife was a mate who controlled the shekels. Heaven help *that* man! "A woman, if she maintain her husband, is full of anger, impudence, and much reproach," predicted Ben Sira.

The book of Ecclesiasticus was relegated to the Apocrypha when the Scriptures were delimited in the first century A.D., but Ben Sira's advice was repeated often in European courtesy books. Similar suspicious utterances and pessimistic views on women were amplified into the doctrinaire misogyny of many early Christian church leaders. Not that Ben Sira was responsible for it, but he certainly made a loud rumble in the thunder.

There were also some words from the Greeks on conduct. In Hellenic times Isocrates, Plato and Aristotle wrote about it. Plato urged parents to instill in their children respect for elders by behaving in a manner to inspire it. In Roman days Cicero dealt with conduct in his *De Officiis;* a 3rd-century A.D. Roman, allegedly called Dionysius Cato, compiled a collection of maxims, *Disticha de Moribus ad Filium,* which contained much common-sense advice on personal conduct and was widely adapted into medieval writings on manners. But in the matter of behavior ethics, the wellsprings of our conduct bubbled up around the Euphrates, not in the shadow of Mount Olympus or the Roman hills.

Woodcut from the Prague Haggadah, 1526. Reproduced in *Ost und West,* 1901.

2 · THE TALMUDIC GENTLEMAN

IN THE 1ST CENTURY A.D. began the intense study and reorganization of Hebrew lore and law, much of which had for centuries been retained by memory and transmitted orally by trained scholars. This reorganization was to lead, around the fifth century, to the codification of the Talmud. Manners and pleasing conduct were traditionally of great importance in Hebrew life, and accordingly an entire section of the Talmud was devoted to them—the *Derek 'Erez Rabbah.*

Decorous behavior, especially at table, was as important in childhood training as learning the lessons of the sages. The great rabbi and teacher Akiba, one of the foremost organizers of the material of the Talmud, made it a point to have his young students dine with him so that he could personally supervise their manners.

In the Talmud, table manners received more than a few passing words. All meals were to begin with a prayer that invoked God's blessing and thanked him for his bounty; the proper behavior that was to follow the blessing was then described down to the smallest detail: "A man should not hold in his hand a piece of bread as big as an egg, but only a piece as big as an olive; otherwise he is a glutton." Bread was broken off by hand, and even this was to be performed without offense to other diners. "A man should not break

22

bread over a dish of food (other than his own, lest crumbs fall into it) nor wipe the plate with a piece of bread, nor gather the crumbs and leave them on the table, because such action is objectionable to men."

A man of refinement (a scholar, the Talmud called him) was expected to be aware of the sensibilities of others at all times, but especially while dining. Licking fingers or belching in the presence of others was so uncouth that the Talmud wasted few words in making the point. Less distasteful errors were covered in greater detail, as in drinking wine at dinner: "He must drink wine with pauses, and not in one gulp. He should not drink from a cup and hand it to his fellow unless he has first cleansed the rim with water." Bad breath was another offense the Talmud took a stand against, especially the controllable kind, "One should not eat garlic, or anything that gives off an offensive odor." To yawn openly was ill-bred. "When one yawns, he should cover his mouth with his hand." Such marks of politeness, while fairly obvious today, were then the refinements that set the *scholars* apart from the commoners.

The custom of giving the right side as a mark of deference is first described in the Talmud, where even its origin is explained: "How does one honor his teacher? When they are both walking along the way, he must place himself at [the teacher's] left hand. . . . If three, and a sage or teacher is among them, the teacher is to be in the middle, the more important of the other two on his right, and the less important on his left. We find it so in connection with the

Woodcut from the Mantua Haggadah, 1560. Reproduced in *Ost und West*, 1901.

three angels who came to Abraham our father, *viz*, Gabriel, Michael and Raphael. Michael was in the middle, Gabriel on his right and Raphael on his left."

Respect for elders was *law* in the Talmud; it forbade young people to be seated until every last elder had taken his seat.

As for women, the Talmudic attitude toward them was nothing like that of Ben Sira in Ecclesiasticus. As in Ptahhotep's *Instructions,* women were to be treated with the utmost tenderness, never to be addressed in a harsh manner, and on the Sabbath eve a husband honored his wife by reciting the description of a good wife, received by King Lemuel from his mother, Bathsheba (Proverbs, Chapter 31). "A woman of valor, her price is above rubies. . . ."

The Talmud went all the way in protecting women from harm and even decreed that if a family were captured by an enemy, always a likely possibility in those perilous days, the wife took precedence over her husband in being rescued. These were not opinions but actions decreed by Hebrew law, in early recognition of woman's right to be treated with dignity and fairness, though this was not her position in all societies, and not adopted by the Western world until recent times.

Close-knit Hebrew family life kept these teachings alive and continued them in an uninterrupted heritage from generation to gen-

Woodcut from an Amsterdam Haggadah, 1695. Reproduced in *Ost und West,* 1901.

eration, just as Ptahhotep had directed more than two thousand years earlier.

Such family life was in great contrast to that of the untutored hordes that rampaged over Europe for centuries. Even when they gentled down, these former barbarians still lacked a heritage of gentle conduct to guide them and had to learn it pretty much from the ground up. Fortunately, lessons and teachers were available as streams of Greek, Hebrew and Moslem learning poured in, on one side from Constantinople and on the other side from Spain—and as the tradition of learning preserved by monks emerged into the light.

Court life in Western Europe grew more sophisticated and ceremonial behavior more important as ruling princes visited Constantinople during the Crusades and took a fresh look at the original pattern on which their courts had been modeled. Theodoric had introduced Byzantine court ceremonials to his Ostrogoths in 471, but at the same time he had rung down the curtain on the old Roman Empire and plunged Western Europe into dark centuries. Now, as the curtain lifted, the Byzantine influence mingled with the Judeo-Christian ethics and spread like fresh gilt over the tarnished remnants of the Roman Empire, from about the 10th century on.

As early as the 11th century Hebrew household manuals were apparently in use in Western Europe, most likely adapted from the Talmud's *Derek' Erez Rabbah,* but probably not known outside Jewish homes. However, monks had preserved and nurtured the tradition of a gentle way of life, with good food and courteous behavior an important aspect of it. The Roman educational system had lingered on inside the walls of monasteries, Roman texts had been studied and handed down, and Latin remained, for centuries more, an almost universal language of communication in Western Europe.

Among the Roman writings studied in the monasteries were the maxims of Cato, now known as the *Disticha Catonis.* Sometime around the end of the 12th century this work was enlarged by a monk or teacher and the inscription *Joannis Faceti* attached to the manuscript. One authority conjectures that the compiler may have been a Joannes Facetus; then again, he may have used *facetus,* the Latin for "affable or polite man," in conjunction with his own name, John. Further rewriting and copying dispersed the work to an ever-widening audience; *facetus* is now sometimes used to designate medieval courtesy texts that seem to have descended from this particular source. But such writings are a far remove from the eloquent poems and texts on courtesy that later followed. The real story begins in the 13th century, when the age of chivalry was at its height and the Renaissance was about to begin.

Title page of a *liber faceti,* Cologne, 1509.

3 · THE ITALIANS LEAD THE WAY

WHEN WESTERN MEDIEVAL EUROPE began to take an interest in social graces, the role of instructor logically fell to the Italians, many of whom had roots that reached back to earliest Roman days. Even the Gothic conquerors of the Romans had become so assimilated that *gentiles homines* (men different from us) had lost its original insulting connotation, and those outsiders, from whom the word *gentleman* is descended, were proudly claimed as ancestors by the ruling class of Italy. There were others in that sunny land who boasted a proud heritage—Tuscans, Venetians, Lombards.

Though not tied together by a common ancestry, nor as yet a common language, the many peoples of Italy did share the common experience of urban society. The Italian way of life, centered in open cities and towns, each of them little states with distinct mores as in ancient Greece, differed from other European countries where life was lived in gloomy castles surrounded by serfs. In point of social-cultural experience the Italians unquestionably had the advantage, and for centuries they led the way. Italy seems to have been at least one hundred years ahead of France, and two hundred years in advance of England in instructing its people in civilities.

One of the earliest writers on civility was a Friulian Italian, Tommasino di Circlaria, in *A Treatise on Courtesy,* c. 1200. Tommasino, also known as Thomasin von Zerklaere—a German version of his name because he later wrote in German and was embraced into that literary fold—had a gift for lively expression that made his *Treatise on Courtesy* highly readable. The *Treatise on Courtesy* is unknown in its original state, but fortunately Tommasino had included excerpts from it in another of his books that survived. He did some moralizing but did it lightly and deftly, and always it was implicit in his remarks on conduct. Carrying tales, betraying secrets and vainglorious boasting were faults that bordered on sin, but waving the arms like a semaphore while talking, or pushing ahead of others in a crowd were only evidence of bad breeding. Many of his sprightly observations were later reground in other literary mills. Compare John Davies' Elizabethan "Beauty's but skin deep" with Tommasino's version nearly four hundred years earlier:

> One must know that false people
> Have not more beauty than in their skins.

Tommasino declared that he wrote the *Treatise on Courtesy* at a lady's request, a standard dedication in days when every red-blooded man performed whatever feats—daring or poetic—to honor his lady. Tommasino, however, may have used this dedication as cover to get off some remarks to the ladies which otherwise they might have resented. A good part of the *Treatise* is taken up with their proper deportment. They were not to walk fast or sit with legs crossed or ride a horse astride. Tommasino also warned them not to display a "roving eye," though he tempered Ben Sira's charge that this was sluttish behavior and said merely that a darting glance was unbecoming to a lady. She should "go forth straightways and not look about her."

He discussed ladylike dress, which meant wearing "her long upper gown," and described the best way to gather her mantle about her. "If she let any part of her body be seen bare, That is quite against Good Breeding."

He objected particularly to those forward ladies who some-times dared to match wits with men. In Tommasino's opinion the entire sex was discredited by such conduct and a lady would be well advised to be less articulate in the company of men. "One does not require her for a mayor," he observed crisply. In general, too much female cerebration did not please men, who wished only that ladies be charming, decorative and easy to manage. As Tommasino put it:

> A woman has enough sense
> In that she be courteous and pliable,

Steel engraving of a noble Italian lady costumed c. 1300. From
Costumes Anciens et Modernes by Cesare Vecellio, 1860.

And also have good gestures
With beautiful speech and a chaste mind . . .
Let her not make a show of what she has in her mind.

Apparently ladies behaved well enough at table. When Tommasino took up those manners he reserved his remarks solely for men.
"One must not eat the bread before the first dishes are brought," he
cautioned; possibly this was to avoid littering the bare table with
crumbs before the meal was served. To drink or to speak "whilst he
has something in his mouth" was uncouth; and to select the choicest
morsels before others had a chance at them was inconsiderate as

well as rude. One interesting rule required ambidexterity: "If the companion sit at your right hand, then eat with your left hand." Since the right side was the honored side according to the early rules of precedence mentioned in the Talmud, and a feature of medieval society, all along the table men would be wielding their spoons and knives (no forks yet) in their left hand in deference to the companion on their right.

Despite the free socializing between men and women indoors, a formal distance was maintained when they met outdoors. "A knight shall not boldly ride up to ladies," said Tommasino. He also forbade knights to "go before ladies with bare legs," a difficult restriction to comply with in the days before private chambers when even the aristocracy lived one on top of another. This passing reference to knights was about the only recognition Tommasino gave of their existence. Indeed they were scarce in Italy, where the feudal system of vassalage and its concommitant, knighthood, never took root. It was a different story in neighboring Germanic kingdoms, where knighthood was deeply entrenched. For that matter, it was deeply rooted in almost all of Europe *except* Italy. By 1215, when Tommasino wrote *The Italian Guest,* he was enough acquainted with knighthood to be critical of its false heroics and its debasement of morality. The hollow pretensions of chivalry should be set aside, he cried in *The Italian Guest,* which considered manners in moralistic terms and argued that a man was only as noble as his deeds; it was time to reexamine so-called noble actions. As the ancient Greeks had said earlier, and Oliver Goldsmith was to say later: "Handsome is as handsome does." For Tommasino, this was the theme and purpose of his book dealing with the meaning of true nobility and manhood.

> To him who is virtuous or becoming so
> To him I give in friendship
> My book, that with it
> He may steer his beautiful manners . . .
> But he who has no good breeding
> And does not know how to act handsomely,
> Let him have nothing to do with it.

Surely one of the potent leaders of Italy's early thrust to the fore-
front in the art of living and social graces was Brunetto Latini, the
13th century Florentine statesman, philosopher, and author. His
Tesoretto (c. 1260) a long, instructive poem, is virtually a conduct
book. Latini was well qualified to write on conduct and is described
as "the initiator and master in refining the Florentines, and cultivating their use of language," by Giovanni Villani, 14th century
chronicler of Florence. As teacher and close friend of Dante, Latini
undoubtedly exerted considerable influence on the great poet.
Dante repaid him with an uncomplimentary portrait in the *Com-
media*.

Latini's *Tesoretto* also was cast as a journey, but unlike the later
one of Dante, Latini's led through a pleasant forest where Lady
Courtesy appeared and expressed Latini's views on conduct. Good
manners were not to be worn like outer garments, put on and
pulled off as the social climate demanded. They should be a per-
manent covering, like one's skin.

> . . . at all hours
> Hold fast to good usage; for that advances thee
>   and makes thee better.
> . . . a good nature [manner]
> Becomes the clearer and more polished if it
>   follows good habits.

The Tesoretto indicates there were social stratifications in the
Florentine Republic despite its claim to equality for all its citizens.
The nobility held themselves aloof from those they considered beneath them—in Latini's time this probably included the *popolani
grassi,* the rich merchants who were growing increasingly powerful
in the government. Like Tommasino before him, Latini declared
that noble is as noble does.

> In sooth there are persons of high condition
> Who call themselves "noble": all others they hold cheap
> Because of this nobility. And, in that conceit,
> They will call a man "tradesman" who would sooner spend a bushel
> Of florins than *they* of halfpence
> Although the means of both might be of like amounts.

. . . He who endures not toil
For honour's sake, let him not imagine that he comes
Among men of worth, because he is of lofty race;
For I hold him noble who shows that he follows the path
Of great valour and gentle nurture,—
So that, besides his lineage, he does deeds of worth,
And lives honorably so as to make himself beloved.

No one, least of all Latini—still speaking through the lips of
Lady Courtesy—could seriously dispute the value of superior birth:
"I admit indeed that, if one and the other are equal in good deeds,
he who is the better born is esteemed the higher." Having reluctantly
admitted this, Latini's better judgment impelled him also to advise
lesser folk to tread cautiously when in the company of the upper
class:

> Know, in such company, to play the prudent part,
> And be heedful to say what will please.

The best course was to stay at one's own social level. In giving
this advice, Latini was in agreement with Ben Sira in Ecclesiasticus,
but for a more sophisticated reason.

> Friend, heed this well: with one richer than thyself
> Seek not to associate—or thou shalt be
>   as their merry-maker,
> Or else thou wilt spend as much as they. If thou
>   didst not this,
> Thou wouldst be mean—reflect always
> That a costly beginning demands perseverance.

No matter what company was kept, the urbane manner was the
one for a Florentine to cultivate. If a man did not know what un-
guarded conduct might tag him as a country bumpkin, Latini told
him:

> I counsel thee . . . to ride decorously
> With head a little bowed, for to go in that
>   loose-reined way
> Looks most boorish; and stare not up at the
>   height

Of every house thou comest to. Mind that
    thou move not about
Like a man from the country—wriggle not
    like an eel:
But go steadily along the road among the people.

Latini left table behavior to other writers, and shortly, around 1290, a Milanese monk, Bonvicino da Riva, wrote what is probably the first book dealing solely with table etiquette, *Fifty Courtesies of the Table*. Perhaps Milan had not yet attained the refinement and urbanity of Florence; some of the behavior Bonvicino warns against would not get by among stable hands today:

> He who eats or is serving, must not blow his nose through his fingers. . . . He who needs to wipe his nose while eating, let him use a cloth. . . . Do not scratch yourself in any foul part while eating. . . . Do not cross your legs on the laid-out table.

Many of Bonvicino's rules were as elementary as those taught little children today: not to loll at table; not to gulp food and liquid in one mouthful; to turn the head when coughing or sneezing; not to lick one's fingers clean of food, or to pick the teeth with the fingers; not to stare in others' plates; and not to talk with a mouthful of food. These had been the basis of the earlier *facetus* work in the 12th century.

Some of the good monk's rules were timeless and changeless, based on consideration for others, and would still apply today. Guests should be given the choice portions; an invitation to dine should be followed by plenty to eat and drink; and guests should never criticize the food they are served.

Table behavior was covered gracefully and tastefully around 1300 by the Florentine writer Francesco da Barberino. He may have been following, or perhaps even initiating, a family tradition as pace-setters in proper conduct. A later Barberino, Pope Urban VIII, inspired the catch saying "If you do not wish to behave like a barbarian, behave like a Barberino." Our Barberino is best remembered as a poet in the great Tuscan literary tradition, and like his contemporaries he sought to guide his countrymen into both elegant thought and elegant behavior. His best known work, *Documenti*

Title page of Barberino's behavior book for women; frontispiece portrait of Barberino. From an 1815 facsimile.

d'Amore, went into considerable detail about proper manners, especially table manners.

Since ancient times the dinner table was the center on which social and political life turned. Here strict rules of precedence pertained, often governing the rules of hospitality. Even more important than the food itself were the seating arrangements. "Place each person in the post that befits him," Barberino instructed, but once the necessary obligations of precedence had been discharged, seating was to be planned for pleasant company and felicitous conversation. What could be duller than two brothers sitting together? "Between relatives it behoves to place others midway," said Barberino.

The usual prohibitions were listed: "Not to maneuver for the best [pieces] but to take the less good"; "Not to sneer at what he does not like." And how to defer to ladies at the table. In Florentine society ladies were treated with great deference, preceded men into the dining room, received assistance into their chairs, and were helped to their food. "With women, I need not tell thee, but thou must help them to everything," wrote Barberino. "Always look to it that thou approach not too close to any of them. Look them in the face but little, still less at their hands while eating, for they are apt to be bashful."

How to greet ladies in public was another topic covered by Barberino, and very early in the history of manners it becomes apparent that there were definite rules for this, which varied from place to place. Tommasino had warned knights against approaching ladies boldly in public. Barberino allowed a "bow without much speaking," and suggested, "In other towns, ascertain the ordinary practice in such cases and observe it. If a man had occasion to greet a female relative, Barberino suggested a harmless piece of deception designed to elevate their stock in other male eyes.

> If you see a female relative in your own town, she being alone or in company with another person, *and if she is handsome,* accost her as though she were not your relative, unless your relationship is a fact known to the bystanders.

With his interest in conduct by, and for, the female sex, it was only natural for such an arbiter of manners as Barberino to prepare an entire manual for them. This he did in his second work, *Del Reggimento e Dei Costumi Delle Donne.* According to him, it was the first work of its kind. "There have been many who wrote books concerning the elegant manners of men, but not of women."

Del Reggimento was divided into twenty parts and covered conduct for females of all ages, ranging from girlhood to widowhood. Constant war made widowhood almost a certainty and Barberino subdivided that stage by numbers and possible types: "How she should comport herself if she marries again; And how if to a better husband; And how if to a worse and less wealthy one; And how if she yet goes to a third."

Barberino drew no class distinction in distributing his advice. Abbesses, countesses, serving maids, "female serf or slave," he instructed them all. "A she-barber must not ogle or flirt with her customers, but attend to her washes and razors," he said. Another fiat declared, "A shrew deserves the stick, nor should that form of correction be spared women who gad about after fortune tellers."

Unmarried females were advised to wear a topaz, "which is proved by experience to be an antidote to carnal desire." Overwhelming temptations might arise in the ordinary daily routine and Barberino warned:

> Beware of a doctor who scrutinizes your pretty face more than your symptoms. Also of a tailor who wants to serve you gratis, or who is over-officious in trying on your clothes; and beware still more of a tailor who is tremulous.

Presumably, all women would be better protected in such situations with a topaz on their persons.

No such cautionary remarks were addressed to the ladies by Agnolo Pandolfini in *Governing of a Family* (c. 1430). He was more concerned with the economics of family life. His audience was the comfortable Florentine middle class, now strengthened by the support and interest of Giovanni de' Medici, himself a self-made businessman, and founder of the Medici dynasty.

Though not a literary light, Pandolfini had held a high government post and had observed Florentine family life for well over a half-century; he was in his seventies—a qualified observer—when he offered his opinions in *Governing of a Family*.

His was the viewpoint of the autocratic family head—patriarchal but affectionate, and immensely practical. He believed in owning a house, not renting it; in buying the best food and clothing because, in the end, "good things cost less than the not good." Manners were best learned in the family circle. The family that eats together stays together and behaves well, was his philosophy, and it made him the advocate of one table for all, at one time.

The table was well laden if the lady of the house took her role seriously. "It is well for every lady to know how to cook and prepare choice viands," said Pandolfini, though he intended her to be an executive, not a drudge. "Not indeed that the lady is to cook; but she should order, teach, and show less skillful servants to do everything in the best way." He advised her how to acquire this skill: "Learn this from cooks when they come to the house for banquets; see them work, ask questions, learn (and remember), so that when guests come . . . the ladies may know how to order all the best things—and so not have to send every time for cooks." Ever practical, Pandolfini pointed out, "This cannot be done at a moment's notice, and especially when one is in the country, where good cooks are not to be had."

An interesting sidelight of Florentine home life is the 15th-century burglar alarm that Pandolfini advocated: a goose and a dog because they are "wakeful animals . . . suspicious and attached; so that one of them, rousing the other, calling up the household, the house might always be secure."

The *Dialogue on Civil Life,* c. 1430, soon followed Pandolfini's book and also dealt with the conduct of family life. Its author, Matteo Palmieri, admired Pandolfini and made him the principal speaker in the book's dialogues—a popular Renaissance method of conveying instruction, patterned after the ancient method of oral teaching and popular long into the 18th century.

Palmieri's topics ranged from the number of guests that would make for successful dinner table talk (no less than three and no more than nine) to disciplining children. Rearing children properly was one of Palmieri's chief concerns. He held some enlightened views on the subject, condemning physical punishment as barbarous—certainly an advanced view for the 15th century. Instead, revoke privileges, he argued. The child who was forced to stay indoors or who had to forgo his supper was more effectively punished than the child who was swatted.

In general, the Italian attitude toward women, children, and family life showed the enlightenment of the dawning Renaissance. It was darker over on the French and English side.

4 · THE LAGGARD FRENCH

IN FRANCE a literature of manners developed slowly and much later than in Italy. When such writings began to appear, around 1380, they were for the most part simple verses about table manners and were known as *Les Contenances de la Table*, exclusively concerned with the civilities of dining.

The deportment that would later establish French authority in the realm of good manners was not yet visible; some of the prohibitions in *Les Contenances de la Table* covered cruder behavior than Bonvicino had remarked on a century earlier. Again the influence of the 12th-century *facetus* work was evident. Diners were warned not to butter bread with a finger; not to blow the nose into the same hand that took meat from a platter (the other hand was apparently permissible); and not to spit on the floor after using the communal water basin (*rince-bouche*) that circulated among the diners after a meal. Courtesy demanded that the water be swallowed; discourteous diners spat it onto the floor, or worse still, back into the basin.

Barring knives from the mouth was a sign of progress in *Les Contenances* and already a rule in many medieval table manuals, but flouted by the lower classes well into the 19th century.

An account of domestic conduct in this period (tag end of the reign of Charles V, whose interest in arts and literature stimulated their development in France) is a household manual, *Le Menagier de Paris* (c. 1380). It was prepared by an elderly Parisian bourgeois to guide his well-born young wife in her new duties—chiefly managing his home and supplying his table with delicacies, though wants of a more personal nature were also discussed.

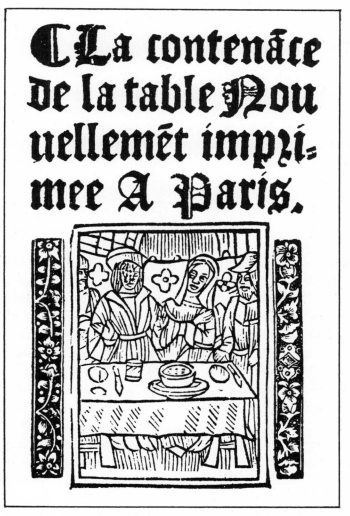

La Contenance de la Table: title page of an early 16th-century book. 19th-century facsimile copy.

To run a home smoothly required good servants and an understanding of them; the *Menagier* is an early statement on employer responsibilities and an intimate glimpse of domestic life in those days. The young wife's supervisory duties included a watchful eye against fleas in the marital bed and hot-blooded youths in the beds of her young domestics. Against the fleas, turpentine, glue, smoke or, in desperation, hand-picking were the best remedies. To safeguard the virginity of her young domestics there was only one sure method:

> Girls or chambermaids of fifteen to twenty years, since they be foolish at that age and naught have seen of the world, do you cause to sleep near to you, in a closet or chamber, where there is no dormer window or low window looking onto the road, and let them go to bed and arise at your own time, and do you yourself (who, if God please, will be wise ere this time) be near to guard them.

Servants' references were to be checked carefully: "Know where their last place was, and send some of your people to get their character, whether they chattered or drank too much, how long they were in the place . . . and why they left." Having satisfied herself that they were fit to employ the wife was to maintain a dignified aloofness, but nevertheless be aware of their personal health needs, give them good food, and "time and space for the repose of their limbs." This meant comfortable beds with a candle nearby, and to make sure they had been "wisely taught how to extinguish it with hand or mouth, and by no means with their shirts."

The greater part of the instructions was given over to the husband's comfort, plus the care of his wardrobe. The *Menagier* discussed virtue and wifely patience, with pertinent examples of the rewards—or the penalties—as the case might be. As one object lesson in wifely obedience he chose Boccaccio's tale of the patient Griselda, a humble lass selected by a powerful lord for the honor of becoming his wife. A dubious honor, it turned out, for her titled husband tested her patience by casting out her children as fast as she bore them, and finally sent her back to her father's hut. In the end he revealed that it had all been done in fun—to test her wifely stamina. Griselda returned to his castle, met her now fully grown children, and sweetly forgave her husband everything.

Not that our elderly *Menagier* expected to pull such tricks on his young wife. All he asked of her was tender, wifely care—the wish of all husbands whose affairs caused them to "go and come, and journey hither and thither, in rain and wind, in snow and hail (sounds like the U.S. mailman!) now dry, now sweating, now shivering." None of this, including lumpy beds in inns, dismayed the husband who could look forward to the joys and pleasures his wife "will do him" on his return:

> To be unshod before a good fire, to have his feet washed and fresh shoes and hose, to be given good food and drink, to be well served and well looked after, well bedded in white sheets and nightcaps, well covered with good furs, and assuaged with other joys and desports, privities, loves and secrets whereof I am silent. And the next day fresh shirts and garments.

Woodcut illustration from *La Vie Privée D'Autrefois; Les Repas,* 1889.

An interesting work on proper maidenly deportment appeared at this time, prepared by a French knight for his daughters and known as the *Book of the Knight of La Tour-Landry* (c. 1371). It overflowed with "do's" and "don'ts" and some dire examples of what the future undoubtedly held in store. The girls were warned against the "wayward eye," to which, by this time, all men had been properly alerted. It seems that nothing could be more of a stumbling block to a good marriage than an inquisitive glance. Eyes should be intent on the ground, like a bloodhound snuffling a scent, the knight told his daughters.

Having instructed them in the maidenly deportment that would secure them husbands, the knight proceeded to their behavior as wives. This called for complete submissiveness to their husbands' wishes. In anticipation of the strain a wife's patience might be put to, the knight offered an example of forbearance paying off in the end. The example was plucked from his own family tree, his aunt the Lady de Languillier.

> She had a knight to her hosbond that was merveilously lecherous, the which had every day in his hous one or two women besides the lady his wiff. And ofte tyme he rose from her to go lye with his leude women, and all way, whanne he come again from hem [them] to bedde, he fonde euer the candell light, and water to wash his hondes, and he saide he come from the priue [privy].

The lady never chided him at that red-hot moment, but waited until

> Atte sum tyme whanne thei were meri and alone she wolde saye, 'Syr I know alle youre doinge . . . but it is youre lust, and that I maye sette no remedie thereon, I will make you nor them never the worse chere; for I were a fole to slee myselff for your sportes.

By being so sensible about masculine "sportes" and asking only that he continue to favor her with a crumb now and then, the lady finally won out. The Knight of La Tour-Landry concluded, "With her goodly wordes he repented hym, and was converted to goodness at the laste, and he dede no more euell; thus with fairnesse she ouercome hym." The conduct of the lady's husband tallied with that of most medieval knights.

Engraving from *La Noblesse de France aux Croisades,* 1845.

5 · THIS IS CHIVALRY?

WHEN TOMMASINO ARGUED that manly daring was not always "noble," he was probably criticizing German chivalry, but wherever it existed chivalry lacked the noble purpose it professed. It conjures up a vision of brave knights protecting the weak and helpless, gallantly aiding maidens in distress, and riding off on holy quests. Unfortunately this was more the fantasy of medieval storytellers and later English writers than a reality of its time.

In their day, knights were the symbols of aggressive masculinity. Like today's he-men and sports idols, they satisfied man's ancient need for heroes to worship.

The actual origins of knighthood are obscure, but in the gradual unraveling of the Roman Empire one can see the eventual need for the institution of knighthood. Before the Empire fell into tatters Roman law and central authority had kept it together, no matter how loosely. Roman legions were on tap when wars had to be fought, and these wars were usually on a grand scale for some imperial purpose, aggressive or defensive. All of this changed as many principalities, some of them no larger than a good-sized farm, took over, made their own laws and mustered their own fighting forces. Wars between rival dukes and barons were more like Indian forays, erupting with little or no warning and enduring briefly. They required much the same type of fighter, not necessarily numerous as highly mobile, and a man on a horse answered that requirement. The chief purpose of knighthood, it would seem, was to supply a guaranteed number of fighting men when needed.

Most knights were really professional fighters, forerunners of the hired mercenaries of later years. Noblemen were automatically knights by definition, it being a title of honor.

In early medieval days a good steed of his own and a promise to serve the lord to whom he attached himself were enough to get a man knighted. With only a knight's word as his bond, and no legal machinery to make him *keep* his word, some device was needed to make him dependable. The chivalric code was the solution.

This involved a mystic ritual that included fasting, purifying baths and a night-long vigil, terminating with a pledge constructed along the lines of a wedding vow—"to love, honor and obey." In the early Middle Ages the vow of the liege knight to his liege lord was sometimes sealed with a kiss on the lips. In later days, and especially in England, knighthood was conferred after a youth had served a novitiate as a squire.

Knights were the heroes of many of the verses and songs composed by troubadours and minnesingers in an ambivalent age when Judeo-Christian ethics and unfettered pagan drives were still in the blending stage. Minstrels sang of knights whose allegorical missions had religious overtones, but whose amorous exploits and clandestine involvements with the wives of other men, as in the Arthurian legends, were remnants of paganism. Illicit love was a part of knightly conduct, not only condoned, but in some quarters demanded. In his scholarly work, *Chivalry*, Edgar Prestage writes, "Under cover of refined manners, [chivalry] concealed and disseminated a code of debased immorality, at its worst in Provence where it elevated fornication and adultery to the rank of social obligation."

Refined manners were indeed the rule at the Provence court of Eleanor of Aquitaine. The colorful queen demanded impeccable conduct from all in attendance there, and from Poitiers *courtoisie*— court conduct, later to develop into *courtesy*—spread to other courts. Adultery was possibly an equal obligation. Eleanor, her ladies, and her daughter, Marie of Champagne, conducted a "love court" at which knights submitted to a mock trial when they defected from their duties as lovers. This "duty" required a knight to spend his free time at court, worshiping his lady love with hands-off detachment, an unlikely relationship which may have been as much myth and fantasy as other alleged knightly performances. One thing is clear: the practical requirements of marriage and the silken demands of romance were not considered a compatible combination, a philosophy later reflected in upper-class European society by the marriage of convenience augmented by a lover and mistress for the wedded pair's amorous dalliance. If a knight married, his obligation as lover was to his lady, not to his wife, which possibly gives some medieval substance to that old vaudeville joke, "That was no lady, that was my wife."

In Germany the rules of conduct among knights were much the same. Minnesingers sang of forbidden love and extolled the heroism

Engraving from *La Noblesse de France aux Croisades,* 1845.

of knights who braved its dangers. The "love watch" was a favorite type of poetic song that described the lovers' accomplice watching from a tower to warn them of the returning cuckolded husband. But seemingly, married knights expected their own wives to be faithful. The romance of the knight Guillem Capestang and his beloved, Countess Seremonda, came to a grisly end when Seremonda's jealous husband, having slain Guillem, had the hapless fellow's heart cooked and then served it to Seremonda. The horrified countess plunged through a window to her death when she learned what she had eaten. Outraged nobles put an end to the vengeful count, and the lady and her knight were buried side by side at Perpignan. In the midst of all this defense and exaltation of illicit love sung by troubadour and minnesinger, Tommasino di Circlaria raised his eloquent voice and called for a new appraisal of true manly conduct.

Chivalry as a code of behavior was defined by Ramon Lull in *The Order of Chivalry*, c. 1300, in what one might call a Talmud for knights. Lull, a Catalan Spaniard, began life as an aristocrat, spent a dissolute young manhood, and ended as a philosopher and Christian missionary. He was stoned to death while in North Africa converting Mohammedans. At what stage of his life he wrote *The Order of Chivalry* is not clear—somewhere in mid-channel, I suspect, for it is a mixture of idealism and exclusiveness.

Lull believed that the worthy motives and sentiments that inspired a knight were beyond the grasp of lesser men. He wrote that "the weariness and toil of his men" should be the source from which the knight "drew his own well-being." If this was not sufficient, it was society's duty, or at least the king's, to provide the knight with adequate income lest he become "A robber, a thief, liar or beggar." Because it was the knight's chief obligation to protect the order of chivalry from disgrace, Lull explained the serious consequences of even petty crime:

> A knight being a thief doth greater theft to the high honour of chivalry in as much as he taketh away the name of a knight without cause, than he doth that taketh away or stealeth money or other things . . . for honour is more worth than gold or silver without comparison.

Frontispiece of *La Noblesse de France aux Croisades*, 1845.

Shakespeare paraphrased the lines in Othello:

> Who steals my purse steals trash. . . .
> But he that filches from me my good name
> Robs me of that which not enriches him,
> And makes me poor indeed.

Knighthood needed defenders such as Lull. Its record was shameful, even in the Crusades with which it was deeply identified. No one will dispute that some knights went on Crusades motivated by genuine religious zeal. But many historians feel that the majority were lured by the side rewards of excitement, adventure and loot. Just about the time Lull's book was written extolling chivalry and its virtues, another ugly chapter was added to knighthood's record. The Knights Templars, the most dazzling of the Crusading orders, and so successful financially that they had aroused the open resentment of other knightly orders, were put to a fiery end—the whole lot of them—in a bloody episode that greatly weakened the institution of knighthood.

The coup de grace was probably dealt by the introduction of gunpowder into European warfare, plus the French disaster at Crécy in 1346, when English archers, firmly planted on their own two feet, unhorsed the pride of all chivalry, the knights of France. The mounted warrior was no longer a fearsome hero. In Germany knighthood degenerated into outright brigandry; in France, Christine de Pisan labeled it corrupt; in Spain, at its tag end, knighthood was satirized by Cervantes as ineffectual and false.

Only in England would the professed principles of knighthood continue to thrive, aided by Caxton's translation of Lull's *Order of Chivalry,* one of the earliest books printed in England, and a keystone in the development of English courtesy books. But that was to come later.

Illustration from *Chaucer's England* by Matthew Browne (pseudonym of W. B. Rands), 1869.

6 · MANNERS MAKYTH MEN

A TRIP ACROSS the Channel to England at this time reveals an awakening interest in manners, or at least an interest in awakening them. Chaucer had an eye for manners. Even if they were not to be widely observed in England—and widely they were not—he had spent ten years abroad, many of them in Italy, and he knew what to look for.

In the *Canterbury Tales* he classified the pilgrims by their manners, "The quality of each of them, and which they were, and of what degree." Madame Eglantine, the prioress, "had been well taught the art of eating, and let no morsel fall from her lips, and set but her finger-tips in the sauce. She knew how to lift and how to hold a bit so that not a drop fell on her breast. Her pleasure was all in courtesy." The young squire also possessed social graces: "Well could he sit a horse and ride, make songs, joust and dance, draw and write." And to qualify him for the heroic ranks, "So hot he loved that at night-time he slept no more than a nightingale."

William of Wykeham, Chaucer's contemporary, and founder of Winchester college in 1394, drew attention to the value of good manners and social graces in the motto he gave the school: "Manners makyth man."

However, for the aristocracy most schooling in manners was carried on in noble households where young people were sent under a kind of "student exchange" that operated among aristocratic English families until well into the 16th century. As children approached puberty, off they went to other noble households where the boys served as pages and the girls as maids-in-waiting. The professed reason was that children might better learn manners and discipline away from home, but a 15th century Italian visitor took a cloudy view of these proceedings and declared that the English were, in fact, cold parents who thought their own comforts "would be better served by strangers than by their own children."

Tender treatment of children was not a medieval English concept, and possibly they fared better away from home. Home or elsewhere, they were expected to perform menial duties, no matter how noble their blood. Girls were in reality chambermaids and seamstresses for the noble ladies they served; and the pages were the bellhops and busboys of those days. Any number of books appeared to help them learn their duties properly; all equated manners with deferential service. The manners *were* important, it is true. And to make certain that the pages behaved politely among themselves, the household ordinances of Edward IV directed that their "maistyr" dine with them, even as Rabbi Akiba had done with his pupils, to see "how mannerly they eat and drink."

Training these aristocratic youngsters to perform their household duties seems to have been the main function of many early courtesy books. The best known and probably the most widely used were four books that come into view around 1460, though they were in all likelihood copies of earlier versions. It is difficult to fix the exact time when such books first came into use in England. Most were compilations taken from other sources—French, German or Italian, for the most part. Until the printed book took over there was no uniformity in copied books. They varied according to the copyist or the wishes of the person for whom the copy was made. However, these four seem to have been in fairly wide use in the 15th century: *Stans Puer ad Mensam* (The Boy Standing at the Table); *Urbanitatis, The Booke of Urbanitie; The Boke of Nurture* by John Russell and *The Babees' Book,* "babee" meaning a much older child than would nowadays be associated with the word.

Each noble household probably had its favorite manual, depending on the extent of the staff and the importance of the lord of the manor. The best-born youngsters probably learned their deportment and duties from *The Booke of Urbanitie* and *The Babees' Book,* both of which adopted a lofty tone. *The Babees' Book* began:

> Oh young babies whom blood royal hath endowed with grace, comeliness, and high ability, it is on you I call to know this book, for it were great pity but that ye added to sovereign beauty, virtue and good manners.

Virtue and manners aside, status was to be protected at all times and the youth was to be aware of his own nobility. *Urbanitie* made that point decisively, coupling it with a moral maxim:

> Play with none but with your peer,
> And tell not all the tales you hear.

With his true superiors, the youth was to observe the deepest respect, as outlined in *Urbanitie:*

> When you come before a lord,
> In hall, in bower, or at board,
> You must doff [your] cap or hood,
> Ere before him you have stood.
> Twice or thrice beyond a doubt,
> Before your sovereign must you lout [bow];
> On the right knee bend you low;
> For your own sake do ye so.

However, rank was the thermostat that regulated the degree of respect. Make sure they *are* your betters, said *Urbanitie:*

> Look wisely to your betters ay
> Do them reverence as you may;
> But do ye none sit all in a row
> Unless ye them for betters know.

Rigid rules of precedence governed all behavior and reflected the layer-cake structure of medieval society. Nothing demonstrates the hierarchal order better than a book on hawking, *The Boke of St. Albans,* printed by Caxton in 1486, but probably handed down from earlier times. It taught the nobility the rules of the sport and paralleled the social status of the birds with the human beings who used them: a gyrfalcon for a king; a peregrine falcon for an earl; a saker for a knight; a lanner for a squire; and a goshawk for "a pore man."

Unquestioning obedience was demanded by all the courtesy books. *Stans Puer ad Mensam* told its young readers:

> Be quick and ready, meek and serviceable,
> Well awaiting to fulfil anon
> What that thy sovereign commandeth to be done.

A hawking party.
Woodcut from *The Boke of Hawkynge, and Huntyng, and Fysshynge,* Dame Juliana Berners, compiler of *The Boke of St. Albans.* Printed by Wynkyn de Worde, c. 1500–1530.

Illustration from *A History of Domestic Manners in England* by Thomas Wright, 1862.

The Babees' Book and John Russell's *Boke of Nurture* described each step of the service they were expected to perform. No matter how ink-blue the blood in their veins, for the moment they were all servants. Says *The Babees' Book:*

> Now must I tell you shortly what you shall do at noon when your lord goes to his meat. Be ready to fetch him clear water, and some of you hold the towel for him until he is done, and leave not until he set down, and ye have heard grace said. Stand before him until he bids you sit, and be always ready to serve him with clean hands.

John Russell's *Boke of Nurture,* though widely used, really guided youths who would make a career of domestic service, as many younger sons of aristocratic families were forced to do if they could not contract a suitable marriage. The duties of a butler, carver, valet, and usher were carefully described. The morning tasks discharged by a chamberlain in his lord's chamber were not unlike the tender ministrations a lesser man might expect of a wife:

> Pray your lord in humble words to come to a good fire and array him thereby . . . and wait with due manners to assist him. First hold out to him his tunic, then his doublet while he puts in his arms, and have his stomacher well aired to keep off harm. . . . Then draw on his socks and hose by the fire, and lace or buckle

53

Illustration from *A History of Domestic Manners in England* by Thomas Wright, 1862.

his shoes, draw his hosen on well and truss them up to the height that suits him, lace his doublet in every hole, and put round his neck a kerchief. . . . Then gently comb his hair with an ivory comb and give him water wherewith to wash his hands and face. . . . Then kneel down on your knee and say thus: "Sir, what robe or gown doth it please you to wear today?" . . . Before he goes out, brush busily about him . . . and see that all be clean and nice.

Once the lord was on his way, to hunt or to dally, the chamberlain (or the youth in training to become one) was instructed to "Return in haste to your lord's chamber, strip the clothes off the bed and cast them aside, and beat the feather bed. And see that the blankets and sheets be clean. When you have made the bed mannerly, cover it with a coverlet."

Personal good manners, the rule at all times, were evidence of superior social position and confirmed the page's gentle upbringing. *The Babees' Book* warned him, "Do not cut your meat like field-men who have such an appetite that they reck not in what wise, where or when or how ungodly they hack their meat; but, sweet children, have always your delight in courtesy."

The Boke of Nurture, long-winded in all other matters, issued a terse order on this point. "I will that ye eschew forever the 'simple conditions' of a person that is not taught."

The manners taught in these early English courtesy books were as elementary as Bonvicino's *Fifty Courtesies of the Table* nearly a century and a half earlier. To pick ears, teeth or noses at table was forbidden. The tablecloth was not to be used as a "nose cloth." "Blackened" nails were uncouth. But additional refinements had been added: "When your pottage is brought, take your spoon and eat quietly; and do not leave your spoon in the dish, I pray you," instructed *The Babees' Book. The Boke of Nurture* frowned on trumpeting with the nose, "lest your lord hear you." Equally disturbing to a lord was "foul breath cast upon him," though *Nurture* suggested no suitable correction for this last problem.

Interspersed with their many household tasks, the pages were coached in hawking, riding and archery, and were given some academic instruction in Latin, French, reading and writing. The schoolroom subjects were taught at a quick gallop, but equestrian instruction was taken at a slower pace; it was most important to the training of a future gentleman.

Less privileged youngsters of mercantile and professional families —those who would some day need to earn their living or who would serve the church—received formal education at the monastic and cathedral schools which were the basis of the early and extensive English school system.

Such learning was considered *beneath* sons of the nobility, though some with an obvious bent for knowledge—and a hunger for it—were given a sound education in the homes where they lodged. Sir Thomas More, for example, "served" in the home of Archbishop Morton, Primate of all England. As a churchman the Archbishop valued education above social graces, though he insisted on both. *The Booke of Urbanitie* was used in his home and probably guided young More in manners. But, generally speaking, the English view was far removed from the earlier one expressed in the Talmud—a "gentleman and a scholar" were not one and the same. More likely they were miles apart in birth, inclination and training.

Life as a schoolboy was much harsher than life as a page serving at table. Teachers used the lash to make learning penetrate more readily, often with the approval and at the direct request of the parents. Mrs. Agnes Paston, the stern matriarchal source of the noted Paston family, whose letters form a chronicle of English life in the 15th and 16th centuries, wrote in a 1457 letter to the teacher of her fifteen-year-old son, Clement, "If the boy has not done well, truly belash him till he will mend." It was a proven method, added Mistress Paston, and the boy had been well conditioned to it by his last master, "and the best that ever he had at Cambridge."

Pupil being whipped.
Carving on a stall in an ancient English church. From *Caricature and Comic Art* by James Parton, 1877.

The Paston family had just begun to climb socially with the marriage of Agnes, the letter writer quoted above, daughter and heiress of Sir William Berry, to William Paston. Agnes, or possibly her sensible father, had preferred an educated youth of ordinary birth, eager to make his own success, to a well-born parasite. William was considered "A right cunning man in the law."

William Paston's children were not candidates for training in a noble's home. However, such families were to produce a new nobility to replace the old one largely decimated by the War of the Roses. Meanwhile, behavior manuals for their children were devoid of descriptions of cap doffing, knee bending, and how to wait on a lord at his table. Instead, in the tone of *The Young Children's Book,* c. 1500, the yeasty rising of the prosperous English middle class at this time is evident. Biblical injunctions with practical everyday application were stated in businesslike language: "Use no swearing or falsehood in buying or selling. Get your money honestly and keep out of debt and sin"—useless advice for young noblemen not destined for "trade," but the sons of mercantile families could heed it well.

Obviously, courtesy books could not have widespread circulation until printing began. The first of the printed volumes was *The Booke of Curtesye,* c. 1477, produced by William Caxton, who forsook the textile business to become England's first printer. Caxton quickly transferred his attention from books used by children in noble households to books for the nobles themselves. In 1484 Caxton translated and printed Ramon Lull's *Order of Chivalry,* declaring, "This book is not requisite to every comyn man to have, but to noble gentlemen that by their virtue intend to come and enter into the noble order of chivalry." Thanks to William Caxton, the ideal of the knight—as codified by Lull in *The Order of Chivalry*—was to become the ideal of the English gentleman.

Caxton was a critic to his age, lamenting the passing of the "good old days" as critics have done in every generation. Of the knights riding around in his day, he complained, "What do ye but sleep and take ease? How many knights be there now in England that have the use and exercise of a knight . . . that knoweth his horse and his horse him?" Because chivalry was so close to his heart, Caxton added a personal exhortation to his translation of *The Order of Chivalry:*

> Oh ye knyghtes of England, where is the custom and usage of noble chyvalry that was used in those days? What do ye now but go to the baths and play at dice? . . . Leave it and read the noble volumes of the Holy Grail, of Lancelot, Galahad, Tristram, Percival and Gawain. There shall ye see manhood, courtesy, and gentleness.

The chivalry Caxton bewailed as lost was a 15th-century view through the rose-colored glasses of imagination and wishful thinking; as we have seen, knights in practice had been somewhat less noble than knights in theory. The battle of Crécy had helped to destroy the myth of invincibility that had formerly surrounded the knight, and the use of gunpowder had further outmoded his style of combat. Besides, knighthood had become an expensive honor because of the obligation to muster fighters. The title could be forcibly conferred as a remnant of the ancient system of vassalage, and in 1439 Parliament was petitioned to allow an unwilling knight to pay the king a fine as a release.

However, the admirable Englishman was still a warrior. Bearing arms was his chief vocation; bravery was synonymous with virtue, and the two words were often used interchangeably. Knight or gentleman—however he styled himself—the two were by now virtually the same man, dissolving into one image.

The following year Caxton gave chivalry another boost (and enriched English literature) by printing the *Morte d'Arthur,* translated and condensed from French Arthurian romances by his friend Sir Thomas Malory. Now there would no longer be any excuse for English knights or gentlemen to be unfamiliar with the gentle conduct at King Arthur's court. As for the popular misconception that there had never been a King Arthur, Caxton wrote a stirring introduction to the *Morte d'Arthur* in which he cited other authorities and pointed out the existence of Arthur's sepulchre at Glastonbury. "All these things considered, there can no man reasonably gainsay but there was a king of this land named Arthur."

If King Arthur's knights were examples too far removed, Caxton suggested more recent examples familiar to all:

> Look in later days of the noble acts since the conquest. King Richard Coeur de Lion, Edward the First and Third, and his noble sons. . . . And also beholde that victorious and noble King Harry the Fifth . . . and many others whose names shine gloriously by their virtuous noblesse and actes that they did in honour of the Order of Chivalry.

Caxton was determined to lead his fellow Englishmen into the paths of proper conduct. If chivalry wasn't for everyone, certainly good manners were. Accordingly, in 1487, he translated and printed Jacques LeGrand's *Book of Good Manners* about seven years after it first appeared in France.

Good Manners, true to the spirit of early courtesy books, was not a guide to politeness, but a collection of moral preachments as stern as any to be found in Ecclesiasticus. Such superficial fripperies as dainty table behavior, which received attention from the light-hearted Italians, were ignored in favor of "How a person ought to think on the day of doom." The medieval goal of grace after death was still the dominant theme of mortal existence, and a virtuous lifetime guaranteed a serene deathbed with nothing to fear on the other side. *Good Manners* proposed to guide the entire family, including the servants, to this happy conclusion of life's voyage, and to prevent them from committing any of the seven deadly sins while in transit. All who dwelt under the family roof were included in the pages of the *Book of Good Manners* under such chapter headings as:

How servauntes ought to maynten [behave] themselves in their service.
How fader and muder ought to teche their children.
How children owe observance and honour to their parentes.
How the Wymen ought to governe themselves.
Of the state of Wymen Widowes.
Of the estate of marriage; how it ought to be governed to have lineage and to love each other.
How Virginitie and Maydenheyde ought to be maynteyned.

Of "Virginitie," which had general application to both sexes, the book observed philosophically, "Such estate ought to be mayntayned right diligently, for it is moche harde to keep, considered human fraylness."

One chapter, "Of The State Of Marchants," cautioned those in trade: "Merchandise ought faithfully to be governed and mayntayned without fraude and without usuary, for otherwise it is not much, but it is deceit, falsehood, and evil."

Another chapter, "Howe The Princes Ought To Be Of Gude Manners," made it clear that ethical behavior was "gude manners" for sovereign and subject alike.

Lest anyone think the subject had been forgotten, there was a chapter on "The Conduct Of Knights." But the social graces which came to typify the English gentleman, and at which Chaucer had hinted a century earlier, were not even touched on in this first manners book printed in England. The design for his future deportment was to come shortly from Italy, the center of social graces. And when the ideal of the English gentleman was finally completed, modeled as he was on the chivalric foundation of Ramon Lull through Caxton's translation, he was also, in large part, the Italian courtier of Baldassare Castiglione.

A detail from the frontispiece, *The English Gentleman* by
Richard Braithwaite. 1633 edition.

PART TWO

Courts and Courtesy

Engraved portrait of Castiglione after a painting by Raphael. Frontispiece of an English edition, 1727.

Title page, *The Courtier* by Baldassare Castiglione. The first edition, Venice, 1528.

7 · THE IDEAL COURTIER

THE NEW MODEL of ideal manhood that replaced the medieval knight appeared in the early 16th century. He sat his horse with the same ease, was equally brave, equally busy fighting wars, and as handy with his sword as the knight with a lance. But this new ideal was a product of the Renaissance. "As fit for counsel as for war," he could thrust with his mind as well as his sword.

Baldassare Castiglione presented him to the world in *The Book of the Courtier* (1528), an account of four evenings of memorable conversation at the court of Urbino. The goal of the conversations was a definition of the perfect courtier. What emerged became a universal model for all courtiers and, eventually, for all gentlemen. The far-reaching and enduring influence of *The Book of the Courtier* in shaping the English gentleman is evident in Samuel Johnson's comment centuries later, when he called it, "the best book that ever was written upon good breeding."

The perfect courtier of Castiglione was urbane, attractive, a sportsman, relaxed, at ease on the dance floor, well-educated and well-read, versatile in the arts even if only in a superficial way, an accomplished conversationalist, and a wise statesman. He was, in fact, a word-portrait of Castiglione himself. Years later the famed Renaissance poetess Vittoria Colonna said to Castiglione, "I do not wonder that you have formed a perfect courtier, since you have only to hold up the mirror to yourself and reflect what you saw there." In a way, Vittoria was responsible for making *The Book of the Courtier* available to the world by circulating the privately printed copy Castiglione had given her. In fear that others might print it after his death, Castiglione had authorized his own public edition, "lest it be much mutilated by the hands of others."

Fate had given the tall, handsome Castiglione all the advantages. As the Bishop of Mantua wrote, prophetically, to Castiglione's father, "He is a young man well-favoured in person, learned, elegant, descreet, of the utmost integrity, and so gifted by nature and fortune that if he continues as he has begun he will have no equal."

Noble birth was another of Castiglione's fortunate gifts. Although in *The Book of the Courtier* the advantages of good birth were debated and no unanimous agreement was reached as to its indispensability for the perfect courtier, it was undoubtedly valuable to Castiglione. His blood ties to the ruling house of Mantua gave him an early start in court experience, and by eighteen he was ready for the brilliant Milanese court of Ludovico Sforza. By the time he reached the court of Urbino—at the invitation of Duke Guidobaldo, who offered him a military command—Castiglione was twenty-six, seasoned in courts and war (he had fought under the banner of his own prince, the Duke of Mantua), and a promising diplomat. Guidobaldo dispatched him to England for six months to represent the court of Urbino. There Castiglione observed the future Henry VIII "growing up . . . under his father, like a tender shoot in the shade of an excellent and fruit-laden tree, to renew it when the time shall come with much greater beauty and fruitfulness." (Later, Henry did exactly that, encouraging the fruits of the Renaissance to thrive in England.)

But no matter where Castiglione went after he had once tasted the joys of life at Urbino, his heart remained at that charming Italian court. Urbino was heaven to him. Its exquisite social amenities delighted him, his admiration for its rulers was nothing short of adoring, and he wrote *The Book of the Courtier* after Guidobaldo's death as a memorial.

The mutual devotion of Duke Guidobaldo and his Duchess Elizabetta, despite Guidobaldo's impotence, was an example, at its highest and truest level, of spiritual love to which Renaissance writers applied the term "platonic." Or perhaps misapplied it, since Plato's ideal love was between men, while Renaissance writers applied it to heterosexual relationships.

Terminology aside, the court of Urbino was lit by chaste, intellectual fires. The rulers set the pattern and any open display or discussion of sensual desire was as ill-bred as nose-picking. But there was excitement in the matching of wits and ideas; in many ways, these verbal encounters between the ladies and gentlemen of the court were as exciting as the physical ones denied the Duke and Duchess. And that is what Castiglione's book is about—the graceful, didactic conversation that was the social pastime of the court of Urbino. It is a testimonial not only to Guidobaldo's memory, but to the art of conversation as well. This is perhaps the first book to call small talk an indispensable social grace.

> [The courtier] should be one who is never at a loss for things to say that are good and well suited to those with whom he is speaking . . . he should know how to sweeten and refresh the minds of his hearers, and move them discreetly to gaiety and laughter with amusing witticisms and pleasantries, so that, without ever producing tedium or satiety, he may continually give pleasure.

However, small talk was by no means idle talk: ". . . one who is ignorant and has nothing in his mind worth listening to can neither speak nor write well." And that included putting on airs by lacerating a foreign language with which the speaker had only a slight acquaintance:

> Our courtier will show grace in all things and particularly in his speech, if he avoids affectation. Many of our Lombards, if they have been away from home for a year, come back and start right off speaking Roman, Spanish, or French, and God knows how! All of which stems from an excessive desire to appear very accomplished.

As a record of the manners of the aristocracy of its day *The Book of the Courtier* has few equals. Castiglione, speaking through the mouths of the characters in his book, also described the conduct at other courts. Perhaps some of the attitudes of his later years were included when he prepared the book for final publication. He was then living in self-imposed exile in Spain and had become a churchman, with an honorary Spanish bishopric. He saw the Spaniard, grave and dignified, as the master of courtiership. The French courtier was too vivacious, clowning with his fellow courtiers, bold in his approach to women, and cunning almost to unscrupulousness in manipulating those who could help him to gain advantages.

The latter part of the book deals with the courtier as a statesman and Castiglione makes it clear that his courtier must be motivated by the highest principles, ready and able to counsel his prince on morals as well as strategy.

Castiglione's attitude was in direct contrast to that of his equally famous contemporary Machiavelli, whose counsel on the conduct of statesmanship by both prince and courtier was undoubtedly truer to actual practice. *The Prince,* written about twenty years before its actual publication in 1532, was a practical blueprint for successful statesmanship which elevated dissembling to a fine art and was attuned to the practical workings of diplomacy. It spoke out as no other book had yet dared—it was a conduct book of a new kind.

To make his point that a prince should be educated realistically, Machiavelli used the fable of the centaur Chiron educating Achilles. Chiron explained that his double form represented the man and beast existing in all men, and those who were destined to govern must know how to use the natures of both. With this Machiavelli agreed completely, and he offered his own choice of beast natures suitable for a prince's study:

> He should make the fox and the lion his patterns. The first can but feebly defend himself against the wolf and the latter readily falls into such snares as are laid for him. From the fox, therefore, the prince will learn dexterity in avoiding snares; and from the lion, how to employ his strength to keep the wolves in awe. But they who rely entirely upon the lion's strength will not always meet with success: in other words, a prudent prince cannot and ought not to keep his word, except when he can do it without injury to himself, or when the circumstances under which he contracted the engagement still exist.

As if he sensed the outrage his words would excite, Machiavelli added, "I should be cautious in inculcating such a precept if all men were good, but as the generality of mankind are wicked and ever ready to break their words, a prince should not pique himself in keeping his more scrupulously."

Outraged cries were not long in coming. Such words fell like boiling lead on the ears of educated Tudor Englishmen, and Italian and French humanists. Consequently more than a century passed before *The Prince* was printed in English (1640). Meanwhile the English made his first name, Niccolò, a synonym for the Devil—Old Nick; and a number of angry books appeared in both France and England denouncing such talk and philosophy as immoral and contrary to the noble principles of the conduct of a prince—or, for that matter, of a gentleman. Not that self-interest was really considered despicable. On the contrary, men in high places had always lived by practical rules. But it was new to express openly what had tacitly been accepted, and to advocate cynicism and hypocrisy as a legitimate means to gaining ends. That Machiavelli dared to attach his name to his book, knowing that it would be unpopular, was certainly courageous.

In one of the many books on court life that followed, there was good advice for the perplexed courtier caught between Castiglione and Machiavelli and not sure which way to turn:

> Truly, he that desires to lead a life altogether innocent and remote from the conversation of men addicted to vice and to their own corrupt inclinations, shall in my opinion do very well to absent himself from that great courtesan, the court, that sometimes corrupts men of the greatest integrity and innocence.

8 · PRICELESS ADVICE

AT ABOUT THIS TIME another Italian book on deportment, *Il Galateo* (c. 1558), made its debut. The Florentine author, Giovanni della Casa, ranks as one of the best Italian poets of the 16th century, although his licentious early poems hampered his later career as a churchman and cost him a cardinal's hat. The highest he rose was to Archbishop of Benvento.

As papal Secretary of State under Pope Paul IV he had observed ceremonious behavior in many quarters, and in experience could match Castiglione, ceremony for ceremony. *Il Galateo* ranks with *The Courtier* as one of the most durable works on polite behavior; it became so popular that as late as 1811 it was still being printed in America as a guide to good manners. In Italy, even today, *Il Galateo* is a synonym for etiquette.

The title is derived from an anecdote in the book. Galateo was a manservant in the employ of an Italian bishop (perhaps della Casa himself?) delegated by his employer to present a parting gift to a guest leaving after a stay of a few days. The gift, Galateo explained, was the sort which would only be bestowed by one gracious gentleman upon another of his own station. If the reader expected a package done up in ribbons he was in for the same disappointment the guest undoubtedly experienced, but there was profit in the incident for both: the bishop's gift was advice. It seems the guest had charmed all with his manners until he sat down to dine. Then, to the distress of all within earshot, he ate with such lip-smacking that ears and tempers alike were frayed by the sound. His otherwise charming manners were completely forgotten and he was rated a lout for his performance at table. To reveal this shortcoming to him with such honesty, said Galateo, was the kind of gift that would

Title page, *Il Galateo* by Giovanni della Casa. American edition, 1811.

only be bestowed out of kindness and friendship. And even today it still is; "Only your best friend will tell you."

Il Galateo was probably the earliest conduct book to take up manners by specific categories, in the style of the etiquette books of later centuries. Della Casa discussed proper dress, table behavior, polite conversation, proper salutations, and how to behave in strange cities. For the many who traveled, he warned that it was fearfully easy to offend local citizens:

> The citizens of Padua were always greatly offended and thought themselves insulted, if a noble Venetian appeared in their streets, not in his full dress gown, but in a short coat; as if he fancied himself taking a walk at his ease, in some country village.

Dress should be "conformable to the customs of the age you live in, and suitable to your condition. It is not in our power to alter the general fashions at our pleasure, which, as they are produced, so they are swallowed up by time. In the mean while, everyone

may make shift to accommodate the general fashion to his own particular convenience." Any egregious deviation in personal appearance distressed him, as he was sure it would others. "If the whole
town wear their hair cut short, I would not have you ostentatiously
display your fine locks." Most of his advice on dress was reserved
for men. Dress like the men you are, he urged. "Neither ought a
man to deck and adorn himself like a lady . . . likewise neither to
smell too sweet, nor the contrary: for a gentleman ought neither to
be offensive like a he-goat, nor perfumed like a civet-cat."

The table instructions were not as detailed as Bonvicino's in the
13th century, but some of the same rudenesses were pointed out:
Not to scratch oneself or spit at table. If spitting was absolutely
necessary, it was to be done in a "seemly" way, and della Casa
pointed out that the ancient Persians had trained themselves never
to spit or blow noses. Fingers were not to be used for picking teeth
—the Italians already had a type of pick to do the job—nor was it
polite to get up from the table with a toothpick in one's mouth,
"like a bird which is nest-building," or worse still, "behind the ear,
like a barber."

I wonder what the recipients of those gold toothpicks occasionally advertised "for the man who has everything" would think if
they could read della Casa's remarks about similar items that apparently go back to the 14th century:

> They are also undoubtedly mistaken in their notions of politeness,
> who carry their tooth-pick cases hanging down from their necks:
> for, besides that it is an odd sight for a gentleman to produce
> anything of that kind from his bosom like some strolling pedlar
> . . . he who acts thus is but too well furnished with every instru-
> ment of luxury, and too anxious about every thing that relates
> to the belly: and I can see no reason why the same persons might
> not as well display a silver spoon hanging about their necks.

The English translator of *Galateo* pointed out that in pictures of
Chaucer, "who had been much in Italy," he had observed a similar
adornment worn around the neck.

Another book on manners and conduct that extended Italian
refinement to the rest of Europe was *The Civile Conversation,*

c. 1570, by the Renaissance intellectual Stefano Guazzo. A member of a distinguished Montferrat family, Guazzo was as qualified as Castiglione and della Casa to describe elegant deportment, having served the Duke of Mantua for many years on diplomatic missions and as ambassador to France and the papal court.

In its day *The Civile Conversation* (Guazzo also intended conversation in the broader sense of social relationships) was as widely known as Castiglione's more lasting work. Shakespeare sufficiently admired it—or perhaps the work of Guazzo's translator, George Pettie, whose translation appeared in 1581—to use much of the material in his own plays, including such examples as "All the world's a stage and we the players." *The Civile Conversation* says: "This world is a stage, wee the players whiche present the Comedie, and the gods, the lookers on," and ascribes the quotation to the ancient Greeks.

Like so many Renaissance works, *The Civile Conversation* is a series of dialogues—between Guazzo's brother and his cousin Annibal. Though written with literary grace, its didactic quality is unmistakable and it is as frankly instructive as della Casa's direct *Galateo* and Palmieri's earlier *Dialogue on Civil Life*. It may seem a smaller-scale work than *The Courtier* because of its limited participants, but in some ways it is a richer feast of talk and a sharper reflection of its times.

Guazzo posed the questions in true Socratic style, and Annibal's replies have lost none of their sprightliness with the centuries. Like most courtesy writers Guazzo despised pretensions about birth. His scornful criticism of folk ashamed of their humble origin brought from Annibal the laughing comparison to "the mule who being demaunded of his birth and being ashamed to say he was an Asses sonne, answered that he was a horses cosin."

Guazzo was equally irritated by those who flaunted the names of relatives or ancestors in order to give themselves importance, another peeve shared by most courtesy writers. "Gentlemen who beeing not by nature endowed with any vertue, make boast of the worthiness of their auncestors: these are to be laughed at, for the more they set forth the worthiness of them, the more they lay open the imperfections of themselves."

Title page, *La Civile Conversatione,* Stefano Guazzo. 1586 edition.

Guazzo sought the polished gentleman just as Castiglione had sought the ideal courtier. The search was for the same man, and one way to recognize him was by his skillful and sensible conversation. "Whoever shall mark the Etymologie of this word Homo, which in the Greek tongue signifieth together, shall perceive that a man cannot be a right man without Conversation," said Guazzo. "For he that useth not company hath no experience, he that hath no experience hath no judgement, and he that hath no judgement is no better than a beast." Intelligent conversation could earn a man wisdom, enhance his dignity, and in many instances earn him riches and worldly promotions. It could also get him into trouble. "The tongue is a little fire which kindleth great matters," said Guazzo, adding an extra morsel borrowed from Ecclesiasticus: "Remember that it is always better to slip with the foot than the tongue."

Guazzo covered much more of the territory of daily life than had Castiglione, or even della Casa. He surveyed marriage, the servant problem; even the time wasted on paying social calls came in for comment and reproof. One can see the Italian ladies displaying the same frantic eagerness to be received in the "right" homes that would be typical of the social striving among the upper middle classes of England and America in the 19th century, and would lead to an elaborate protocol of calling cards:

> I cannot be restrayned from speaking of this Cytie, where a manne shall see nothing else all day long, but women in the streets, which go from house to house, visityng some of courtesie, and other some (who before have vysited them) of duty, though without occasion; not by reason of some mariage, or of some friendes death, but if some one have had but a fit of an ague, or have kept her a chamber a few dayes, all the women in towne runne thyther of a ranke, as it were a procession.

The Civile Conversation discussed the timeless servant problem, with some hints on how to improve it. Employers were first to take a long look at themselves if they would know why their servants turned rotten.

> It may well be sayd that the faults of the servaunt belong in a maner to the mayster; for if the Proverbe be true: that like man like mayster . . . a fish beginneth first to smell at the head.

Those who did not treat their servants well would find themselves changing staff often—with the added danger of releasing a swarm of gossip with each departing employee:

> When a servaunte departeth from his mayster . . . whether contented or discontented, hee cannot refrayne from reporting wheresoever hee goe, the lyfe and behavyoure of hys former mayster; and though wyth one truthe hee myngle a hundred lyes, yet there bee many that wyll beleeve him.

If an employer was lucky enough to have a good servant, Guazzo advised, "Keep him always like a precious thing, remembering that the servaunte is in a certayne sorte one part of the mayster, and that there is nothing in his life more necessary than a good servaunte."

This, as we shall see, was overwhelmingly the attitude of all courtesy and etiquette books.

On wives and marriage Guazzo's views were astringent. Leave romance out when you choose a mate, he advised. A wise man chooses with his head, not his heart. Besides, a marriage fueled by love alone could burn low quickly:

> When these husbands that marry for love only, consider with themselves how their wives have brought nothing unto them, their love beginneth to waxe cold, and repenting their folly they begin not to [treat] them like wives, but like kitchenstuffes.

A sizable portion was sure to give more lasting pleasure, and with most men it was

> Bring somewhat with thee,
> If that thou mean to live with me.

To be beguiled by mere beauty was folly. "It is yet an ordinary saying," said Guazzo, "that he that hath a white horse and a faire wife, is never without trouble." But who wanted to gaze across the beaker of morning wine at an ugly mate? Guazzo and Annibal agreed on a safe choice after volleying the subject back and forth a few times: "One that is neyther fayre nore foule." And a wife should be of suitable age, said Guazzo, who frowned on marriages of great disparity:

> Methinks it is an unseemly thing to see a yong woman matched with a man that carryeth the countenance rather to be her father than her husband, and I am persuaded that yong dainty damsels go as willinglye to such husbands as they would doe to their graves.

In a gratuitous comment on marriages in 16th-century France, he added: "In France there happen no such disorders [mismatching] where the maydes as well as the men have free liberty to say yea, or nay, as their fancy serveth them." It would seem, from this comment, that "arranged" marriages were not then the prevailing mode in France, which is surprising. Guazzo may be stating only his opinion, and how well founded it is I cannot say. But it is another interesting sidelight.

Do women dress to please their husbands? This question, not infrequently heard from modern husbands who never notice a wife's new dress, was also asked by Guazzo. And answered: "I thinke the gorgious apparell they put on when they go abrode, is rather to please those which are abrode, than the husband that is at home."

In another bit of dialogue on wives, Guazzo asked, "What do you think of those husbandes who beat their wives?"

"Mary as I do of sacrileaggers and churcherobbers," replied Annibal.

"Yet I remember I have read, I know not where, these verses," said Guazzo:

> A woman, an asse, and a walnut tree,
> Bring the more fruit the more beaten they bee.

Guazzo's work, though it was widely read in England, was not typical of the prevailing attitude on women and marriage expressed by English writers at this time. Women were given more sensitive and respectful treatment, at least in the pages of courtesy books, during the great era when a queen headed the realm. Edmund Tilney spoke for some Englishmen in his *Brief and Pleasant Discourse of Duties in Marriage* (1568): "As meet it is that the husband obeys the wife, as the wife the husband . . . for women have souls as well as men, they have wit as well as men." That was a gentleman talking.

Henry VIII and his jester.
Original letters illustrative of English history, 1825.

9 · THE TUDOR GENTLEMAN

THE FUTURE ENGLISH GENTLEMAN came into sharper focus as Tudor England moved along the corridor that led from medieval times to the beginning of its modern history. He emerged from a new aristocracy based on wealth that Henry VII had encouraged into existence when the old nobility dwindled away in the War of the Roses.

In this new aristocracy, learning was less disdained than it had been earlier. Some gentlemen now read Latin and Greek classics, studied the works of Italian and Spanish humanists and knew Hebrew. And they saw to it that their children did likewise.

Possibly the most important factor in making education acceptable to the English aristocracy was Henry VIII's endorsement of the new learning, which belatedly brought the Renaissance to England, and in its trail such noted humanists as Erasmus and the Spanish philosopher Juan Luis Vives. Henry engaged Vives to tutor his daughter Mary. When he lost his taste for Mary's Spanish mother, Catherine of Aragon, he also lost his taste for the Spanish philosopher, especially when Vives opposed the divorce.

76

But nothing dampened Henry's enthusiasm for learning, and later he provided a liberal education for young Elizabeth as well. This proved to be an excellent investment for England's future. Elizabeth became an excellent scholar and carried on her father's tradition of respect for learning, and during her reign the literary fruit of the Tudors ripened into luscious perfection.

Not all English aristocrats shared Henry's enthusiasm for learning, nor were all of them pleased to see the old values set aside. Many still saw education as weakening—unfit for men of action and suited only to scribes and clerics.

One 16th-century diehard observed to Richard Pace, dean of St. Paul's, "I swear by God's body I would rather my son hang than study letters. For it becomes the sons of gentlemen to blow the horn nicely, to hunt skilfully, and elegantly train and carry a hawk. But the study of letters should be left to the sons of rustics."

Woodcut from *A Jewel for Gentrie,* 1614.
A manual for Tudor gentlemen, "Being an exact dictionary, or true method, to make any man understand all the art, secrets, and worthy knowledges belonging to Hawking, Hunting, Fowling, and Fishing."

However, Roger Ascham warned that such thinking was removing noblemen from the seat of authority: "The fault is in your selves, ye noble men's sonnes, and therefore ye deserve the greater blame, that commonlie the meaner mens' children cum to be the wisest councellors and the greatest doers, in the weightie affaires of this Realme."

Though instruction in social graces, polite manners, and sports remained vital in preparing a boy to become a gentleman, it was now deemed important to stretch his mind as well as his muscles. There were even some who did not frown on educating females; after all, Henry VIII had set the example with his daughters, and many prominent men had done likewise. Sir Thomas More gave his daughters the same scholarly supervision received by the boys in his home. The prioresses of England were distinguished for their learning, and one of them, Dame Juliana Berners, prioress of Sopwell nunnery, was the compiler of the *Boke of St. Albans,* a definitive work on falconry.

Wherever the Renaissance was infusing its spirit, the training of youth came in for greater attention, and inadequate teaching was assailed by many humanist thinkers. Rabelais poked satirical jibes at the bad manners of his times and at what he considered to be faulty methods of instructing children. His own quite serious ideas on improving manners and education were conveyed in the first book of his series, which describes the birth and education of Gargantua.

Perhaps the most influential of the humanists bent on improving the education of youth was the great Erasmus. His influence was widely felt in England, where he was Professor of Divinity at Cambridge from 1511 to 1514. Erasmus, who particularly objected to the fashion for codpieces, "the bright and wanton gardying of the breche," was more inclined to brighten the mind. And this he wished to do for all youth whether "future monarchs or the sons of mechanics."

Lessons in good manners were integral to Erasmus' educational theories and the home was the first school: "Children oughte to be taught and brought up gently in vertue and learnynge, and that even forthwyth from their nativitie." One of the most important courtesy books of the 16th century is Erasmus' *De Civilitate Morum Puerilium* (1526), which covered not only manners but also supplied some rules for hygiene.

> Cleanliness of teeth must be cared for, but to whiten them with powder does for girls. To rub the gums with salt or alum is injurious. . . . If anything sticks to the teeth, you must get it out, not with a knife, or with your nails after the manner of dogs and cats, or with your napkin, but with a toothpick, or quill or small bone taken from the tibias of cocks or hens. To wash the mouth in the morning with pure water is both mannerly and healthful; to do it often is foolish.

On proper deportment at table, Erasmus advised a smiling face, clean nails and a comfortable bladder—all of this out of consideration for the feelings of others.

> At table or at meat, let mirth be with thee, let ribaldrie be excised; sit not down until thou have washed, but let thy nails be prepared before, and no filth stick in them, lest thou be called sloven and a great nigard. Remember the common saying, and before make water, and if need require, ease thy belly, and if thou be gird too tight, to unloose thy girdle is wisdom, which to do at table is shame. When thou wipest thy hands put forth of thy mind all grief, for at the table it becomes mete not to be sad, not to make others sad.

Two Englishmen, Sir Thomas Elyot and Roger Ascham, also stand out like beacons in English education as it expanded under the influence of the humanists. Along with the new Greek learning, both men advocated renewed attention to gentle manners.

Elyot had been one of the fortunate children taken into the home of Sir Thomas More, and from that gentle but dynamic teacher he absorbed an appetite for less rote and more attention to the spirit of studies. This he expressed in *The Boke Named The Governour* (1531), the first English work on educating children. Elyot compared children to precious herbs that would grow to perfection with careful tending. For boys, however, after the first tender growth was completed, he preferred a hardier environment, away from the company of women and into the hands of a wise, experienced tutor—a recall of his own early youth spent under Sir Thomas More's roof.

Many of Elyot's views, radically advanced for his day, are modern enough to guide educators today—for example, using toys and pictures to instruct the very young, and studying languages with less attention to grammar and more to the spirit of the text. He made a particular point of searching out and cultivating any special aptitudes, a philosophy that Plato had expounded in ancient times:

> Do not train boys to learning by force and harshness; but direct them to it by what amuses their minds, so that you may be the better able to discover with accuracy the peculiar bent of the genius of each.

Good teachers—gentle in spirit and able to understand and reach children—this was the greatest need of all in Elyot's view, and he bewailed their lack: "Lorde God, how many good and clean wittes of children be nowe a dayes perished by ignorant schole maisters."

Roger Ascham, Elyot's contemporary, had similar freewheeling ideas which he expressed in *The Scholemaster* (published in 1570 shortly after his death), "specially purposed for the private bringing up of youth in Gentlemen and Noble mens houses."

If anyone was qualified to speak on "private bringing up," it was Ascham, former tutor to the young Princess Elizabeth. In his opinion, children were better off taught at home. He was an outspoken critic of the schools—of their harsh methods and merciless birchings. But his loudest salvos of disapproval were directed against parents who sent their sons to Italy to round out their education. Italy, as the center and source of most of the new learning, presumably attracted students in pursuit of scholarship. But Ascham suspected there were other lures, and he labeled Italy's intellectual centers, Florence, Padua and Rome, "The Courts of Circe," responsible for degrading English morals and the mannerly discipline so carefully learned in youth.

"I know divers that went out of England, men of innocent life, men of excellent learning, who returned out of Italy, not only with worse manners, but also with less learning."

However, he had no objection to Italian learning studied in the safety of English surroundings, and he heartily recommended *The Courtier* as required reading. "Advisedlie read, and diligentlie followed, but one yeare at home in England would do a yong Jentleman more good, I wisse, than three yeares of travell abrode spent in Italy."

Many of the social accomplishments lauded by Castiglione were considered proper, even necessary training for Englishmen of good birth. Dancing and instrumental music ranked high because of Elizabeth's own interest. Even the roughest knights had been proud of their ability with the lute; the Elizabethan warrior-gentleman was no exception. He danced as gracefully as he rode a horse, but nothing exceeded expert horsemanship as the crowning accomplishment of a gentleman, unless it was skill with the rapier. Whether on the battlefield or to settle a point of honor, self-defense was the most manly art of all.

Though the Italians failed to win Englishmen over to the use of the fork until the late 17th century—it was laughed at in England as a silly refinement not worthy of a man's grasp—they won quick approval for the new Italian dueling weapons, the foil and the dagger. *Il Duello,* by Girolamo Muzio, had become popular in England in 1565, and gradually the graceful foil was substituted for the sword and buckler with which English duelists had formerly hacked away at each other.

Elaborate rules and regulations governed dueling between gentlemen, and proficiency was graded: Master, Provost, or Scholar, not unlike a progression through karate belts. Vincentio Saviolo's *Of Honour and Honourable Quarrels* (1595) usurped the place of the Muzio work, freely pirating from it—an act that logically should have involved Saviolo in a duel with the original author. But perhaps plagiarism was not provocation for a duel. The process leading to involvement was so elaborate, and the preliminary sparring with insults so formalized, that Shakespeare gleefully satirized it in *As You Like It:* "Oh sir, we quarrel in print, by the book:—we met, and found the quarrel upon the seventh cause."

This was obviously modeled on Saviolo's chapter "Diversity of Lies," which tabulates them as: the Lie Certain; the Conditional

Duel with rapier and dagger.
Vincentio Saviolo his practise, 1595.

Lie; the Lie in Particular; the Foolish Lie; and the Returning Back of the Lie. Of course it was better not to provoke a duel in the first place, and avoiding such provocation was a fundamental purpose of courtesy books. Courtesy could save a gentleman's life.

One Elizabethan volume, *A Health to the Gentlemanly Profession of Serving Men* (1598), was concerned with a vanishing species which apparently gave a sound historical background to the phrase, "A gentleman's gentleman." The author, who signed himself I. M., lamented the falling standards and rising demands of all household servants, and recalled the time when "Gentlemen thought mete this helpe or servaunt should be made of their own mettal, even a loafe of their own doughe. . . . The Gentleman received even a Gentleman unto his service."

As we have seen earlier, the personal service that in modern times is performed by a valet was part of the training of all well-born youths. Service was not looked down on as demeaning. On the contrary, because of primogeniture and the lack of suitable means of livelihood for youths who were not first-born, personal service often offered security when an advantageous marriage had not been secured.

The gentleman's gentleman often functioned as a type of maitre d'hotel who made wheels turn in regal style for his employer, but alas, in Elizabeth's day the supply was diminishing. And who was to blame if gentlemen could no longer find their own "mettal" and "doughe" to fill the mold of serving men? The gentleman employer, of course. He no longer maintained his household with his old liberality, chiefly because he (or his wife) now insisted on handling the household money—an unthinkable practice in the past, when "Gentlemen of worth spent their whole Rentes and Revenues in hospitalitie and good housekeeping . . . never troubling themselves with the art of Arithmetique to add and subtract. They . . . held Coyne in utter contempt, not vouchsafing to touch, handle, or dispose of it. That care they committed to the consideration of their Servantes."

Furthermore, in those good old days, "If one gentleman invited another to his house . . . the serving-man's diligence to do his maister's friende service and honor" was suitably rewarded and "some pence redounded to his profit." Unfortunately, in the leaner days of 1598, "Many are slack in performance of this gentlemanly liberalitie and gratitude." This is one of the earliest references to tipping, or vails, as they were then known in England, where the plague of the outstretched palm seems to have started.

Regardless of the lavish style that some "serving men" still provided for them, as a lot the Elizabethan gentlemen were a coarse, ill-mannered company. Not surprising, with a queen who was often in her speech and actions as coarse as a man. Though Elizabeth was greatly educated, a student of Greek and Latin, and a distinguished bibliophile as well, she could make many a man blush. Sir Robert Cecil spoke from intimate knowledge when he said, "She was more than a man, and (in troth) sometyme less than a woman."

This could also be said of the ladies surrounding Elizabeth, who imitated her elegant handwriting, followed her in the study of ancient tongues, and kept up with her in oaths and ribaldries even as they bent over their dainty needlework. Those were rough times for gentlemanly behavior, and Elizabeth was a rough queen who commissioned pirates to plunder in her name.

Nevertheless, as Chaucer had done before them, some Elizabethan writers tried to demonstrate gentle manners through their writings. Some followed Thomas Dekker and Ben Jonson and chose satire as the most effective way to make points. The fop and the coxcomb, who seem to have put in their first appearance in the late Elizabethan period, were favorite targets of derision.

Few works were as explicit about the gross conduct of those days as *Grobianus,* a stinging satire by the German poet Friedrich Dedekind, written in 1549 and translated into English in 1604. The title is derived from Grobian, the patron saint of ignorant boors (*grobbe narren*). A fair example of the vulgarity described by Dedekind and offered as a warning to Englishmen is contained in the heading to Chapter VII of the Third Book of Grobianus:

> Some few more examples of Orators
> Who fart, and belch, and stink like nasty curs:
> Of keeping in our waters when they press,
> And exemplary Acts of Boorishness.

The chapter dealt in detail with breaking wind in public and, worse still, using the wide top of a boot to surreptitiously relieve oneself while seated at the table. Mischievous remarks were also addressed to "Girls," told by the wind-breaking "Orator" to ease themselves publicly like a man: "To fart and fizzle in the Time of Need; Those who retain stale wind are nasty sluts, And feel tenfold confusion in their guts."

Some critics of Elizabethan behavior attacked such vices as "Dicing, Dauncing, Vaine Plaies, or enterludes with other idle pastimes." Many treatises appeared denouncing gambling. George Whetstone shuddered out an indignant description of what was to be found in "The bowels of this famous citie . . . the wicked playes of the dice, first invented by the devil, and the nurses of these hellish exercises, places called ordinary tables, of which there are in London, more in number to honour the devil, than churches to serve the living God." Not a man to tangle with temptation, he asserted, "I constantly determine to cross the streets, where those vile houses—ordinaries—are planted, to blesse me from the inticements of them, which in very deed are many, and the more dangerous in that they please with a vain hope of gain."

The most polished and explicit voice of all was that of Edmund Spenser, who sought to revive the ideal of chivalric perfection that Caxton had imbued with new life a century earlier. The grand example is, of course, Spenser's allegorical *The Faerie Queen*, dedicated to Elizabeth. In it the gentlemanly ideals are presented through the courteous Sir Calidore, said to have been inspired by the man considered to be the prototype of the chivalrous gentleman: Spenser's close friend, the poet Sir Philip Sidney.

Sidney, who was a great admirer of Castiglione's *The Courtier*, was one of the luminaries of Elizabeth's court and as well qualified as Castiglione to symbolize the archetype of the perfect courtier by birth, breeding, accomplishments, and handsome appearance. His fame rests largely on his poetry though he was active in Elizabeth's councils.

There is no question that he followed Castiglione's line, and anything that smacked of Machiavelli would have been repugnant to him. His personal integrity and moral commitment, as much as his writings, helped him to achieve immortal fame. Even his untimely death from a battle wound at thirty-two fitted him to the specifications of the ideal hero, and his final act was a glorious example of courtesy, recorded by his friend Lord Brooke:

> As he was returning from the field of battle, pale, languid, and thirsty with excess of bleeding, he asked for water to quench his thirst. The water was brought and had no sooner approached his lips, than he instantly resigned it to a dying soldier, whose ghastly countenance attracted his notice—speaking these ever-memorable words: "This man's necessity is still greater than mine."

This was certainly one of the most chivalric episodes of the Elizabethan period, but it is the tale of Sir Walter Raleigh, who threw down his cloak to protect his queen's shoes from the mud, that is the popular legend of the Elizabethan age. Gentle Sir Philip Sidney could never have perpetrated such brutalities against the

Funeral Cortege of Sir Philip Sidney.
One of thirty engravings by Thomas Lant, c. 1588.

Irish in the Munster rebellion as had Raleigh, but both men became immortal examples of an age that nurtured the chivalric legend in its quest for the ideal gentleman. Chivalry was then—as it had been before—more concept than reality, more hope than fulfillment. Its ideals were still only a mirror before which men could stand and study their actions and adjust their imperfections—each probably seeing the reflection he chose to see. Between such dissimilar ideal gentlemen as Sidney and Raleigh the image was bound to appear blurred. The seventeenth century would make it sharper.

10 · THE COMPLEAT GENTLEMAN

THE WORD GENTLEMAN had descended through centuries of linguistic change, from a derisive connotation, the *gentiles homines* that Romans had used for their Gothic conquerors, to a meaning clearly desirable, but not easily defined. A satisfactory definition continues to be complicated and elusive. The word was already the object of study and debate in the 16th century; it was the old argument—what constituted true nobility?—with *gentleman* replacing *nobility* as the contested word.

Though there were linguistic links with the Italian *gentilhuomo*, the Spanish *gentil hombre,* and the French *gentilhomme*—and the English gentleman, like Portia's suitor, had "learned his behaviour everywhere"—the English gentleman became, in the final analysis, the particular and peculiar product of England. He was native to it, as are fragrant Kentish meadows and Devon gardens. Just as those meadows and gardens need the English climate to reach their perfection, so the English gentleman needed England's political, social and economic climate to mature into that model admired by the world for principles, sportsmanship and politeness. The winds of social revolution blew earlier in England, creating a strong middle class. From this matrix, more than from ancient noble lines, the model Englishman eventually emerged. Turning the pages of 16th and 17th century courtesy books, one can see him breaking out of the medieval chivalric code and into the practical ideas of the modern world.

In the 14th century, when English peasants led by John Ball, early champion of socialism, revolted against their overlords, the answer to their marching chant was easy to define: "When Adam delved and Eve span, who was then the gentleman?" He was the nobility, the ruling class—and if he belonged to that class, good or bad he was called a gentleman. Nobility still claimed that right in the 16th century, but now they shared it with descendants of the ragtag band that had chanted John Ball's couplet.

"Of gentlemen, some be called Gentle Gentle, others Gentle ungentle, the third sort, ungentle Gentle," said *Institucion of a Gentleman* in 1568. The Gentle Gentle and the Gentle ungentle were the perennials, blooming on the well-rooted growths of entrenched gentry. The ungentle Gentle could be likened to annuals, except that, in time, they too would become perennials. They were easily identified as recent plantings and they bloomed with the vigor of marigolds. As the author defines them:

> Born of a low degree of a poor stock . . . which man taking his beginning of a poor kindred, by his virtue, wit, policy, industry, knowledge in laws, valiancy in arms, or such like means, becometh a well-loved and high esteemed man. . . . In like manner that man which through honesty raiseth up his small cottage and deviseth to make thereof a high castle, is in my opinion much worthy of praise, and may be called Gentle ungentle, that is to say, ungentle by his father, and not by lineage made noble, but by his own knowledge, labor, and industry becometh gentle.

"This word Gentleman is a compound word," said the author of *Institucion*. It was also a compound problem in definition, and most writers who dealt with conduct had a try at it.

Gervase Markham in *The Gentleman's Academie*, 1595, divided gentlemen into "Four manner and nine sorts." "Four manner" covered the main classifications. "To wit: one of ancestry, which must needs be of blood and three of coat-armour, and not of blood." It was the right to coat armor that made a man a gentleman in Markham's day. As Shakespeare put it in *The Taming of the Shrew*, "If no gentleman, why then no arms." But arms were easy to come by and gentlemen were as readily made as knights had been in former times. Armorial insignia were acquired from the king's herald, a post which vaguely and falsely implied that the arms were granted by the crown. Actually, for a suitable fee the heralds could convey an armorial shield and the status of gentleman to almost anyone who sought it, a practice which later brought the whole affair of family arms into disrepute. The distinguished Elizabethan writer and statesman Sir Thomas Smith had commented acidly on this in *The Commonwealth of England*, 1583, and the comment was often reprinted in the 17th century.

> As for gentlemen, they bee made good cheape in England. For whosoever studieth in the Lawes of the Realme, who studieth in the Universities, who professeth liberall Sciences: and to be short, who can live idly and without manuall labour, and will beare the port, charge, and countenance of a Gentleman hee shall be called Master, for that is the Title which men give to Esquires and other Gentlemen. . . . And (if need be) a King of Heralds shall also give him for money Armes newly made and invented the title whereof shall pretend to have been founde by the saide Herald in perusing and viewing of old Registers, where his Ancestors in times past had been recorded to beare the same.

Perhaps this explains why the study of heraldry occupied so many emerging gentlemen. Studious snooping might reveal the inaccuracies of roundels, bezants, or rampant beasts in a neighbor's proudly displayed armorial bearings.

Quite coincidentally, the 17th century's successor to Castiglione as an authority on polite conduct was also somewhat of an authority on heraldry. Henry Peacham, author of *The Compleat Gentleman* (1622), one of the best known of all courtesy books, was apparently not endowed with family arms but moved, for a good part of his life, among those with the most impeccable genealogies. Such first-hand observation certainly qualified him to lead aspiring gentlemen in the right direction, and his book was the *vade mecum* of 17th-century Englishmen.

Peacham, born around 1576, was the son of a cleric and well-known classical scholar who was still vigorously conducting his affairs as rector of the parish of Leverton, Herfordshire, in 1605. Young Henry was brought up in the best educational traditions of English churchmen; he graduated from Trinity College, Cambridge, and embarked on a career as a teacher, and later a tutor to the sons of aristocrats whom he prepared for university entrance. Teaching gave Peacham the time to pursue his chief loves, painting and heraldry; his first book was on pen and water-color drawing, a gentlemanly accomplishment endorsed by Castiglione and pursued as zealously as hunting by 17th-century gentlemen.

When Peacham eventually began to devote himself to a literary career he attracted the attention of several titled patrons and soon moved in the company of the accomplished wits and writers of his day. He was obviously one of them—a talented fellow who could turn an epigram or sing a madrigal with equal ease. He traveled widely and had a talent for making friends. One friend, a Frenchman, M. de Ligny, suggested the idea for *The Compleat Gentleman*. English youth, said de Ligny, needed to be directed to an interest in the arts; Peacham, who knew the arts from active practice and who had already written his successful book on drawing, was just the man to do it. When it was completed, Peacham dedicated it to the eight-year-old William Howard, Lord Stafford, whose father, Lord Arundel, was a leading art collector in England.

In the foreword to *The Compleat Gentleman*, Peacham modestly acknowledged that the efforts he was about to undertake put him in such company as Plutarch, Erasmus, Vives, Sir Thomas Elyot, Roger Ascham, "And sundry others: so that my small taper among so many torches were as good as out, as seeming to give no light at all." His taper, too, became a bright torch. Its enduring light radiated all the way to America, where it continued to shine even when later authorities appeared. Washington Irving's Squire Bracebridge, "from early years took honest Peacham for his textbook, instead of Chesterfield."

Most courtesy books included a discussion of true nobility. Peacham's was no exception. Performance, not birth, was the criterion, said Peacham, and as for possessions, "Riches are an ornament, not the cause of nobility." All the same, he was sharply aware of social stratification and did not hesitate to speak out, usually in support of it. He did think that physicians deserved more respect; the time was past when they should be looked upon as servants. However, he added, "I here intend no common Chirugians, Mountebanks, unlettered Empericks, and women-doctors (of whom for the most part there is more danger, than of the worst disease itself). . . ."

Merchants were then surveyed: "Concerning merchantes," he

Frontispiece, *The Compleat Gentleman* by Henry Peacham.
First edition, 1622.

began, "the exercise of merchandise hath been (I confess) accounted base and much derogating from Nobility." He went on to
cite the historical precedents. "Romans had to disparage Tarquinus
Pricus . . . and make him odious to the people with his being a
merchant's son. . . . Aristotle speaking of merchants and mechanickes saith, 'this kind of life is base and contrary to virtue.'"
There was no disputing it, Peacham was forced to agree, merchants
and "mechanickes" (tradesmen and those who worked with their
hands) were pretty base; they could not be considered gentlemen.

However, he raised his voice in defense of those merchants who
risked their means, to say nothing of their lives, to go to remote
regions for commerce. For this he had ancient Tully as an authority. "The merchant of ordinary Petty things is to be accounted base
and ignoble, but of great things, fetcht from many places and publicly vented for the use of many men, without fraud and guile, is
not much to be found fault with." At least members of the recently
chartered East India Company could rest easy.

Possibly mindful of his own days as teacher and tutor, Peacham had some harsh comments for those parents who were stingy in paying these:

> Is it not commonly seen that most gentlemen will give better wages and deal more bountifully with a fellow who can but teach a Dog or reclaim a hawk, than upon an honest, learned and well qualified man to bring up their children? It may be that dogs are able to make syllogisms in the field when their young masters can conclude nothing at home.

Whatever a parent or teacher had failed to provide in the way of instruction, Peacham urged his gentleman reader to study on his own. *The Compleat Gentleman* covered all subjects from poetry, music, drawing and painting in "oyl" to fishing, fighting, and the proper care of books, with a survey of necessary academic subjects sandwiched in, and special emphasis placed on geometry and cosmography. A gentleman, especially a young one, should know his universe and his nations, said Peacham, suggesting a pleasant French study aid: playing cards decorated with maps of various countries. The cards used contemporary rulers for kings and queens, and peasants typical of their lands, for knaves—"Which ingenious device cannot be but a great furtherance to a young capacity, and some comfort to the unfortunate Gamester," said Peacham, "when, what he hath lost in money, he shall have dealt him in Land or Wit."

This lighthearted, urbane approach was typical of Peacham. He could sprinkle classical allusions and Greek quotations through his book as frequently as any of his contemporaries, but his belief that learning was one of the great pleasures of life shone on every page. He concentrated on telling the English gentleman how to *think,* not how to conduct himself at table. *His* reader knew that; and if by chance he didn't, he could consult della Casa's *Il Galateo.* It seems a shame that so pleasant a gentleman never married, and sad indeed that his final years were spent in poverty.

An equally prominent 17th-century molder of gentlemen, Richard Braithwaite, author of *The English Gentleman,* 1630, went at his subject like a serious schoolmaster and Puritan, though he was neither. Like Peacham, he was a Royalist. He was born to the estate of a gentleman, attended both Oxford and Cambridge, indulged his literary aspirations with some minor poetry and eventually settled into the leisurely routine of a born gentleman's life. As a justice of the peace he was an influential figure in his small world. He liked it small, had no ambition for court life—or perhaps no taste for it—and advised his readers to control *their* ambitions as well. His philosophy of moderation in all things, and his preference for the contemplative life, paid off in a serene life. He died in 1673, a contented old man of eighty-five.

Where Peacham urged a gentleman to live in the world and enjoy it to its fullest, Braithwaite exhorted him to think of the end, never missing an opportunity to make his point. If a gentleman diverted himself with a game of chess he gave him much to ponder:

> There is no one game which may seeme to represent the state of man's life to the full, so well as the CHESSE. For there you shall find Princes and Beggers, yet when the game is done, they are all truss'd up in a bagge together; where then appeares any difference betwixt the poorest Begger and the Potentest Peere?

However, Braithwaite was as class-conscious as the next gentleman and of no mind to make all men equal in *this* world. In case the reader had misunderstood, he clarified his position.

> While we are here . . . wee are according to our severall rankes exteemed; and fit it should be so, for else should all degrees bee conspicuously confounded: but no sooner is the game done, than wee are throwne into a bagge, a poor shrowding sheet.

A vocation was the best means of keeping out of mischief while tarrying on this planet. Every man needed one, and there were vocations to fit all types, gentlemen and lesser men. Unfortunately, as Braithwaite saw it, there were many who were not willing to accept vocations suitable to them, especially those ambitious to perform beyond their own sphere. Much trouble and dissension resulted and it was time the human race, at least the English members of it, took a lesson from the human body:

> The nose it smels and tastes not; the eare it heares and walkes

93

not; the foote, it walkes and heares not . . . contrariwise, how itching are men after imployments as least concerns them: the Drayman he will play the Divine; a Dairy maid the Physician; a Collier the Informer; the Farmer a Lawyer. Wherein surely I have observed no small inconvenience redounding to the Publike State.

Recreation was desirable, but in moderation. Recreation was "for refreshing the minde and enabling the body to perform such offices as are requisite to be performed. It is not to bee made a Trade or Profession." Hawking was one recreation that gentlemen followed with professional zeal. While it could easily fill a man's day, it could also strain a lean purse. Once limited to kings and nobles, hawking was now widely popular with the gentry and had become the elite sport of the 16th and 17th centuries. "This pleasure, as it is a princely delight, so it moveth many to be so dearly enamored of it, as they will undergoe any charge, rather than foregoe it," said Braithwaite, warning how the costs compounded.

Hawking compared—in initial cost, upkeep, and snob appeal—with polo today. Like ponies, good hawks were costly. One gentleman, Sir Thomas Monson, paid a thousand pounds for a cast of hawks, and any decent goss-hawk or tassel-hawk went for at least one hundred pounds. And the hawks were only the beginning. Hawkers needed horses to ride (at least several—horses tired more readily than hawks or riders), dogs to retrieve the fallen game, and a staff of servitors to care for the avian, equine and canine menagerie. It was a bankrupting sport for the gentleman who could not afford it but insisted on flying with the best. I suspect that this sport gave rise to the phrase "high flyer," used by Samuel Pepys to describe one given to extravagant tastes.

Braithwaite went through a whole list of sports that a gentleman could pursue without straining his purse or, for that matter, his vocation. There were swimming, fishing, riding, or just plain running, and any one of them would keep a man fit.

In general, Braithwaite's views followed the Puritan line, but at a dignified distance that permitted a gentleman a bit of innocent roistering. He did object to the excessive drinking of "healths"—the ancient Anglo-Saxon custom of toasting everybody in sight plus all members of the royal family, a custom which enabled serious drinkers tȯ get roaring drunk in a hurry—but Braithwaite had no objection to a little convivial drinking and saw no need to follow such drastic examples as that of Thracius, "who cut down all his vines lest he should bee drunken." A nip here and there was actually good for the man who knew how to limit himself. "Use wine or any such strong drinke to strengthen and comfort nature, but not to impaire or enfeeble her," ruled Braithwaite.

However, one popular "Recreation" was strictly out of bounds:

> There are some gentlemen, and these for the most part of the higher sort (I could wish they were likewise of the better sort) who repair to the *House of the Strange Woman*, sleeping in the bed of Sinne, thinking so to put from them the Evill day. And these are such as make *Whoredom a Recreation*.

Harsh words were also addressed to those gentlemen who spent extravagant sums on their appearance. Indeed, the laces, velvets and feathers of the Royalist Cavaliers added up to princely costs, causing

"An English antick, his codpiece open tied at the top with a great bunch of riband."
17th-century satirical sketch, reproduced in *Humour, Wit and Satire of the 17th Century* by John Ashton, 1883.

a decrease in what Braithwaite regarded as more worthwhile expenditure:

> Hospitality, which was once a relique of Gentry . . . hath lost her title . . . whither are these Great Ones gone? To the *Court,* there to spend in boundless and immoderate riot what their provident ancestors had so long preserved. . . . They have abridged their familie, reduced their attendants to a small number . . . none but a Page, a Coachman, a Lackey and perchance a Cooke. . . . Now if you ask me how their meanes should be so consumed when they [live so cheaply] my answer is: the lesse they bestow on their *Caterer,* the more they bestow on their Taylor.

This complaint was reminiscent of I. M., who had shed printed tears in *A Health to the Gentlemanly Profession of Serving Men* over the same lack, in 1598.

One last recreation—painting—to which Peacham had devoted several chapters, received a scant few words from Braithwaite. Most of what he had to say on the subject concerned paints that were being applied to the wrong areas—ladies' cheeks, for example. Gentlemen were well advised to avoid *that* type.

Next to Peacham and Braithwaite, Richard Allestree was probably the third most important conduct guide for 17th-century gentlemen. In *The Gentleman's Calling,* 1660, he dealt almost exclusively with the gentleman's spiritual needs and dwelt on the responsibilities of fortunate birth. "Gentlemen are distinguished from the Vulgar, not only by empty Names and airy Titles, but by real [gifts] distributed to them by God." These gifts—particularly wealth—were meant to be shared, and the possessor was merely the lucky conduit through which they passed. "God in his wisdom, discerning that Equality of Conditions would breed Confusion in the World, has ordered several States, design'd some to Poverty, others to Riches, only annexing to the Rich the care of the Poor."

The gifts of education and leisure should be used with greater care than gentlemen currently exhibited, complained Allestree. Leisure especially, which should be used "in preventing or curing spiritual maladies," was being wasted in "contracting or increasing them."

Allestree, a great sermonizer, devoted his numerous books almost entirely to the Christian duties of men and women and, in fact, titled two of them *The Whole Duty of Man* and *The Whole Duty of Woman*. Addison, in the *Spectator,* referred to *The Whole Duty of Man* as "one of the best books in the world." The chief difference between it and *The Gentleman's Calling* was that *Whole Duty* was offered to all men, "Especially the *meanest* reader." *The Gentleman's Calling,* a more select version of the same preachments, pointed to the man who had everything and needed to be reminded that it was only a temporal loan.

The gentleman who followed the counsel of Peacham, Braithwaite, and later Allestree, could hope to measure up to the ideal. There were many such men in England. There were also, in the feckless Stuart days of the 17th century, many who rejected the conception.

It was a time of great contrasts, underscored by the political and religious dissensions that led inevitably to civil war. Puritan gentlemen in somber dress and soup-bowl haircuts contrasted with Royalists in the ostentatious garb condemned by Braithwaite, their long hair in the "lovelocks" ringlets that angered many contemporary critics. Heartless frivolity in one faction contrasted with stern Calvinistic condemnation of such simple pleasures as "Maypoles, Christmas keeping, and dressing houses with ivy" in the other. (Objections to these harmless festivals were specified in the indictment against William Prynne, the articulate Puritan pamphleteer. For this, along with his denunciation of plays in general and male actors dressed as women in particular, Prynne had his ears sliced off in 1634.)

The absence of the strong Tudor hand was felt throughout England, and after a century of strong commitment to the nation's good, the court under James I had become a weak shambles of immorality and duplicity, where favorites replaced statesmen in the councils of the king. It was no less true at the intrigue-filled court of France, where Richelieu manipulated the strings controlling young Louis XIII. It was the age of the court favorite, and time for a new book on courtiership to appear.

11 · PLEASING PRINCES

Traicté de la Cour (Treatise of the Court) resembled Castiglione's book in only one respect: it, too, was written to guide a courtier. Otherwise, the attitudes of the two authors could not have been more dissimilar. The presumed author of *Traicté de la Cour* (1616), a courtier named Du Refuge, wrote in the spirit of Machiavelli, and while he favored the cultivation of social graces, he consistently adopted the realistic 17th-century approach to getting ahead amidst fierce competition, stripping away the idealistic pretense that courtesy books and chivalric writings had so long maintained. While it did not make attractive reading, it was sound advice for the courtier who sought success in a system somewhat similar to that in which the organization man moves today.

If principles kept getting in the way, a courtier's life was not advisable, said Du Refuge. However, there were undeniable advantages for the man with a strong stomach who could calculate his every move: "I do not deny but a courtier's life will be far more difficult to an honest man than to another, but withal I must affirm that the advantage of glory and content of mind that will arise from it will recompense the trouble of it."

Quite a few modern tycoons come to mind who fit the description of the prince Du Refuge's courtier sought to please:

With such a prince . . . a lover of ceremony and respect . . . a condemner of all men's opinions that differ from his own . . . one must always have his eyes and ears open, that he may readily understand and obey the first beck, without making any reply or delay, lest . . . the prince come to suspect him . . . as one that would seem to think himself wiser than he.

Figuratively the courtier was to be always on his knees "patient of injuries and no ways mindful of them, but after a wrong, so much the more officious."

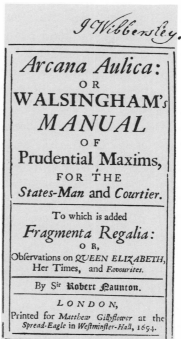

There were many routes to a prince's favor. A circuitous one, but perhaps the most direct in the end, was through someone already close to the prince—an approach requiring ingenuity, a talent for showering an April rain of flattery on the viable seeds of human vanity, and, most of all, great patience.

> You must note by the way that access to the great ones is not suddenly obtained, we must by degrees gain that; and to this end, all that have any interest in him whether they be strangers or domestics, even the dependents of these (according to their usefulness)—are to be won by you.

Some years after its first English translation, *Treatise of the Court* reappeared with a new title, *Arcana Aulica,* or *Walsingham's Manual of Prudential Maxims for the Statesman and Courtier.* This title was as sly as the machinations recommended to the courtier. The publisher, by omitting Walsingham's first name, implied that it was the work of the powerful Elizabethan statesman Sir Francis Walsingham, though the author was really a relatively obscure contemporary Walsingham named Edward. The new edition was apparently issued as anti-Royalist propaganda, for at that particular moment Cromwell was running England. But when courts and courtiers returned, Du Refuge's work with its own title continued to be popular well into the 18th century. Such prominent latter-day courtiers as Lord Chesterfield borrowed liberally from its pages.

Meanwhile other new works for the courtier had followed *Treatise of the Court,* most of them originating in France, which now was assuming the role of conduct arbiter to Europe. One author, Nicholas Faret, compiled a work in 1630 called *L'Honneste Homme ou L'Art de Plaire a la Court* (The Honest Man, or The Art of Pleasing at Court), a contradictory title since Du Refuge had demonstrated that the two were incompatible. Faret offered nothing new and had, in fact, combined portions of Castiglione with bits and pieces of Du Refuge's book. Thus the honest courtier could follow Castiglione, but if he wanted to succeed he could switch to Du Refuge, all in one volume. The Faret book received an English translation in 1632.

Jacques de Callières, a Marshal of France, contributed a work in 1658 that dealt with French court manners, possibly based on the Marshal's own firsthand experience. It was translated into English in 1675 as *The Courtiers Calling.* Some of the Marshal's observations have the ring of ancient Ptahhotep's maxims. Where the good Egyptian advised his readers to please a great man by amusing him and laughing at his jokes, Callières told the courtier to share his master's games and, whenever possible, give him the pleasure of winning. Callières didn't endorse blatant flattery, but he was all for such subtle tributes as praising what the prince liked. To his mind a courtier's most valuable asset was an amiable disposition. Few people failed to lower their guard in the face of amiability; thus it had the added virtue of disarming even enemies at court, making it easier to flush them out. Once flushed out, the Marshal gave them no quarter—enemies were to be ruined. He agreed that this might sound unchristian, but, after all, we could not be asked to love our enemies to our own destruction. His courtier was to be tough, practical, and with it all, elegantly mannered. Manners became more elegant as courtiers became more cynical.

12 · COUTH FRENCH; UNCOUTH ENGLISH

A royal court is in a sense the family living room of a nation; the conduct prevailing there influences subjects in the same way that parental conduct influences the behavior of children. When Louis XIV insisted that the manners of his retinue be as exquisite as the food at his table, and himself set the example, the influence of his court reached far beyond the châteaux of his immediate circle, into the bourgeois homes of France—and eventually into other lands. Elegant manners, like elegant food, became the supremacy of the French.

Louis XIV was following the example set for him in a court under the influence of Italian elegance since the mid-16th-century days of Catherine de' Medici—a court whose social authority Richelieu and Mazarin had made absolute because of the power they had preserved for the crown.

By the time Louis XIV's reign was established, France had become the acknowledged headquarters of 17th-century *civilité*, and the natural source of a 17th-century manners book that added elegant touches to the simple rules of good conduct offered by such previous authorities as della Casa in *Il Galateo*. Those behavior rules were now too simple to meet the demands of a more sophisticated society in which courtiers were openly counseled to machinate, but to do it as surreptitiously as possible, and to conduct their amorous indiscretions with the same caution. For the latter, Louis XIV himself set the example, taking care never to publicly acknowledge his mistresses by any word or gesture. Manners and outward decorum were everything—the yardstick by which the king, and his followers, measured human worth.

The newer rules of decorum were defined in *Nouveau Traicté de la Civilité (The Rules of Civility)* (1670), attributed to Antoine de Courtin, a first step toward later etiquette books. The author ex-

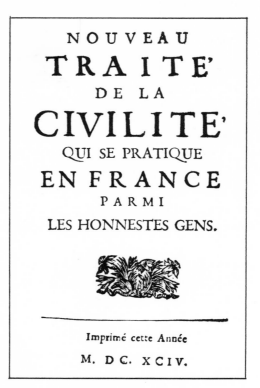

Title page, *Traité de la Civilité,* 1694 edition.

plained that his treatise on civilities had not been intended for publication: "It was only an answer to a gentleman of Provence . . . who begged some few precepts of Civility for his son come newly from the Academy and designed for the Court." Therefore, it would seem that knowledge of these new refinements was as yet confined to a select inner circle, probably the court and the French aristocracy. Those without firsthand contact with it were not familiar with the newer nuances of polite conduct. As later etiquette authorities would do, Courtin decided to share the ways of the aristocracy with the emerging bourgeoisie.

The book was concerned with such precise details as how to fold note paper, and the correct way to help oneself to olives—"To be taken out of the dish with a spoon, and not the fork, which mistake I have seen the occasion of very good laughter." Greater delicacy was evident in the language: "Be as hungry as we may, we must not gormondize," and in the demands upon the diner: "We are to wipe our spoon every time we put it into the (main) dish, some people being so delicate they will not eat after a man has taken with his spoon and not wiped it."

It was bad manners to display a finicky appetite and to say, "I eat no rabit. . . . I cannot endure pepper, nutmeg, or onyon." "Those kind of repugnancies are to be concealed," said the author sternly, explaining that the diner need not eat what offended him, but he was not to decline anything served him, and to be silent and unobtrusive about the matter.

In earlier times classes had been broken down into the simple divisions of superiors, equals and inferiors; a much more subtle gradation was now evident in *Rules of Civility,* which steered its reader to the proper salutation for a count, marquis or duke, and warned that it was rude to inquire after a man's spouse as his "wife." If he were an important man, his wife was to be referred to by the important man's full title, as for example, "How is Madame la Présidente?" There were even degrees of condescension proper for addressing chambermaid, parlormaid, and kitchen helper.

Medieval undertones continued to be evident. Courtin warned, "Never turn your back on people of quality." This applied particularly when traveling in coaches, when the lesser folk were never to take a seat that would present them rearwards to higher personages in the carriage.

Civility called for gracious hospitality to all, but in the case of a superior arriving for a visit, the host was to drop everything and dash out to greet the visitor before he dismounted from his coach or steed. And there was to be nothing casual about the host's attire at this moment of greeting: "Have either our cloak upon our shoulders, our sword by our side, or both when we receive him, it being indecorous for a gentleman to appear without either."

However, Courtin felt that the ceremonious visit (obviously one of the oldest of established customs) was getting a bit out of hand and decried it as had Guazzo a century earlier, complaining of "the extravagances of certain people who consume the greatest part of their lives in visiting others, to oblige them to a return." Such antics were not "for a person who knows how to employ his time," though there were certain "indispensable occasions which we cannot omit."

La civilité de la table.
La Vie Privée D'Autrefois; Le Repas, 1889.

Courtin's list of these would be the same today: congratulations, condolence, and inquiries after an ill person's health. And being practical, Courtin also advised his reader, "A great man is to be visited often, and his health to be inquired after, if for no other end than to preserve ourselves in his favor."

Nothing could halt the growing importance of the ceremonious visit as a means to social and personal advancement, and about this time calling cards seem to have been introduced in France, to be left in case a host was absent. These earliest calling cards were decorated with garlands, verses and the visitor's name and were apparently similar to greeting cards used today.

In the concluding chapter of his book Courtin surveyed the changing pattern of manners and called to his reader's attention some customs that had been acceptable "not long since," and were now sternly proscribed. Where it had once been excusable to hawk or spit, provided the offensive matter was ground into the dirt, such a practice was now "intolerable." Once it had been acceptable to dip bread into a sauce, and ill-bred only if the bread had been gnawed beforehand—now, *all* sauce dipping was bad manners. And it was no longer permissible to openly pull something unswallowable from the mouth, though this had once been permissible if done "dexterously." The same fate would probably befall many of the customs he advanced as civilities: "No question but that time will have the same influence upon our present, as it has had upon former proceedings," Courtin observed philosophically.

Though the English promptly translated Courtin's *Rules of Civility* in 1671, their manners lagged far behind those of the French, in spite of their prolonged exposure to French ways and French influence during the reign of Charles I's French queen, Henrietta Marie, and later during that of her son, Charles II, upon his return from French exile.

The "parental" influence of the English court had been reduced by defiance of the crown and the turbulence of the 17th century when rival factions, like parents with opposing natures, wrangled over the behavior of the English. While Puritans tried to pull them toward rigid austerity, the Royalists, a good many of them at any rate, tugged in the opposite direction.

Natural English stubbornness also played a part in their open resistance to all French cultural influences, from kitchen to parlor. And in the end Charles II proved himself more an Englishman than blood kin to Louis XIV in the coarse behavior that he adopted and that was followed by his court.

Not that English manners had ever been very elegant, as we have seen. The upper class still swore lustily, and ribald language filled the air at all aristocratic gatherings.

The repeated drinking of "healths" at social functions literally imposed drunkenness on the upper classes. Bishop Burnet, who dared publicly reprove Charles II, complained that the honor of house and host seemed at stake if a guest left it sober. The Restoration poet Sir Charles Sedley defecated into the street from a balcony while drunk and thus made history of a sort by establishing what is apparently the first recorded case of indecent exposure as a common-law offense. Upon receiving a lenient sentence of one week in jail and a fine of "2000 marks," Sedley declared he believed himself to be "the first man that paid for shiting."

About this time "healths" also became known as "toasts," derived from the custom of placing a toasted apple or slice of bread in hot ale or sack (or the wassail bowl). One day at Bath, a celebrated beauty was in the waters, damply receiving attentions and "healths" from her admirers, as was the custom. One wit filled his glass from the water in which she stood and drank her health to the company.

CHAP. VI.

Some more Examples gives; of making Water,
Of Vomiting, and other goodly Matter.

WHEN Guefts on Supper too much Time
　　　　　　　　　　　　　　[beftow,
　　Their Urine preffes for a Vent below;
Some Men indeed, whom Shame can overpow'r,
By Force will keep it in a tedious Hour;
Imprudent Wretches! prodigal of Health,
They diffipate their fole intrinfick Wealth.
O Friend! fuch foolifh Modefty forbear;
May Length of Days become your greateft Care!
Get up, tho' in the Middle of a Feaft,
And let your loaded Bladder be releas'd :✳

　　　　　　　　　　　　What-

---

* That the learned Reader may be thoroughly appriz'd how bene-
ficial a due Difcharge of Urine is, in fome Cafes, I have fubjoin'd
the following Aphorifm of the divine Ceam: 'Ο Κλοσιζιν ἐκ τεαγ-
γυεἰης ωλεὸς ὁπιγ/νεται, ἐκ ἰπἰα ἡμἐρησιν ἐπἰλλωταις, ἰυδ μὴ
συρεπἰ ὁπιφυριαιν ἀλισ τι ἰεριν ρυἰη. Moreover the celebrated Dr.
Baynard tells us in his Hiftory of Cold Baths, that a Strangury, with
all its terrible Confequences, will not unfrequently fupervene if we
retain our Urine too long.

Whatever Man obftructs you while you rife,
Bid him remove, tho' noble, grave, and wife.

　Or rather, as you keep your Seat, contrive
To let the Current of your Water drive;
Till rowling onward with lafcivious Pride,
All o'er the Room the fweet Meanders glide.
Severely rigid, and by much too nice,
Are thofe that deem Rufticity a Vice;
Learn by a Pattern that the Deed is juft,
Or, if you trefpafs, you are not the firft.

　To an illuftrious Feaft there fally'd forth
A bidden Gueft, of no ignoble Birth:
In royal Luxury were all Things plac'd,
And with ambrofial Fare the Tables grac'd.
They took their Seats, a Woman and a Man;
And foon the hungry Combatants began

R 3　　　　　　　To

From the 1739 edition of Grobianus.

Another, tipsy but not to be outdone, declared that while the beverage did not appeal to him, he would have the "toast."

Gambling, possibly the most popular English pastime, ran a close second to drinking as an upper-class vice. Temporarily curtailed under the Commonwealth when strict punishments penalized all betting, from cards and dice to shovelboard, the gates were again swung open when Charles II encouraged public lotteries.

Still there were attempts to hold the line on decorum to which even Charles gave his approval, though it was only a signature and not an act of faith. A handful of his subjects managed to have him sign "An Act for the Better Observation of the Lord's Day, Commonly Called Sunday," which declared drinking, gambling, swearing and whoring illegal on that day. The act was on the books, but action lagged until sedate William III (and Mary) reached the

English throne in 1689, William gave his blessing to the Society
for the Reformation of Manners, organized in 1692 by a handful
of lay members of the Church of England, and issued an order to
the bishops of the land to preach against "the keeping of courtesans,
swearing, and gambling," and to enforce the ecclesiastical laws.
The Society members were simply informers—self-appointed spies
who lurked in the streets, taverns, and coffeehouses and turned
over the names of offenders to be punished.

By 1699 the Society claimed to have obtained thousands of con-
victions for "Cursing, drunkenness, and profanation of the Lord's
Day." But to judge from the continued decline in public conduct
their efforts were as effective as a cannonade of soap bubbles. As a
universal model, the gentleman was temporarily in the background,
considered by many to be out of step with his times if he held
strictly to the old courtesy rules. There may have been a tendency
to confuse "gentleman" with "Puritan." Puritanism was still at
work, hoping to recapture the brief, sober intermission England had
known during Cromwell's rule. However, eleven years of the severe
propriety displayed at the seat of power had evidently been enough
for most Englishmen, to judge from their response to the Restoration, and the influence of Charles II's court on English manners.
The English preferred Charles's lusty ways to roundhead propriety.

But despite the vulgarity and lack of restraint, there was a
natural, honest quality to English manners and considerable moral
strength underneath the coarseness. And it would be false to ascribe
unlicensed behavior to all Englishmen at this time. Many clung
to decent behavior as earnestly as they rejected those manners they
considered affected. When the English eventually refined their
behavior, many had learned to juggle the demands of ceremony
with much of the genuine courtesy implicit in the ideal of a gentleman, though this was not accomplished for nearly a century.
Meanwhile, in the chaotic factionalism of the 17th century many
Englishmen, from aristocrats to middle class, were more concerned
with guiding youth into future security than into mastering the
rules of ceremony. Parental guidance was a duty mentioned by almost all conduct books. The obligation led, in turn, to a special
type of conduct book that appeared in England in the 17th century.

17th-century woodcut illustration.

13 · CUNNING GARDENERS

Those who would rear a child successfully should be "wise and cunning gardeners," wrote Thomas Elyot in the days of Henry VIII. By the beginning of the 17th century many parents were gardening in earnest, judging by the numerous books of parental advice that appeared, indicating a real interest in this fertile soil.

Many of these early works were by distinguished parents for their own children and had not originally been written to be published; consequently they were more direct in what they had to say. What really set these parental writings apart was the way in which they combined earlier courtesy ideals with the realistic attitudes necessary in the more sophisticated society that was developing. While they did not openly advocate cunning and scheming, still a good many of them advised their young readers to learn how to turn—if necessary to forcibly twist—situations to their advantage. Certainly there had always been ambitious men who fawned on the powerful and sought to ingratiate themselves, but such behavior had never been held up to *young* eyes as a model. Not until the 17th century.

This is not to say that all books of parental advice fell into this pattern. However, it is clear that many of them did. And essentially, all of them strove to prepare youth for the practical requirements of life.

The most illustrious of these parental writers was James I of England, whose *Basilikon Doron; or His Majesty's Instructions to his dearest Sonne, Henry the Prince,* was published in 1604, just after James ascended the throne of England. James had written it in 1599 when he was ruler of Scotland and the young prince five years old, meaning it to be an intimate communication. However, his accession to the English throne made it a timely document to set before his suspicious new subjects since it expressed some comforting views on the conduct of royalty. Englishmen could breathe easier when they read James's idealistic professions on the duties and responsibilities of a king. Any royal sin was so serious that it could cause "the whole multitude to be guilty of same." A ruler, said James, must remember always, "Glistering worldlie glory of kings is given them by God."

Unhappily young Henry died in 1612 at eighteen, still too young to have put much of his father's good counsel to work. And later events proved that James did not practice his own precepts. His court became one of the least virtuous in England's history despite his advice to his son: "Make court and companie to bee a pattern of godliness and all honest vertues."

Some of the golden nuggets of advice dealt with such daily and commonplace matters as table conduct and personal attire. The young prince was to eat "Neither uncivill like a gross Cynicke, nor affectedlie, like a daintie dame, but in a manlie, round and honest fashion." (With his hands, James probably meant.)

Young Henry was told not to clothe himself "Sluggishly, like a country clowne, nor over lightly like a candy soldier or a vaine young courtier, nor yet over gravely like a minister, but proper, cleanly . . . keeping your clothes in middle forme." Too bad James didn't take his own advice: his appearance is reputed to have been as oafish as that of any "country clowne."

Later on in *Basilikon Doron* he unburdened himself of some views on commerce.

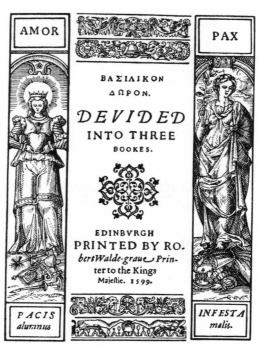

ΒΑΣΙΛΙΚΟΝ
ΔΩΡΟΝ.

DEVIDED
INTO THREE
BOOKES.

EDINBVRGH
PRINTED BY RO.
bertWalde-graue Prin-
ter to the Kings
Majeſtie. 1599.

AMOR

PAX

PACIS
alumnus

INFESTA
malis.

Title page of *Basilikon Doron,* privately printed for James I
in 1599. 19th-century facsimile edition.

The merchantes think . . . it their lawful gaine and trade to
enrich them selves upon the losse of all the rest of the people.
They transport from us things necessarie, bring back sometimes
unnecessary things, and at other times nothing at all. They buy
for us the worst wares, and sell them at the dearest prices. . . .
They are also the special cause of the corruption of the coyne,
transporting all our own and bringing in forraine, upon what
price they please to set on it.

James had his solutions for these problems and he passed them
on to young Henry for his future consideration.

Permit and allure forraine merchantes to trade here, so shall ye
have the best and best cheape wares, not buying them at third
hand. And set every year downe a certain price of all things; considering first how it is in other countries, and the price being set
reasonably down, if the merchants will not bring them home on
the price, cry forrainers free to bring them.

As for "coyne," "Make your money of fine gold and silver," said
James. That was excellent parental advice for a future king.

At about this time some sensible parental advice was also offered by William Shakespeare in Hamlet—Polonius bidding goodbye to his son Laertes. Polonius is supposed to have been modeled after Queen Elizabeth's great chancellor, William Cecil Lord Burghley, who by this time was dead—but his paternal advice to his own son, Robert Cecil, *Certain Precepts Left by a Father to His Son,* had been published in 1615, enabling Shakespeare to go right to the source for his inspiration.

It is doubtful that Lord Burghley ever meant his private views to be published. They were far shrewder than Shakespeare presented them, and they included How to choose a wife (not a poor one, "Because a man can buy nothing in the market without money"); When to marry off daughters ("Betimes, lest they marry themselves"); and a precept that every successful politician knows: win friends in all walks of life, but especially among inferiors because this "Gains a good report, which once got is easily kept."

Some friends might turn out to be mere "glow-worms, parasites, and sycophants." These he was advised to "shake off." The most useful friend was a "great man" and Burghley made quite a point of this "Be sure to keep some great man thy friend. . . . Compliment him often with many small gifts . . . and if thou hast cause to bestow any great gratuity, let it be something which may daily be in sight."

Reversing his father's advice, Robert Cecil bestowed, rather than received, the benefits of his friendship with a great man. He was instrumental in securing for James I the throne of England. A suitable match with a baron's daughter produced a son and daughter for Robert Cecil, but he failed to instill in his own son the drive to greatness his father had instilled in him. He left behind no book of parental advice.

Sir Walter Raleigh also left a legacy of advice, *Instructions To His Son And To Posteritie,* published in 1632, long after he came to an end under the headsman's ax. One Instruction wisely urged his son to "Remember the divine saying: *he that keepeth his mouth keepeth his life.*" But many of his remarks seem extremely cautious for one so dashing and adventuresome. And somehow Raleigh doesn't quite register as a timid drinker. Yet he advised his son, "Take especial care that thou delight not in wine; for there never was any man that came to honor or preferment that loved it." Perhaps Raleigh's long imprisonment in the Tower had changed him.

Many high-born fathers were tossed into the Tower to await the ax during the turbulent Stuart century, and the waiting period seemed to act as a catalyst for parental advice. In 1641 Sir Thomas Wentworth, Earl of Strafford, left a book-size letter of parting advice to his son, which suggested none of the tyranny and stubbornness Strafford had displayed in ruling the Irish, nor his resourcefulness and ambition at the court of Charles I. Strafford's parting words were as anemic as Raleigh's. He urged his son to devote himself to knowledge, virtue, and religion, "And not to seek revenge for the wrongs done to his father."

Another who left his head in the Tower, along with a publishable statement to guide his children's conduct, was Sir Henry Slingsby, a Royalist supporter. He composed *A Father's Legacy* in 1658, just before his death, urging his children to lead a quiet life if they would know security.

The Duke of Argyll, head of the Campbell clan, met a similar fate and wrote *Instructions to a Son* while waiting for the unhappy event. The book was published later that year (1661), with an introductory verse:

> Lo here, the Genius of the great Argyle
> Whose Politicks and Ethicks in one pyle
> Like Anchor buoys, appear to teach thee Wit
> To shun those rocks on which himself was split.

It proved of no value to Argyll's son, who was himself beheaded in 1685 for political activities.

So many heads were lopped off by both factions during those tumultuous years that William Tipping wrote *The Father's Counsel* (1643): *Certain useful directions for all young persons, especially older brothers, whose portion it may be, in these perilous daies, to be left in a fatherlesse or friendlesse condition.*

All parental advice was not necessarily written by fathers on the way to the block—or by fathers only, for that matter. Such books as *A Mother's Blessing* by Dorothy Leigh (1616) and *The Mother's Legacie to Her Unborn Child* by Elizabeth Joceline (1624) were two popular works by women. They dealt chiefly in spiritual advice.

One prominent father who managed to keep his head was Sir Francis Osborne. His *Advice to a Son* (1656) is significant for its open cynicism, and perhaps his cynicism helped him to survive. Lord Chesterfield, who is usually considered the most cynical of parental advisors, was merely a lengthened shadow of Osborne.

Osborne deliberately prepared his son for a world of greed and perfidy where, in his view, even hunting was a dangerous sport because an enemy could shoot you and claim it to be an accident. He had great respect for bribes: "A small drop of silver will carry you more safe than a sword," said Osborne.

He approved of cultivating influential people for personal profit and saw no sin in serving a man who had risen to power through a crime. Conscience, that built-in monitor, was best regulated as each occasion warranted. "Conscience must serve our own honest, safe, and wholesome conveniences." And this meant putting one's own safety first: "In seeking to save another beware of drowning yourself," he warned.

Hardheaded formulas for maneuvering through life were replacing the biblical quotations that had formerly filled the pages of courtesy books. These were now rarely used unless they fitted practical needs; there was the good book itself, in a new authorized version, for those who wished to hear directly from the Bible. The most familiar piece of biblical advice still retained in 17th-century behavior books for youth was on surety. Lord Burghley restated it in his own words, and Shakespeare in turn later paraphrased Burghley: "Neither a borrower, nor a lender be."

Parental books scarcely touched on social behavior. Della Casa's *Il Galateo* remained the best authority for young people until about 1640, when Sir Francis Hawkins translated a French work compiled c. 1595 at the Jesuit College of La Flèche—*Youth's Behaviour, or Decency in Conversation Among Men* (using "conversation" in Guazzo's broader sense of human association). It was really an altered version of *Il Galateo* with additions from Erasmus' earlier rules of civil behavior. Civility books (and later, etiquette books) were monotonously alike; often the only change was the title.

Youth's Behaviour is of special interest because evidently it served as a manners guide for young George Washington more than a hundred years later. Young George, fifteen at the time, prepared a personal notebook, titled it *True Happiness, or Rules of Civility,* and filled it with maxims on moral and social conduct, many of them copied directly from *Youth's Behaviour.*

However, if these were the rules of politeness among the upper class, imagine the behavior of the lower!

> Spit not in the fire . . . nor set your Feet upon the Fire, especially if there be meat before it.
>
> Kill no Vermin as Fleas, lice, ticks, etc., in the sight of others.
>
> Cleanse not your teeth with the table cloth, napkin or knife. If others do it, let it be done with a tooth pick.

Youths of the middle class received a "father's" counsel from Caleb Trenchfield in *A Cap of Grey Hairs for a Green Head, The Father's Counsel to his Son, an Apprentice in London* (1688). Trenchfield felt that practical advice was more valuable than talk about manners; accordingly he warned his reader of the evils of bad company, especially bad women, and most especially of maidservants, who were most dangerous of all.

If the young man was personable he was encouraged to reach higher, and one way was to master dancing. This would make him more desirable in social gatherings. Trenchfield also recommended fencing, probably for the youth's own protection. Horsemanship would prove too expensive for a young apprentice, so why waste time on it? As for a wife some day in the future, Trenchfield took up this matter, as a responsible "parent" should. Choose a pretty one, he advised. This was contrary to most advice given young men of the upper class, who were told to look aside when beauty was presented, and instead to carefully consider the finances and family background of their intended bride. Trenchfield reasoned otherwise for his middle class reader. If a daughter resulted from the union and she inherited her mother's good looks, she would be easy to marry off, and possibly advantageously. It never occurred to Trenchfield that his apprentice reader might be a homely fellow with the bone structure of a dray horse, and that the daughter might favor *him.* Trenchfield struck a delightfully ingenuous note amid the cynicism of his times.

"Matrimony—a man loaded with mischief." An old English
tavern sign presents a wife as baggage.
From *Caricature and Comic Art* by James Parton, 1877.

14 · WOMEN, THE BAGGAGE OF LIFE

To be a gentleman *and* a husband—ah, that could be a rub—
though all odds were seemingly stacked in favor of the 17th-cen-
tury husband. There was St. Paul's gospel: "Ye wives, be in sub-
jection to your own husbands," reiterated and paraphrased in numerous courtesy books and marriage manuals offering advice on how
to make marriage bearable. But wives, it seems, were not always
willing to follow Paul's command, to judge from the many complaints in these same manuals citing the perils of matrimony more
frequently than its pleasures. Wives, and women in general, were
looked upon as an exasperating lot, well and briskly summarized by
the poet Sir John Suckling, in the early 1600s:

> Women are the baggage of life; they are
> Troublesome and hinder us in the great march
> And yet we cannot be without 'em.

The tendency in Italy and France had always been to treat marriage as a practical institution devoted solely to continuing the

blood line through the propagation of heirs, while maintaining and increasing family estates. Love and romance were as nonessential to marriage as they had been in the days of chivalry; a man was expected to attend to such needs outside of matrimony. His wife did likewise, if not always so openly. But not so in England. There, extramarital supplements were frowned upon. A *gentleman,* said the courtesy books, should satisfy all his requirements, romantic and otherwise, within the boundaries of marriage. For an all-purpose wife a man certainly needed the right kind and most 17th-century courtesy books stood ready to help him make a wise choice and to live in harmony with her. Many books devoted themselves exclusively to the problem, with such titles as *A Discourse of Marriage and Wiving* (1615); *a Happy Husband* (1619); *A Bridebush* (1623); and *Crown Conjugal* (1623), to name a few and to show in which direction the wind blew in the early 17th century.

All men longed for that rare find, a compliant wife. Unfortunately she was not only rare, but difficult to discern, "For the devil can transform himself into an angel of light," warned Alexander Niccholes, whose book, *A Discourse of Marriage and Wiving: . . . How to choose a good wife from a bad,* was one of the first to offer a working guide for a man seeking a proper mate. He cited the important features to look for in a sound wife, and at times his book read like a guide for choosing sound horseflesh. At best, and even with careful study of his manual, choosing was a chancy thing, Niccholes warned, for there was the unpredictable transformation that could come over even the genuine angel. This bonafide creature might be the very paragon St. Paul specified—as patient as Griselda, as modest as Lucrece, but as yet untried by the fires of temptation. Suppose, said Niccholes, a man had chosen "A country damsel . . . who can scarce think of marriage but that she blushes to think what shame it is to lie with a man." Transplant this paragon of modesty from her rustic surroundings to the city with its seductive influences, and the upright wife might become unexpectedly horizontal: "Not blush to do unlawfully, which before she was bashful to think on lawfully."

The important thing was for a gentleman to keep his eyes open, his pulse under control, and to take note of certain infallible warn-

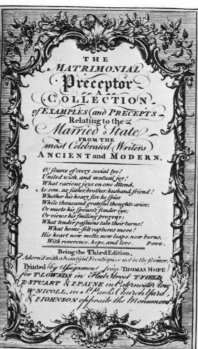

An 18th-century collection of writings on the joys and tribulations of marriage.

ing signs. Taking his cue from Ecclesiasticus, Niccholes warned against "wandering eyes or a coquettish gait" and pronounced a caveat: "An honest woman dwells at the sign of an honest countenance."

The man foolish enough to be dazzled by beauty had only himself to blame if he wound up a cuckold. A beautiful wife would expose him to "every carnal eye. Every goatish disposition shall level to throw open thy inclosures . . . thy wife shall be harder to keep than the garden of the Hesperides." Whereas, said Niccholes, the man who used his head, "And a fit wife to himself doth wed . . . keeps long a quiet bed."

In a chapter headed "Whether it be Best to Marry a Widow or a Maid," Niccholes declared that most widows sought "lust and ease, more than affection or love." Experienced in the ways of the connubial bed and eager to resume what had long been denied them, they would prove "as insatiate as the sea, or rather the grave," to which new husbands might soon be carried because of the lusty demands of an experienced wife. "At the decease of their first husbands they learn commonly the tricks to turn over a second or third." To summarize them, Widows were "navigable without difficulty, more passable than Virginia, and lie at an easier road." But the risks outweighed the pleasures of the voyage.

Despite the tone of these writings, seemingly indicating some element of free choice, marriages were rarely founded on anything but practical considerations. Marriage for love was a luxury only the poor could afford. For the gentry it was a serious, unromantic business arrangement, usually arrived at by the parents of both parties and designed to consolidate or perpetuate family fortunes, and based on such mutual interests as politics or religion, both of which could have great bearing on family fortunes in 17th-century England. Prosperous merchants and farmers with ample fortune but no status as gentry and no armorial bearings could often realize their own social ambitions by dowering their daughters into marriage with a second son of a titled or at least crested family. The law of primogeniture made it necessary for many younger sons to seek such marriages for their own financial security. While the marriage did not alter the status of the bride's father, at least he had the pleasure of knowing that his grandchildren would be gentry.

Often marriages were arranged without consulting the young couple, and not infrequently while they were still children. However, by English law the marriage could not take place until the bride was at least twelve and the groom fourteen. At this tender age many couples were legally united, though their actual residence together might be postponed a few years. Most marriages, when finally solemnized, were between consenting parties. Only the most flint-hearted parents would push a young daughter into a marriage she detested. There were some of these, it is true, and most courtesy books warned a man against embarking on such an alliance.

When it came to a choice of a wife, Richard Braithwaite set himself up as an expert—for that matter, an expert in the entire field of marital counseling. His several books on the subject bore such sentimental titles as *Ar't Asleepe Husband? A Boulster Lec-*

A BOVLSTER LECTVRE.

This wife a wondrous racket meanes to keepe,
While th'Husband seemes to sleepe but does not sleepe:
But she might full as well her Lecture smother,
For ent'ring one Eare, it goes out at t'other.

From *Humour, Wit and Satire of the 17th Century* by John Ashton, 1883.

ture; *A Ladies Love Lecture;* and *The Turtle's Triumph.* His approach to marriage was the same in all his books—love, understanding and mutual respect. His basic advice to a gentleman was: "Ground your choice on love. What miseries have ensued on *forced marriages* there is no age may record." Nevertheless, he also took a practical view of the matter of dowry: "If she be a good wife, a good Portion make her no worse; and if an ill one, shee had need of a Portion to make her better."

If the rich wife came from a prominent family, well and good, provided the husband's family tree sported similar foliage. "Match with your equal," Braithwaite warned, adding that the worst examples of marital discord were those where "the wife will not sticke [hesitate] to twit her husband with her parentage and brave him with repetition of her descent."

In most marriages the dowry was all-important, and heaven help the unfortunate lass of good birth but limited fortune. At best she could only hope for a mate much inferior to herself. Many ended as spinsters, finding genteel employment as companions or nursery governesses. In France a pretty face might capture a rich lover and from such a liaison future financial security might result, but the lot of a mistress in England usually ended dismally. "Keeping," while practiced in England, was widely regarded as a sinful irregularity. There was little chance of landing a desirable husband solely because of a pretty face; warnings against such an error continued to be dinned into gentlemen long after Alexander Niccholes provided his acerbic guide to selecting a mate.

Once married, the usual problems of adjustment presented themselves, but there was no easy out via hasty divorce. Marriage, good or bad, was to be worked out somehow. Marriage counseling was offered by the Reverend William Whateley in *A Bride-bush* (1623), which the good reverend presented as "A direction for married persons, plainly describing the duties common to both, and peculiar to each of them, by performing of which, marriage shall prove a great help to such as now for want of performing them doe find it a little hell." In a second manual, *A Care-cloth* (1624), the Reverend Whateley offered "A treatise of the cumbers and troubles of marriage, intended to advise them that may, to shun them." For those who could not successfully shun such "cumbers" as a drunken husband or a sharp-tongued wife, there was unfortunately only one answer: "Well and patiently to beare them."

Most of the responsibility for bearing "cumbers" fell on wives, a burden which it seems they were beginning to bear with less docility toward the end of the 17th century. Richard Allestree, who had already provided *The Gentleman's Calling* (1660), along the lines of Peacham and Braithwaite, now called wives to order in *The Ladies Calling* (1674), though he used more conciliatory language than most of his contemporaries.

The Ladies Calling instructed females from virginity through widowhood, but devoted most of its space to the duties of wives to husbands, "First to his person; Secondly to his reputation; Thirdly to his fortune." For his person the word was *obedience,* "A word of very harsh sound in the ears of some wives," Allestree admitted, "but it is certainly the duty of all." Furthermore, there was no weaseling out of this duty on *any* grounds: "Whatever is the duty to the husband is equally so, be he good or ill." However, Allestree suggested, if *love* was regarded as the first duty, affection

THE

Ladies Calling.

IN

TWO PARTS·

By the AUTHOR of the *Whole Duty of Man*: The *Caufes* of the *Decay* of *Chriftian Piety*, and The *Gentleman's Calling*.

Favor is deceitful, and Beauty is vain: but a *Woman that feareth the Lord, she shall be praised.* Prov. 31. 30.

OXFORD, Printed at the *THEATRE*.

M. DC. LXXIII.

Frontispiece and title page, *The Ladies Calling* by Richard Allestree, 1673.

would ease all the other duties of marriage and "make the yoke fit so lightly that it rather pleases than galls."

Certain "fashionable maxims"—particularly the vogue for mixing couples at social functions—were a threat to marital stability. "'Tis pronounced a piece of ill breeding, a sign of a country gentleman, to see a man go abroad with his own wife," he complained, damning this fashion as an ill-conceived design "to make men and their wives the greatest strangers to each other."

Of her husband's reputation a wife was to be "extremely tender." She was to make "All that is good in him as conspicuous, as public as can; setting his worth in the clearest light, but putting his infirmities in the shade." Even better than shade, said Allestree, "Cast a veil upon those infirmities to skreen them from the eyes of others";

for that matter, "from your own too." Nothing was to be gained by studiously contemplating a husband's shortcomings; besides, he was hers, "good or ill."

The duty to a husband's fortune was not as easily defined. As Allestree explained, the husband's fortune "is not ordinarily the wife's province. But where the husband thinks fit to make it so," she was to muster her best talents in preventing waste and defrauding, especially in that most likely place, the household. Not that the household was by any means her clear-cut province. However, "though the wife be not supreme," Allestree explained that she could operate with the "delegated authority" received from her husband.

Allestree complained that *both* husband and wife were often guilty of shirking their household responsibilities preferring the "Fashionable thing . . . for the Master to resign up his concerns to the Steward, and the Lady hers to the Governant." Allestree cautioned that "These officers serve themselves instead of those who employ them; raise fortunes on their patron's ruines, and divide the spoil of the family; the housekeeper pilfering within doors, and the bailiff plundering without."

What with calling the servants to prayer, supervising the children, seeing to it that the servants kept hands off the family stores, and studying her husband's whims, a wife had her day cut out for her and little time to get into mischief. "I have now run through the several obligations consequent to the married state," said Allestree. "If they were all duly attended to, Ladies need not be much at a loss how to entertain themselves, nor run abroad in Romantick quest after forreign divertisements, when they have such a variety of engagements at home."

Many of Allestree's comments document the social life and fashions of the Restoration. "Such a degenerous age do we now live in, that everything seems inverted, even sexes; whilst men fall to the effeminacy and niceness of women, women take up the confidence and boldness of men." The passing of the blush told a lot, in his opinion. "Formerly considered the color of virtue, it is now accounted worse manners than those things that ought to occasion it." Women were not content merely to abandon blushing: "Some women think they have not made a sufficient escape from their sex till they have assumed the vices of men too." Swearing was one of these—"A sober modest dialect is now too effeminate for [women]." Drinking was another, and Allestree doubted that a woman who lost her sobriety could retain her chastity, since she was then "at the mercy of every assailant. . . . He that means to defend a fort must not abandon the outerworks, and she that will secure her chastity must not let it come too close to siege," he warned.

But worst of all was the alluring example this conduct set for innocent young women, who saw "the gay people of the world" acting in this way, accepted it as the fashion "and upon peril of that formidable calamity of being unfashionable, conform to it."

Lady Compton, a 17th-century noblewoman, was surely one of the "gay people" who angered Allestree, and it seems safe to conclude that she had not read his book when she penned her premarital list of demands to her future husband, the Earl of Northampton. Her letter began with a request for a generous cash allowance, and how she spent it was to be entirely her own affair. Then she itemized the retinue she expected to have attend her.

My sweet life [she began] . . . I will have three horses for my own saddle that none shall dare to lend or borrow. Also, I would have two gentlewomen, lest one should be sick. Also, believe me, it is an indecent thing for a gentlewoman to stand mumping alone when God hath blessed their lord and lady with a great estate. Also, when I ride a hunting or a hawking, or travel from one house to another, I will have them attending; so, for either of those said women, I must and will have for either of them a horse. Also, I will have six or eight gentlemen: and I will have two coaches, one lined with velvet for myself, with four very fair horses; and a coach for my women, lined with cloth and laced with gold, other-wise with scarlet and laced with silver, with four good horses. Also I would have two coachmen, one for my own coach, the other for my women. Also, at any time when I travel, I will be allowed not only caroches and spare horses for me and my women, but I will have such carriages as shall be fitting for all, orderly, not pestering my things with my women's, nor theirs with either chambermaids, nor with washmaids. Also for laundresses, when I travel, I will have them sent away before the carriages, to see all safe. And the chambermaids I will have go before, that the chamber may be ready, sweet and clean. Also, for that it is indecent to crowd up myself with my gentleman usher in my coach, I will have him to have a convenient horse to attend me, either in city or country. And I must have two footmen.

Nor would Lady Compton have had much use for the stern language addressed to wives by John Stevens in 1694 in *The Government of a Wife,* which Stevens translated from the c. 1660 Spanish work of Francisco de Mello. The book evidently aroused a storm of protest before its publication, for Stevens added a defensive foreword. "This book being yet a manuscript was slandered as too severe upon the woman . . . but [its] design was not to raise trouble and jealousy, but to shew the way to prevent them."

The way was as simple as keeping a baby out of mischief: watchful supervision. A wife safely padlocked behind the curtains of her home was not likely to get into any scrapes; and home was where *Government* proposed to keep her. In this the Puritan attitude conjoined neatly with that of the Spaniards.

Two rules of thumb for keeping a wife's virtue intact was passed along by *Government.* One: A wife should never attend balls, which "were invented so that men might encompass forbidden waists by the only means available." Two: She should not be present among her husband's male guests. "The husband who delights to have his wife among other men, takes pleasure that she should be admired and consequently merits the ill consequences that are likely to follow."

The husband should be like the sun, the wife a moon, said *Government.* "Whatever light she gives must be borrowed from him." This planetary balance was to be maintained at all odds, even if the wife possessed the superior fortune. Her money should be in her husband's hands. Money could be as lethal as henbane if entrusted to a woman, and it should be measured out to her in small quantities. Extravagant wives should not be permitted to handle the stuff at all. "They are like children and fools, who should have keepers," said *Government.*

Government of a Wife also offered a few asides to husbands on self-government, especially to those husbands "who suffer their affection to stray toward their maids." If the husband thought he could sneak in and out of a maid's room at night without having it known, he was mistaken. "The disorderly proceedings of the master is known to the Family," *Government* warned him. Worse still was the danger that "The maids finding themselves belov'd by their master, plot against their mistress." Husbands were advised to do their straying elsewhere and to learn from "Birds of prey [who] generally go far from home to find their Food. Why should men be less cautious and wary?"

Fidelity, it goes without saying, was expected of all wives. "Some women believe that because they are true to their marriage bed their husbands are obliged in all respects to bear with whatsoever they will impose upon them. This is a very gross mistake," said *Government.* "A husband is no way beholding to an honest woman for performing the duty she owes to God, to nature, and even to her own safety."

Husbands needed all the patience they could muster to govern a wife, for in many cases a good wife was as headstrong as a good horse or a valuable servant. "Each of them, sensible of their own value, follow their own will and not that of the master or owner." A husband was advised to choose a young wife for "Tender years are free from ill customs, because such as are there, having taken no root, are easily removed."

It was one thing to manage a wife once the halter was slipped over her neck, but acquiring her was the first order of business. As the 17th century neared its end, the method seemed to be changing. Courtship was becoming more of an accepted procedure, evident in such volumes as *Advice to Lovers* (1680), which offered "certain rules of behavior, shewing them how to demean themselves so as not to miscarry in the grand affair of love"; *The Academy of Complements* (1685), which promised "a new way of wooing" (with love letters); and *The Mysteries of Love and Eloquence* (1685), which concentrated on "the arts of wooing and complementing."

Courtship grew more cynical in the 18th century, and leaden tongues could learn to drip honey with help from *The Amorous Gallant's Tongue Tipp'd with Golden Expressions* (1741). The amorous gallant was sometimes bent only on dalliance; the lady on the receiving end would be well prepared if she had read *The Whole Duty of a Woman—An Infallible Guide to the Fair Sex* (1737), for which William Kendrick had lifted most of the text of Allestree's *The Ladies Calling*. Kendrick had updated his version to include warnings against just such golden tongues. "Women should remember that men who say extreme fine things, many times say them most for their own sakes. It is as safe to play with fire as to dally with gallantry," he warned. "The humble gallant, who is only admitted as a trophy, very often becomes the Conqueror . . . and from an admirer grows into a master, for so he may be called from the moment he is in possession."

Whether a gallant seeking a conquest or a suitor seeking a bride, mastery of the "baggage" was the ultimate goal once the lady had capitulated. But women grew more assertive as the 18th century unfolded. When Lyttleton penned his *Advice to a Lady,* in which his metric demands seemed far too repressive to Mary Wortley Montagu, she summarized his verses with the tart couplet:

> Be plain in dress and sober in your diet,
> In short, my deary, kiss me and be quiet.

And surely a woman's pen dashed off this verse (Anon.):

> . . . Let us scan
> The coward insults of that tyrant man,
> Self-prais'd and grasping at despotic pow'r,
> He looks on slav'ry as the female dow'r.

"Conversation at Midnight"
A view of his times by William Hogarth

PART THREE

Courtesy into Etiquette

A N
ACCOUNT
OF THE
PROGRESS
OF THE
Reformation of Manners,
I N
England, Scotland, and *Ireland,*

And other Parts of *Europe* and *America.*

With some Reasons and plain Directions for our hearty
and vigorous Prosecution of this Glorious Work.

In a Letter to a Friend.

To which is added,

The *Special Obligations* of MAGISTRATES,
to be diligent in the Execution of the *Penal-Laws*
against *Prophaneness* and *Debauchery,* for the Effect-
ing of a *National Reformation.*

The Twelfth Edition with considerable Additions.

L O N D O N,
Printed and Sold by *Joseph Downing* in *Bartholomew-Close*
near *West-Smithfield,* 1704.

A pamphlet issued in 1704.

15 · A QUEEN, TWO KINGS, AND A BEAU

IN THE 18TH CENTURY there began a profound alteration in manners. By the end of the century the basic ethics of polite behavior had been garnished over, almost beyond recognition, with the pretentious rules of etiquette. In large part this grew out of social, political and economic changes that had been gathering for a long time and now accelerated, creating a mobile society that was like a bed of disturbed embers, sending numerous sparks up the flue to the society above.

This upward draft, felt wherever the Enlightenment penetrated, was particularly pronounced in England. As a result, the 18th century there saw the beginnings of greater class distinction and social wariness than ever before

Little cause had existed for social vigilance when everybody knew his place and was reasonably content to remain in it. But now the social structure grew more intricately stratified as the upsurge from below increased steadily and the middle class expanded. "The excellent middle," Voltaire called it, comparing the English to their ale: "frothy at the top, dregs at the bottom, but in the middle excellent." As in any beaker of ale, the expanding middle sought to merge with the froth at the top.

The upper class struggled to prevent this and evolved a code of manners—regulations really—modeled on those that governed court life, but composed also of numerous private ceremonials observed in certain cliques and sets. Each ceremonial was an invisible bar against intruders, and by the end of the century these had been codified into the rules of etiquette.

The century began with the English as ill-behaved as ever, particularly those who comprised the froth, often indistinguishable from the dregs. Some hoped that when Queen Anne picked up the scepter of authority in 1702 she would improve English conduct by setting a queenly example of elegance and run a court the English could take pride in. But Anne was a disappointment. Her court was lusterless, her tastes as simple as a housewife's, and her preference for privacy so great that she refused to dine with the court as was the custom of most monarchs, and nervously gnawed at her fan when she held informal audiences. Conceivably, bearing seventeen children occupied some of her time and interest. But her moral, prim attitudes would have been better suited to the end of the century than they were to its beginning, and she had little to offer a nation that still hankered after a lighthearted monarch.

Officially Anne did little to further decorum in England. However, at the request of the Society for the Reformation of Manners, now larger than ever and reinforced by a few additional reform groups, she issued a proclamation calling for stricter observance of the acts already on the books. Failure to do so would mean answering to "Almighty God, and upon pain of Our highest displeasure." God's displeasure was a meaningless threat in light of the widespread irreverence. Much of this irreverence, and some of the rude behavior, was traceable to the continuing feud between contending religious interests, as well as to the lax attitude of the Church of England. Religion was treated with almost airy disregard and even the queen had prayers read to her while she dressed, though her chaplain refused to mumble them if her dressing-room door was closed, complaining, "I will not whistle the word of God through a keyhole."

To please the reformers, Anne forbade the sale of even a cup of tea or chocolate on Sunday, lest stronger stuff be sold in seemingly innocent containers. But such irreverent acts as knitting in church went unchallenged except by anonymous letter writers, one of whom complained to the press that it was done "in the immediate presence of both God and her Majesty, who were affronted together! !"

If Anne's court was thought dull, even greater disappointment was in store when George I took over. He, too, disliked court life.

A satirical comment on lack of decorum in church.
William Hogarth, 1736.

He had no grace or social charm and no taste for the niceties displayed across the Channel in the French court. Even in the matter of choosing a mistress, his choice ran to lumpy German ladies whose ineptness made even his subjects blush. A more sophisticated example was set by his son, later to become George II, who held his own court in another palace, with attractive English mistresses. The friendship between his flexible wife, Caroline, and his mistresses now gave "keeping" public approval. The kept mistress was an open feature of upper-class English society in the 18th century and many of the mistresses were callously abandoned when their lovers tired of them. London was crowded with such unfortunate women, who had no means of support and certainly no matrimonial prospects. In an article "Matrimony and Keeping Compared," the popular 18th-century *Gazetteer* urged Englishmen to abandon "keeping" because of "the fatal influence such an example may naturally have on the morals of youth; for how should that appear a shame to them, which they see openly practised, perhaps by their fathers, uncles, or master . . . ?"

The example set for morals by the court was no better than the example set for manners. Unfortunately, Hanoverian crudeness suited much of the English upper class, and there was little interest in improving manners. Aside from a few translations of French works and some pamphlet sermons by reformers, writings on conduct were virtually absent from English bookstalls for the first twenty years of the 18th century.

Queen Anne's influence on the manners of her subjects was negligible; the first two Georges merely encouraged prevailing behavior, but the reign of Richard (Beau) Nash at Bath changed many established customs.

Nash successfully broke down caste lines at Bath, mixing rustic country families with the aristocracy at the public assemblies where they shared the gaming tables and danced together. The Whartons, 19th-century historians, later hailed this as the beginning of the modern English middle class, perhaps too ambitious a claim, but there is no question that Nash swept aside the respectful reserve that ordinarily existed between the classes. John Wood, writing in 1749, reported that with the building of an assembly hall at Bath, "Rank began to be laid aside, and all Degrees of People from the Private Gentleman Upwards, were soon united in society with one another."

Aristocratic London ladies danced the stately minuet and informal country dances with rough squires and Liverpool tallow dealers. And if Beau Nash observed a lady offering her hand gingerly in this contact, he promptly rebuked the offender.

The guard rails went up, however, the moment the participants departed from the spa. "This is so scrupulously maintained," wrote

Tobias Smollett, "that two persons who lived in the most intimate correspondence at Bath and Tunbridge Wells shall, in four and twenty hours, so totally forget their friendship, as to meet in St. James Park, without betraying the least token of recognition." A century later Sir Walter Scott added, "No intimacy can be . . . more transitory in its endurance, than that which is attached to a watering place." It became a tacit rule of etiquette to treat vacation friendships as temporary. Later, etiquette books spelled out the rules governing chance meetings even under the roof of a mutual friend. Strangers were to be as friendly as they pleased with each other while the visit lasted, "But the acquaintance ceases the moment you have left the home."

Nash's democratic ideas may have proceeded from his own unpretentious background—decent enough, but hardly aristocratic. After explusion from Oxford for an amorous misadventure, Nash unsuccessfully tried both law and soldiering before he found his true calling as a professional gambler, a socially acceptable pursuit in a gambling-mad nation. (Bet-making is still a respectable occupation in England.) In this capacity Nash came to Bath and headed for immortality as the century's leading arbiter of manners.

When he arrived, around 1705, and shortly afterward took over as Master of Ceremonies, the spa badly needed overhauling in physical matters as well as decorum. Nash soon achieved both. The assembly hall was erected, the streets and landscaping were beautified, and the seedy lodging houses were forced to adopt better standards.

Nash imposed a strict code of polite behavior on the entire community. Banned now was all-night gambling by disgruntled players hoping to recoup their losses. Country dances (similar to today's square dances) were now an occasional diversion in the assembly hall, instead of a feature in outdoor tents that had given the town a carnival atmosphere.

Nash insisted on proper evening dress in the assembly hall. Ladies were forbidden to wear aprons. When the Duchess of Queensberry was forced to remove hers and protested that it was of costly Point Venise and she a duchess, Nash replied "None but Abigails [servant maids] appear in them," starting their decline after centuries as a fashionable accessory. His ban on swords started a trend "of real historical importance . . . reflecting and sustaining the pacific habits that were growing in society," says William E. H. Lecky, Irish historian. Nash's ban produced tangible results away from Bath as early as 1720, according to Lecky, when ". . . young men of fashion in London had begun in their morning walks to lay aside their swords, which were hitherto looked upon as the indispensable signs of a gentleman." And necessary, for the 18th-century gentleman was always ready to duel, despite such works as *Discourse of Duels* by Thomas Comber, "Shewing the sinful nature and mischievous effect" of such encounters.

By 1780 the fashion of leaving off swords (and aprons) was general. Nash well knew the risks of sword wearing, and how often a rashly drawn sword was used to settle a gambling argument. He had received his own post as Master of Ceremonies when his predecessor, Captain Webster, was fatally wounded as the result of such a settlement.

Nash's numerous reforms at Bath were soon the talk of England, and the spa's popularity increased steadily because of the pleasures Nash had created there for all classes. It was a marriage mart for well-born young men not fortunate enough to be firstborn, seeking to match their blue blood to the redder stuff that pounded through the veins of merchant's daughters. Ambitious commercial families with marriageable daughters were there in even greater numbers, with the same objective.

In their efforts to act like gentlefolk these commercial folk from England's provincial mill towns were often more polite than the aristocracy and gentry, and at times to such an exaggerated degree that the *Spectator* waspishly commented, "One may know a man that never convers'd in the world, by his excess of good breeding." It expressed the same disdain that Elizabethan gentry had shown for "rustics." But under Nash's rule at Bath rustics learned the nonchalant ways of upper-class society—a lesson perhaps so well learned that etiquette was forced to step in.

16 · 18TH-CENTURY LESSONS IN MANNERS

THE "SMALL TAPER" Henry Peacham had held aloft to light the way to courtesy in *The Compleat Gentleman* flickered low in the 18th century. The most influential voices on social conduct were now satirists, polemicists and sharp-tongued poets, who replaced the homilies and ancient quotations in the courtesy books with caustic ridicule. The few books that employed straightforward language spoke mostly to the middle class, and often in terms many of them were ready to reject.

Among the first to appear was Adam Petrie's *Rules of Good Deportment* (1720). It still clung to some of the older precepts of courtesy but was more notable for the deference it recommended. Petrie, after an unsuccessful try for the church, became a tutor in an aristocratic family where he apparently learned to be self-effacing and was now ready to teach others how to do the same. His book was studded with references to "superiors" and "persons of quality" who were to be given the wall or right side when walking, the best seat in a coach when traveling, aid in dismounting from their horses if a groom was not handy, and deferential silence when they conversed.

Those who provided all this deference had *their* inferiors as well; Petrie was aware of the stratification developing in the middle class. Ladies received a kiss on the lips when greeted by their equals—but "Ladies give their inferiors their cheeks only." However, Petrie ruled against one widespread and coarse habit even in the presence of the lower class: to break wind in company was rude, "even tho amongst inferiors."

First glimpses of the ultramodesty that would develop later can be seen in *Rules of Good Deportment*. Though it certainly was not true as yet, Petrie rated all ladies as modest and proposed to spare

Frontispiece, *Rules of Good Deportment, or of Good Breeding* by Adam Petrie, 1720.

them embarrassment while traveling. Male companions were not to expect ladies to announce their need; it was to be anticipated by stops at regular intervals with the explanation, "Let us allow the horses to breathe a little." To give the real reason "would put [the ladies] to the blush." Lest his counsel be ignored, Petrie warned, "I know of a modest lady who in riding with an inconsiderate person lost her life."

Devoid of such primness, but equally class-conscious was Sir John Barnard's *A Present for an Apprentice* (1741) which announced to its middle-class male readers that in offering them a book on conduct it was the first book "to stoop so low."

Barnard ranged from the evils of drinking to the techniques of proposing marriage, and displayed a lively wit and topical awareness in everything he discussed. On drinking he advised: "When you are most inclined to stay another bottle, be sure to go." For a proposal he saw no need to kneel, even verbally. Make the proposal as light as a joke, he advised—then, if the girl turns you down you *can* pass it off as a joke.

Actually, much of the wisdom Barnard offered was similar to

Caleb Trenchfield's *Cap of Grey Hairs for a Green Head,* but if Barnard was acquainted with the earlier book he failed to acknowledge it. His attitude was condenscending, whereas Petrie treated his readers as equals. But Petrie's book was a model for exactly the kind of obsequious behavior the *Spectator* criticized as provincial. Not for Addison or Steele such laborious civilities. Said one of them, "This rural politeness is very troublesome to a man of my temper, who generally take the chair that is next to me, and walk first or last, in the front or the rear, as chance directs. Nothing is so modish as an agreeable negligence."

This "agreeable negligence," was dealt with in *The Rudiments of Genteel Behavior* by F. Nivelon (1737). Illustrations of ladies and gentlemen in elegant attire, apparently in the midst of festive entertainments, were supplied to clue the readers on "the method of attaining a graceful attitude, and easy air, and a genteel behaviour." To judge from the expressions of elegant disdain on the men's faces, and the frozen haughtiness of the ladies', the "easy air" was achieved through studious affectation and was about as natural as the wigs people wore.

Most writers ignored the way a man wore his face and dealt instead with his vulgarities. Their remonstrances were often cruder than the habits they sought to curb, but strong stuff was needed to deal with such grossness as that of an eminent peer who spat into the hat of unsuspecting Lord Hervey to win a wager. Only Lord Hervey's extreme courtesy prevented a duel. Or the fishwife vocabulary of Lady Northumberland, who, finding a drawing room too crowded for passage, loudly exclaimed, "I wish I could get my arse through!"

Grobianus, a milestone in explicit vulgarity, was reissued in 1739 and dedicated by its new translator to Jonathan Swift, who could hold his own with the best of the vulgarians.

Many of the satirists turned their attention to foppish attire, still as irritating to men with plainer tastes as it had been in the previous century. A monthly fashion journal, *Delights for the Ingenuous,* warned men not to dress themselves in finery more becoming to women or to arrange their hair like women. *The Man of Taste* (1736), *The Modern Fine Gentleman* (1746), and *The*

Pretty Gentleman (1747), jibed at the mounting effeminacy of men.

An articulate and widely published clergyman, John Brown, achieved fame through *An Estimate of the Manners and Principles of the Times* (1757), which also earned him the nickname of "Estimate" Brown. The free use of vulgar language by upper-class women and the "vain, selfish effeminacy of its men," would bring ruin to England, predicted Brown, who saw only catastrophe ahead with such an unnatural reversal of the sexes.

Brown found something to carp about in everything the upper class did. Their food was too French; they drank too much; they could give the Sybarites lessons in indolence; and for all that Englishmen presumed to look down on Frenchmen as strutting peacocks, the French were actually the more manly, asserted Brown. But his chief scorn and denunciation was reserved for England's young men of privilege: their educations were either neglected or of the wrong kind. And when a youth's learning was topped off with a trip to the continent, that *really* finished him off.

Brown's criticisms attracted much attention; there was agreement, and some rebuttals as well. One defense, entitled *The Real Character of the Age,* gave a long list of eminent nobility whose actions refuted Brown's free-swinging criticism. And since Brown failed to suggest specific remedies for the evils he complained of, the author of the rebuttal suggested that Brown curb his pen.

When the "Macaronies" appeared in the 1760s, they seemed to support Brown's unfavorable estimate of English young manhood. Pampered, well-traveled youths, apparently affecting a taste for continental foods, especially macaroni, the "Macaronies" adopted continental styles and mannerisms, wore their hair in long, tight curls, and seem to have carried "spy glasses" and two watches —"One to tell us what time it is, the other to tell us what time it is *not*," said one irritated critic.

But Brown and all the others only repeated what had been said for nearly two centuries. Englishmen had been censured for sending their sons abroad since 1570, when Roger Ascham had labeled Italian cities "Courts of Circe" because of their "degrading" effect on young English visitors. Nor was effeminacy or overdressing by men a new complaint. The coxcomb appeared on the English scene

in the 16th century, The 17th-century fop aroused the same complaints. And in the 18th century "beau" was frequently used in a
pejorative sense. (The dandy arrived in the 19th century.) But
in each period these young men represented only a conspicuous
minority; and while they tend to give an entire generation its
coloration at the moment, eventually the distortion falls into historical perspective.

The social spectrum of the 18th century embraced many types,
as every period does. There was the "fast" crowd—each century
had its particular version, usually dictated by the conduct at court—
there were the severely proper, the merely proper, the witty, the
learned, the shallow. There were truths both in Brown's Estimate
of the times, and in his opponents' refutation of it.

For what distinguished it—or rather, for what failed to make it
distinguished—upper-class English social life in the 18th century
could be compared to life among the affluent country-club set today.
English society occupied itself with much the same pastimes: drinking, cards, casual amours and gossip. With one important difference: there was far more time for such idle pleasures in the 18th
century. Social life, and especially gambling, was the entire career
of many gentlemen. As one letter in Georgian archives put it, "A
man of taste must play all the morning, or at least four or five
games before dinner [then served at mid-day] . . . idleness and
debauchery [have] taken possession of all ranks in society . . . all
knowledge is at the gaming table." Horace Walpole complained
of "the innundation of breakfasts and balls that are coming on."
Social life in the 18th century was a round of superficial pleasures

"The female Coterie." Ladies gambling.
Old Times by John Ashton, 1885.

and frivolity, set down in the words of many contemporary writers and brilliantly drawn by William Hogarth, who also commented sharply on much of its debauchery.

Cards were the most compelling social magnet, with loo the favorite game. Loo players were so addicted that it was customary to have games at the home of lying-in ladies while waiting for the birth to occur. Horace Walpole suggested that players seeking a game, "should send to Dr. Hunter's, the man mid-wife, to know where there is Loo that evening."

Among the few social gatherings which did not feature cards were the "levees" of influential men. These were morning receptions, patterned after the royal custom of having members of the court in attendance when the monarch awakened. For non-royalty the custom apparently began in the late 17th century and was the rage in 18th-century England. The man who could muster a sizable gallery of admirers to watch him sip his morning chocolate and receive his matinal barbering was a social leader. Ladies, too, prepared to meet the day before an audience, and many a duchess had her false curls anchored while admirers whispered compliments in her ear.

Levees were favorite fawning places for all who sought social contacts for whatever reason, and aside from being morning functions, they resembled today's sprawling cocktail parties and attracted the same kinds of people, from the socially ambitious to the hangers-on.

Attractive appearance, complete self-possession and a witty tongue were latchkeys that could open the right doors, as has always been true. Wit was important, but it seems that the art of conversation was at a low point in England in the 18th century. While French society was equally enamored of card-playing and amorous dalliance, a higher value was placed on intellectual achievement, and French salons hummed with good conversation. The *salonnier* had been an established adjunct to French society since 1607 when the Marquise de Rambouillet, then a mere nineteen years old, but already married for seven years, had gathered around her a circle of friends to practice the fine art of conversation as at the court of Urbino in Renaissance days. No Castiglione emerged to immortalize the graceful conversations, but the splendid literature and memoirs of the period, influenced by the frequenters of the Hôtel de Rambouillet, have their own immortality. The *salonniers* helped greatly to elevate and expand the questing spirit of French intellectualism.

Nothing comparable existed in England until the 1750s when Mrs. Agmondesham Vesey and Lady Elizabeth Robinson Montagu (a cousin by marriage of Lady Mary Wortley Montagu), both of them weary of the eternal drinking and card-playing that passed for social life, organized similar salons. The two ladies were joined by others of similar persuasion and adhered to Lady Montagu's declaration that at *her* entertainments "cards could not be thought of."

Lady Montagu arranged her guests in one large circle and allowed each to speak in turn, while Mrs. Vesey preferred to separate her guests into small groups and let them talk as they would. But in whatever formation the hostesses chose, the shuffle and slap of cards at whist, loo and bassett were replaced by the buzz of entertaining talk, often led by such masters of it as Benjamin Stillingfleet.

Stillingfleet, a noted botanist and essayist, had established a reputation for brilliant conversation, and he praised its charms and rewards in his *Essay on Conversation* (1737). As a close friend of both Mrs. Vesey and Lady Montagu, he may have stimulated the ladies to found their salons. His preference for bluish-gray cotton hose, when the evening hour of the salons dictated black silk hose as the proper choice, is supposed to be the origin of the term "blue stockings," a deprecatory name, as had been *Les Précieuses* when applied to the Marquise de Rambouillet's followers.

This version is disputed by Elizabeth Montagu's great-great-niece and biographer, Emily Climenson, who claims that her aunt's salon was patterned after the Countess de Polignac's in Paris. *That* group adopted the blue stockings fashionable at the time and thus became known as the *bas bleus*. Whatever the origin of the name, the influence of these ladies is beyond debate. The English literary salon, thanks to them, helped to place English women on an intellectual level with men and lured the male literati out of the coffeehouses which had been their gathering places.

At the moment, however, the "blue stockings" drew very few upper-class Englishmen away from their gambling. Conduct books were consulted more for information on how to behave in company at a card table than how to converse. While such works as Pierre Ortigue's *Art of Pleasing with Conversation* (1736), *The Conversation of a Gentleman* (1738), and James Burgh's *The Art of Speaking* (1758) did appear, more pertinent information was offered in Sir Richard Hill's *An Address to Persons of Fashion Containing Some Particulars Relating to Balls; and a Few Hints Concerning Play-Houses, Card-Tables, and the Like* (c. 1755). This small volume pointed unmistakably in the direction of the future etiquette book.

Jonathan Swift could plainly discern the proliferation of elaborate rules governing deportment and applied his sandpaper wit to *A Treatise on Good Manners and Good Breeding* and *Hints on Good Manners* two works which were published after his death in 1745—in 1754 and 1765 respectively. They were not guidance manuals, as their titles might imply, but ironic indictments. At one point Swift set aside sarcasm to observe, "Ignorance of forms cannot properly be styled ill manners; because forms are subject to frequent changes. . . ." In the same mood he stated the principles of true courtesy as early courtesy books had taught them: "Whoever, from the goodness of his disposition or from understanding, endeavors . . . to contribute to the ease and comfort of all his acquaintance; however low in rank, or however clumsy he may be in his figure or demeanor, hath, in the truest sense of the word, a claim to good breeding."

These generous sentiments no longer squared with the growing class consciousness of the 18th century, nor with the cold formulas that were beginning to stand for good breeding. It was a time when footmen were sent around to make personal calls—"How do ye's" —on sick friends of a master or mistress too socially occupied to come in person. Swift himself received a number of "How do ye's" from footmen bobbing in and out of his bedroom when he lay ill. Such an age had forsaken much of the old spirit of courtesy, and the courtesy book gradually disappeared in the 18th century, as Peacham's ideal of courtesy was replaced by Chesterfield's etiquette.

17 · CHESTERFIELD,
THE SPIRIT OF ETIQUETTE

I CANNOT WRITE about etiquette without going into some detail about Lord Chesterfield, who, in a way, sponsored its entrance into the English language. It was on March 19th, 1750, to pinpoint the date precisely. Chesterfield used the word in one of the famous letters to his illegitimate son, Philip Stanhope, then eighteen and visiting in Rome. Eager that Philip savor every experience that the city had to offer, Chesterfield wrote: "Pray get somebody to present you to him [the pope] before you leave Rome; and without hesitation kiss his slipper or whatever else the *etiquette* of that court requires."

No one was better qualified than Chesterfield to escort *etiquette* into the English language, and its general spirit into manners. He was the 18th century's prototype of the experienced courtier, even more analagous to the corporation man of today than Du Refuge's earlier courtier. In dress, talk, actions, even to having been schooled at "the best courts," the 18th century's courtier matched the others at the court he frequented in the way today's executive fits the corporate image of his company. In a 1749 letter that would prepare his son for a similar career, Chesterfield described court life. It would seem to explain some whys of etiquette as well.

Nothing in courts is exactly as it appears to be. Courts are the seats of politeness and good-breeding; were they not so they would be the seats of slaughter and desolation. Those who now . . . embrace, would affront and stab each other if manners did not interpose: but ambition and avarice, the two prevailing passions at courts, found dissimulation more effectual than violence; and dissimulation introduced that habit of politeness which distinguishes the courtier from the country gentleman. In the former case the

Engraved portrait of Lord Chesterfield. From an 1800 edition of the *Letters*.

strongest body would prevail, in the latter the strongest mind. A man of parts and efficiency need not flatter everybody at Court, but he must take care to offend nobody personally: it being the power of very many to hurt him who cannot serve him.

As a product of one of England's most aristocratic families, Lord Chesterfield had been in attendance at all of the important courts of Europe. But it was as a young blade at the court of Louis XIV that he acquired his impeccable manners and his libertine tastes. In his exquisite behavior and his attention to the formalities of politeness he remained always more a Frenchman than an Englishman.

While a social amenity was inviolable, feminine virtue was another matter. Chesterfield was, in fact, a first-rate lecher. But, according to his own account, only with the best ladies. He constantly stressed to his son that affection or even attraction rarely motivated him, and that he went to "great pains to make many a woman in love with me, for whose person I would not have given a pinch of snuff." With his goal only to "grow in fashion and popularity," the conquest of well-born ladies gave him "the reputation of having had some women of condition: and that reputation, whether true or false, really got me others."

That reputation was indeed false, declared his contemporary, Lord Hervey. Chesterfield's boasted ladies were not from the better boudoirs: they were for hire by any man, whether a handsome youth or an ugly blacksmith. "In fact and in truth he never gained anyone above the venal rank of those whom an Adonis or a Vulcan might . . . for an equal sum of money." Such talk would ordinarily have led to drawn swords. Fortunately, Hervey's *Memoirs* (of the Court of George II) were published long after the deaths of both gentlemen.

Chesterfield encouraged his son to try for the best ladies, especially at the French court where a lover "is as necessary a part of a woman of fashion's establishment, as her house, table, or coach." In a subsequent letter Chesterfield elaborated further on the subject, proposing to discuss it on a man-to-man basis, not as father to son. Personally, *he* never paid for "female favors." It was senseless to buy what could be had free, especially "in such a place as Paris where [affairs] are both the profession and the practise of every woman of fashion." There were hygienic advantages as well: "Low company and low pleasures are always more costly than liberal and elegant ones."

Aside from his exquisite manners, the reasons for Chesterfield's own amorous successes were not immediately detectable. He had a squeaky voice, a short, ungainly, thickset body, and was described by George II as a "dwarf baboon," while his fellow courtiers called him "Little Stanhope."

This lack of stature may have triggered overcompensation in the direction of ladies' boudoirs. Chesterfield was obviously sensitive about his lack of height and expressed excessive concern over a similar lack in his son. As the boy went through adolescence the

father's letters touched often on this concern: "Your riding, fencing, and dancing, constantly at the Academy, will, I hope, lengthen
you out a little; therefore, pray take a great deal of those exercises;
for I would fain have you to be, at least, five feet eight inches
high. . . ."

As a statesman Chesterfield stood tall and played an active mod-
ernizing role in English politics and government. He put England
in step with the rest of Europe when he brought about the adoption
of the Gregorian calendar in England (1752); most of Europe had
already adopted it since the 15th century.

Early in his political career, as ambassador to The Hague in 1732
he met Mlle Elizabeth Du Bouchet, an attractive young French-
woman of good family but meager resources employed as a governess in a wealthy Dutch household. When off duty, Mlle Du
Bouchet got around in the better social circles, where she heard
much talk about Chesterfield's amorous exploits.

One day, fed to the gills with hearing about him, or possibly
to bring about the predictable outcome, she denounced his lechery
before a group of his friends, proclaiming that *she* was one he
couldn't tumble. Naturally, the incident reached Chesterfield's
ears, and the leading rake of the day could not afford to ignore
such a public declaration of impregnable chastity. At least so the
story goes.

Mlle Du Bouchet proved pregnable indeed, and one year later
bore Lord Chesterfield his only child. When Chesterfield returned
to England she followed and remained there, supported by him
during his entire lifetime. Though he did not choose to marry her
and give his son a legal mother, his correspondence contains many
respectful mentions of her to the boy. In one he wrote: "The tea-
things which Sir Charles Williams has given you, I would have
you make a present of to your mamma. You owe her not only duty,
but likewise great obligations, for her care and tenderness; and,
consequently, cannot take too many opportunities of showing your
gratitude." At another time he wrote: "Remember to bring your
mother some little presents; they need not be of value, but only
marks of your affection and duty for one who has always been

tenderly fond of you. You may bring Lady Chesterfield [his own wife] a little Martin snuffbox of about five louis."

Perhaps Chesterfield had hoped for more children with the legal mate he took the year after his son's birth, Melusina de Schulenberg, "niece" of George I's mistress, the Countess of Kendall and rumored actually to be the daughter of George I. She was obviously of good pedigree, bore the title of Countess of Walsingham, and seemed in every way a suitable match for Chesterfield.

Melusina continued to live in her own establishment, and Chesterfield fluttered, beelike, between the two ladies for a while in the fairly standard arrangement of those days. Just when Mlle Du Bouchet ceased to be a part-time couch partner and became merely a full-time dependent is not clear.

One fact *is* clear: from the beginning, Chesterfield undertook the rearing of his illegitimate son and spared no cost or attention to mold him into a suitable Chesterfield. "From the time that you have had life it has been the principal and favorite object of mine to make you as perfect as the imperfections of human nature will allow," he wrote, repeating it often in the famed correspondence that began when the boy was seven and continued until his untimely death at thirty-six.

The letters were a mail-order course in how to win friends (male and female) and use them influentially. "The art of pleasing is a very necessary one to possess: but a very difficult one to acquire," wrote Chesterfield when the boy was fifteen. He advised him to "observe carefully what pleases you in others, and probably the same things in you will please others." Few letters were without a paragraph or so on the importance of charming manners.

> Remember always what I have told you a thousand times, that all the talents in the world will want all their lustre, and some part of their use too, if they are not adorned with that easy good-breeding, that engaging manner, and those graces, which seduce and prepossess people in your favour at first sight.

As Philip grew older, the instructions became more direct. When the boy was sixteen, Chesterfield, still urging him to learn the social graces by careful observation, gave him other reasons to keep his eyes open around people who could be of help to him.

> Observe carefully their manners. But . . . go deeper still; observe their characters, and pry, as far as you can, into both their hearts and their heads. Seek for their . . . predominant passion, or their prevailing weakness; and you will then know what to bait your hook with to catch them.

By seventeen, Philip was being instructed in "an innocent piece of art—that of flattering people behind their backs, in presence of those who (for *their* own advantage) will not fail to repeat, and even to amplify, the praise to the party concerned."

His father now inducted him further into the mysteries of how to handle women. Since they could make or break a man at court through their influence, "it is absolutely necessary to manage, please and flatter them." But with a cool head and a cold heart: "A man of sense only trifles with them . . . he neither consults them about, nor trusts them with, serious matters." In dealing with women flattery could never be carried too far, "nor too high or too low for them . . . you may safely flatter any woman."

As an example that a man was never too young to profit by skillful handling of women, Chesterfield cited the Duc de Richelieu, though it would seem the *Duc* had been handled a bit himself. ". . . Women alone formed and raised him. The Duchess of Burgundy took a fancy to him, and had him before he was sixteen years old: this put him in fashion among the *beau monde;* and the late Regent's eldest daughter took him next, and was near marrying him."

Despite the many advantages provided for him, and the reams of advice written by his father, young Philip matured into a disappointingly gauche young man who ate like a glutton and had no instinct for the correct people. Especially, he lacked an instinct for choosing the right females—the very area where his father's advice should have served him best. He married an obscure young woman also of illegitimate birth, Eugenia Peters, said to be the daughter of a wealthy Irishman. Out of fear, or perhaps out of consideration, he kept the marriage a secret from his father, who learned about it only after Philip's death in 1768.

Philip's widow made the letters available for publication in 1774, a year after Lord Chesterfield's death, motivated possibly by financial need, though some thought she did it out of malice because her father-in-law had reacted so icily when he discovered her existence.

The letters caused a storm that thundered all the way to America (where a watered-down version "suited to the youth of the U.S." was later published). Samuel Johnson called them a pernicious influence, instilling "the morals of a strumpet with the manners of a dancing master." Actually, the letters were models of wisdom and erudition except for their cynical observations, but they exposed nothing in conduct and attitudes that had not already been reviled by pamphleteers, satirists and novelists. Chesterfield's moral philosophy was matched by that of many of his contemporaries, and perhaps by many of his critics who, fortunately for them, had not written sheaves of letters.

The storm of criticism was soon spent and Chesterfield emerged as the single most important influence on manners, the personification of the new etiquette, which the increasingly prosperous middle class was eager to master.

George III and Queen Charlotte depicted as homebodies.
Satirical drawings by James Gillray, 1791.

18 · GEORGIAN DECORUM

WHEN GEORGE III came to the throne of England in 1760, decorum finally swept into England in the wake of the shy, unworldly, overprotected young king. The crown was scarcely settled on his head when George was married to the equally reserved Charlotte of Mecklenburg.

George and Charlotte were disinclined to pomp and ceremony and behaved more like Darby and Joan than a king and queen. Satirical cartoons of the period show them toasting muffins and frying sprats like a pair of homebodies. In contrast to that of the two earlier Georges, their family life was a model of correctness that encouraged the rebirth of the Puritanism still lingering in England. In slightly altered form it bloomed again in John Wesley's Methodism, as George and Charlotte steered the English court back to propriety.

Despite his recurring mental illness, George III had one of the longest reigns in English history, and his court exerted perhaps the most enduring influence on English conduct. The propriety later credited to Victoria was incubated at her grandfather's court long before she was born, and for more than a century it influenced English behavior.

Other factors, or the lack of them, affected English conduct. A particular loss was the French influence on English manners which had seeped in despite the many howls of protest against it. With the decline of the French court, followed by the upheaval of the French Revolution, privileged young Englishmen no longer topped off their education with travel to the continent and particularly to France. Along with French laces, the import of French graces was temporarily suspended.

But the most important factor was the rise of the urban entrepreneurial class. English social life changed from small centers of village society, where the manor house was a small court of its own, to crowded, aggressive centers of urban life with Society at its core. (It was around this time that "society" took on the special meaning of a fashionable elite group.) Etiquette eventually became the banner word of the social side of the Industrial Revolution and dominated the lives of all socially ambitious families.

The first English work to call itself an etiquette book was *The Fine Gentleman's Etiquette; or Lord Chesterfield's Advice to his Son Verified* (1776) by an unidentified author. The book was not an explicit guide in the sense of the later etiquette book but it deserves mention as the first manners book to use the word "etiquette" in its title.

A more popular work, widely read and reprinted, was *Principles of Politeness* (c. 1775) by Dr. John Trusler, an eccentric minister who preferred the editor's chair to the pulpit. Trusler professed to have extracted the juice of Chesterfield's correspondence and now offered it handily arranged to guide those who would emulate the manners of Chesterfield's aristocratic circle. In those circles, Trusler confided, "custom has lately introduced a new mode of seating; a gentleman and lady sitting alternately at the table."

Some conduct banned by Trusler—"Smelling the meat whilst on the fork before you put it in your mouth"—would surely have been beneath Chesterfield's notice, but, according to Trusler it was a common practice. "I have seen many an ill-bred fellow do this, and have been so angry that I could have kicked him from the table," he complained. "If you dislike what you have, leave it."

An obvious withdrawal to attend to "the necessities of nature, particularly at dinner," was another frequent indelicacy. "Endeavor to steal away unperceived, or make some excuse for retiring that may keep your motives secret," he said. The same secrecy was to be observed upon returning from the errand; there was to be "no adjusting of your clothes, or re-placing of your watch, to say whence you came."

However, some of Trusler's *Principles* were indeed those of Chesterfield. "Flatter delicately. Study the foibles of men, and observe certain rules applying to these foibles. Be choice in your compliments. Seem friendly to your enemies." It had all been said over and over in the *Letters*.

Trusler also included a few *Principles* for ladies which he certainly had not gleaned from Chesterfield and which show manners changing under George III. The ladies of Chesterfield's correspondence had thought nothing of bearing illegitimate children or seducing sixteen-year-old boys. Trusler's ladies would have swooned at the thought, and though they were still of the 18th century, they were already ankle-deep in the ways of the mid-19th. "Seem not aware of improper conversation," Trusler advised his ladies. "Don't even *hear* a double entendre." Ladies turned deaf and purple at such words as belly, breast, and tail, now excluded from polite conversation in the spreading ultra-respectability of the late 18th century. "Ass" was forbidden as a reference to the animal. As for applying it to the anatomy, that was definitely in the same category as a gentleman fastening his trousers as he returned to the dinner table. "Dare to be prudish," was Trusler's rallying cry to the ladies, possibly an admission that *all* were not yet won over to the newer fashion of decorous behavior.

Respect for majesty and for titles continued in England, despite great economic changes that impoverished the aristocracy at the same time that it enriched the middle class. Such performances as ladies backing out of the king's presence clear through a doorway so as never to turn their backs on majesty was a rigorous exercise which foreigners viewed as symptomatic of English class rigidity.

Some of this rigidity was forced to bend and yield under the in-

"A modern belle going to the Rooms or Balls—1796."
Old Times by John Ashton, 1885.

flationary pressures caused by the American Revolution and the Napoleonic wars. The fixed incomes of the established gentry and aristocracy contracted alarmingly under these pressures, while the same ballooning worked to the advantage of the business class, their social ambitions now fired by increasing affluence.

One of the easiest ways to stoke these fires was to provide the lavish entertainment which the established upper class could no longer afford in the light of their reduced incomes. For a while, by this means, admission into society was as easy as presenting a pass at a half-filled theater hungry for an audience, but it was to prove a brief performance. Mary Berry, whose life spanned ninety years (d. 1852) could take a long backward glance for her *Social Life of England and France from 1660–1830,* and she offered some first-hand glimpses into the temporary relaxations which were soon rudely withdrawn. She wrote of the wondrously lavish balls and fetes where "often the masters of the house were strangers to three-fourths of the company." Eventually "Top society grew bored with these crowded affairs and withdrew into small groups. All those who thought that by their former entertainments they had purchased the freedom of the company to which they were ambitious to belong, now found themselves cruely thrown out."

Even the lavish homes of the upper class were taken over by rising entrepreneurs happy to pay an extravagant rental for the

153

use of such charmed premises. The practice of subletting houses dates from the early 19th century, when it was an emergency means of supplementing fixed incomes. And the newly moneyed class delighted in the authentically upper-class background such houses gave their new wealth.

The changes in the social structure of France were equally great, but in France the social field had been completely leveled and re-plowed; little trace was left of the old nobility, and the new plant-ings of society grafted from the bourgeoisie took root easily, unim-peded by such resistance as entrenched "society" offered in Eng-land.

French bourgeois attitudes showed considerable resemblance to the propriety that England had adopted, and in many matters of conduct France was to take its cue from England for a time. The gallantries of former times were no longer the fashion; young men were "no longer taught to consider the reputation of a libertine as either graceful or distinguishing." Instead, secure family life now earned the highest premium of outside approval, just as colorful extramarital arrangements had elicited it in the elegant days of the Louis'. Eventually the remembered spirit of those days—the ele-gance, the artistic drive and the open acceptance of liaisons as a necessary corollary of the *mariage de convenance*—revived in the French upper classes, but the immediate post-Revolutionary devel-opment placed the emphasis in France on stable family life and the kind of morality that some observers tagged as the ultimate bour-geois expression. The influence of the bourgeoisie was undeniably pervasive in both France and England. After all, it held the purse strings; its mark on manners and general behavior had to be felt.

The sheer size and continued growth of the middle class caused stratification within it, each layer intent on keeping the one beneath from rising too close for comfortable exclusiveness. Even the serv-ant class, which had greatly enlarged to meet the demands of the expanding middle class, now increased *its* stratification. As a society in itself with its own rigid hierarchy, and because of the effect it exerted on the character and comfort of the middle and upper class, it deserves a passing examination—especially because nu-merous books were written to guide its conduct.

19 · CIVILITIES FOR SERVANTS

THERE HAS NEVER BEEN an age free of the servant problem. In different ways it has been the burden of those who could command service and of those who were commanded to supply it, but in the 18th century it reached greater degrees of mutual exasperation and settled into its modern outlines.

Few courtesy books in the past had failed to advise the employer to treat his servants with consideration. Richard Allestree, in *The Ladies Calling,* had told the 17th-century wife that her husband's comfort depended on contented servants. "For these are the wheels of a family . . . if they stop or move wrong, the whole Order of the House is either at a stand, or discomposed." To this end she was to keep the servants' path strewn, if not with roses, at least with kind words. Furthermore, if she had any understanding of the stuff that mules were made of, she would know that a haughty tone to servants "begetteth an aversion in them, of which the least ill effect to be expected is that they will be slow and careless in all that is enjoined of them."

Even Ecclesiasticus had observed (33.31), "If thou have a servant, intreat him as a Brother for thou hast need of him as of thine own soul." But in the 18th century this soul brother (more often a sister) became more mulish than ever. Courtesy books redirected their aim. Numerous volumes now appeared to tell servants how to behave to their masters, and among themselves as well; the servant class had become a highly stratified society with strict respect for precedence among its own members. Its aristocracy of butlers, footmen, and French-trained cooks looked down on lesser servants, refused to take their meals with them, and made it a point not to frequent the same pubs and taverns. The jobs to be performed were sharply defined and lines were rarely crossed, much as in craft unions today.

One of the earliest behavior books for servants was an anonymous volume, *The House-Keepers Guide* (1706). The "house-keeper" was an employee, not a housewife, and it was her duty to instruct those under her management in their proper attitudes toward life in general and employers in particular. As a guide, a Servant's Prayer was provided:

> I humbly submit to the State wherein thou 'hast been pleased to place me, below many others in the Low Condition of A Servant; and as my Talents are few, so at the day of Judgement my Accompt shall be less. . . . Help me to demean myself so humbly, and whatsoever I do to do it so heartily, that I may obtain Favour in their Eyes. Or if they be Froward and hard to please, O God, preserve me from all unseeming Passions, and disrespectful Behaviour toward them.

There is a hint of tongue-in-cheek about this prayer in view of the actual circumstances. Trained servants were in short supply. This fact they used to their advantage, demanding high wages and many more privileges than unsalaried noble pages and maids-in-waiting of earlier days had dared to expect. Employers complained that servants new to the city soon learned its ways. Said one, "When a country girl arrives in London she becomes a fine London Madam, and can drink tea and take snuff with the best. Indeed, she bargains for her tea twice a day before she takes a place."

Daniel Defoe, more widely remembered for Robinson Crusoe (who had the perfect servant in Friday) than he is for his numerous political and social writings, let go a blast at servants. A short work with the long title of *The Great Law of Subordination considered: or, The Insolence and Insufferable Behaviour of Servants in England, Duly Inquired into* (1724) examined the servants of England and found them all wanting. "They're bamboozling the entire nation," cried Defoe. "Yet with all these inconveniences, we cannot possibly do without these creatures." With servants' wages rising like mercury, he suggested a law to limit the wages, and these to be based on the servant's experience.

Furthermore, he wanted laws to regulate and limit their personal finery.

Servant-maids' pretensions to elegance angered him particularly: "They are so puffed up with pride these days . . . it is a hard matter to know the mistress from the maid by their dress, nay, very often, the maid shall be the finer of the two." He spoke from actual experience, said he, having once "kissed the chamber-jade by mistake," thinking her the daughter of his hosts.

This urge to be well dressed and to compete among themselves for the best males caused many maidservants to turn to other means of supplementing their incomes. Defoe described it:

> Streets swarm with strumpets who have turned to whoring and thieving. Some rove from bawdy house to service, and back again. This amphibious life makes 'em fit for neither and hard to please in each way . . . so in effect they neither make good whores or good servants. . . . Those who are not thus slippery in the tail, are light of finger. . . .

But worse than this, declared Defoe, servant maids used their charms, snakelike, to hypnotize young men. "If the upstart [serving wench] be tolerably handsome, with any share of cunning, the apprentice or his master's son is entic'd away and ruin'd by her. Thus many good families are impoverish'd and disgrac'd by these pert sluts who take advantage of a young man's simplicity and unruly desires."

Sir John Barnard in *A Present for An Apprentice* bore out Defoe's words and warned his readers to keep clear of servant maids; they were all seductresses in starched uniforms. Because of their alleged boldness, serving maids and parlormaids were declared to be a threat to decent young men; warnings came from pulpits, the press and novels.

Jonathan Swift offered some of his sharpest mockery in *Directions to Servants* (1745), a satirical manual that told ladies' maids to empty a mistress's chamberpot at the exact moment a gentleman caller arrived, and if possible, to empty it right under his nose. Swift told the maids how to turn a gentleman's caress into coin: "Never allow him the smallest liberty, not the squeezing of your

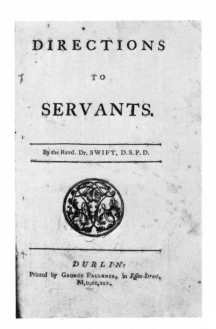

Title page, *Directions to Servants* by Jonathan Swift, 1745.

hand unless he puts a guinea in it. Five guineas for handling your breast is a cheap penny worth, altho you seem to resist with all your might."

There were those who thought matters were the other way around; that the master's son had his eye out for a tasty wench, and hang the consequences where she was concerned. The servant-maid controversy—were they vixens or were they victims?—was widely debated, with excited voices raised for both sides. The hazards of the serving-maid's profession can be glimpsed in some chapter heads from *A Present for a Servant Maid* (1743), ascribed to that outspoken 18th-century feminist, Eliza Haywood:

Observance	Carelessness of Children
Avoiding Sloth	Of Fire, Candle, Thieves
Sluttishness	New Acquaintance
Staying on Errands	Fortune-Tellers
Telling Family Affairs	Giving Saucy Answers
Secrets Among Fellow-Servants	Liquorishness
Entering into their Quarrels	Apeing the Fashion
Tale-bearing	Dishonesty
Being an Eye-Servant	The Market-Penny

Delaying to give Change	Mispending Time
Giving away Victuals	Publick Shews
Bringing in Chair-women	Vails
Washing Victuals	Giving Advice too freely
Quarrels with Fellow-Servants	Chastity
Behaviour to the Sick	Temptations from the Master
Hearing Things against a Master	If A Single Man
or Mistress	If A Married Man
Being too free with Men-servants	If from the Master's Son
Conduct towards Apprentices	If from Gentlemen Lodgers

Mrs. Anne Barker, a housekeeper with many years of experience, encouraged maids to dream of more than a passing pinch from the master if they plied their craft wisely and well. She began her manual, *The Complete Servant Maid* (1762), written for "those members of her own sex whose circumstances oblige them to live in servitude" with these encouraging lines:

> Be honest and trusted—be prudent and prais'd
> Be mild to be pleasing—and meek to be rais'd
> For the servant whose Diligence strikes Envy dumb,
> Shall in place be admir'd—and a Mistress become.

The angry outcries over servant maids were second only to those that rose over tips, or vails, lamented back in 1598 as too slender by *A Health to the Gentlemanly Profession of Serving Men,* but now of such robust proportions that they were the talk of the century among the English and scandalized visitors from other countries. One French traveler reported: "You'll find all the servants drawn up in the passage like a file of musketeers, from the house steward down to the lowest livery servant, and each of them holds out his hand to you in as deliberate a manner as the servants in our inns on the like occasion."

A nobleman leaving the home of the Duke of Newcastle after a dinner party found, as expected, the cook waiting at the door. He offered the man a crown. "Sir, I do not take silver," said the cook, nose in air. "Indeed!" replied the irate noble. "Well, I do not give gold."

All visitors were not as defiant as the duke's dinner guest. In many cases Englishmen found it too expensive to visit each other's estates because of the vails that would be exacted. One host, his invitation refused by a guest who confessed he could not afford the cost, supplied the gratuities because the guest's visit would serve an important purpose. Many visitors brought along their own servants.

The most conspicuous adornments of a household staff were the footmen, maintained in some luxurious households in units of eight or ten, all of them as nearly matched in height and appearance as a set of Queen Anne chairs. The running footmen were the most exceptional. The term "footman" originated in their chief duties: running on foot to neighboring estates to deliver messages and packages. When a family traveled by coach, the footmen preceded the horses, running at a steady pace of seven miles an hour, watching for ruts and obstructions that might endanger the vehicle. On festival occasions in the city they sometimes ran before the coach holding aloft a cane with a liquid-filled cup in the top. If their pace was steady enough, not a drop of liquid would slosh over the edge.

Roads improved and postal service eventually took over, making running footmen obsolete, but the household variety remained, at least in title, though often more valet or butler than footman.

The most famous footman was a late 18th-century manservant, John MacDonald, who introduced the umbrella to rainy London. Not until 1778, when MacDonald first carried an umbrella about the streets of London to shield his head on rainy days, was this

"A Rain-beau."
Old Times by John Ashton, 1885.

accessory adopted by Englishmen in lieu of the sword. Footmen were forbidden such adornments, and this may have moved Mac-Donald—who had observed Frenchmen occasionally carrying umbrellas—to assert his right to swing a useful accessory at his side. MacDonald took up where Beau Nash left off and was bracketed with him by W. E. H. Lecky for "the peaceful revolution that substituted the umbrella for the sword."

Despite the need to reduce their staffs, imposed on many aristocrats because of heavy taxes and rising expenses due to the cost of the French-English wars and the American Revolutionary War, there was no decrease in the demand for servants, who could find more than enough employers in the affluent mercantile class—nor in the servants' demands. Their conduct continued to arouse as much outraged criticism at the end of the 18th century as it had at the beginning.

Angry employers often aired their grievances in the London *Times,* and the complaints had not changed. One "Constant Reader" of 1795 called on "every good master and mistress to stop . . . the present ridiculous and extravagant mode of dress in their domestics," as Defoe had nearly a century earlier. "On a Sunday, see a tradesman's family coming from Church, and you would be puzzled to distinguish the porter from the master, or the maid from her mistress," complained the correspondent.

If employers had already taken a stand on their servants' lavish attire, he warned them of another practice: "Houses open on purpose where those servants who do not choose their mistresses shall see them, carry their dresses in a bundle and put them on." In all this robing and disrobing, Constant Reader suspected, "Many a poor deluded creature has been disrobed of her virtue."

Few employers looked upon servants as "poor deluded creatures." The shoe was on the other foot, and pinching noticeably. Said another correspondent in the *Times:* "Tell a servant now, in the mildest manner, they have not done their work to please you and you are told to provide for yourself, and, should you speak again, they are gone." In the face of such terrorist tactics the wise employer observed the rules of courtesy preached by Ecclesiasticus, and "intreated" his servant as a Brother.

"A Scene in Kensington Gardens, or Fashions and Frights of 1829."
Etching by George Cruikshank, 1829.

20 · KNOW YOUR PLACE

WHEN ENGLISH SOCIETY hedged itself in with etiquette in the 19th century it did so as "a shield against the intrusion of the impertinent, the improper, and the vulgar." This was its fundamental purpose, explained Charles William Day in *Etiquette and the Usages of Society* (1836): "Etiquette is the barrier which society draws around itself as a protection."

Etiquette proved to be as effective as a barberry hedge. Any outsider who tried to crawl through its prickly thicket of unfamiliar rules could emerge scratched and bleeding from the snubs.

Until *Etiquette and the Usages of Society* was published, to be quickly followed by a number of similar manuals, the current rules of etiquette, like the ceremonies Courtin had described a century earlier, were "inside" information. Those who moved in the inner circle of society knew the rules, but unless some kind friend already settled there was willing to extend a hand, there was no way for outsiders to learn etiquette accurately. The point of it was, you were supposed to *know* it, not learn it.

Furthermore, a helping hand from a friend already arrived in fashionable society was a most unlikely gesture. As *Etiquette and the Usages of Society* pointed out, "The English are the most aristocratic democrats in the world, always endeavoring to squeeze through the portals of fashion and then slamming the door in the face of any unfortunate devil who may happen to be behind them."

How then was the "unfortunate devil," or his wife, to learn that absolutely *nobody* served coffee at the dinner table (unless, of course, the guests were going on to the theater) or that the joint was never carved at a fashionable dinner table? (It was served already sliced or carved at a sideboard.) And how were the hopeful pair to know that introducing their callers to each other was "bad form" and would cause those they wanted to receive never to return again? Members of fashionable society recognized each other by the correct practice of these various rites. But how was one to learn them? Charles William Day rode to the rescue.

Masked in the borrowed name of Count Alfred D'Orsay, and wrapped in flowing rhetoric, Day extended a helping hand to uninitiated aspirants to society. "This is not written for those who do, but for those who do not know what is proper," he proclaimed at the outset. The know-nots he recognized as "comprising a large portion of highly respectable and estimable people, who have not had an opportunity of becoming acquainted with the usages of the (so termed) 'Best Society.' " The parentheses and quotation marks are Day's.

Like the traveler setting out for Coblenz for the first time with the first Baedeker (a guide to that city) in hand, the newcomer to society could now pick up his etiquette book and study the route to follow. Interestingly, both etiquette books and Baedeker guidebooks appeared at the same time.

"The upper ranks of the middle classes in London," knew their way all right, said Day, but not so the country people in the "mercantile districts." These were increasing like cowslips in the spring, but in case his readers thought of themselves as special cases, Day confided, "In a mercantile country like our own, people are continually rising in the world. Shopkeepers become merchants, and mechanics manufacturers. With the possession of wealth, they acquire a taste for the luxuries of life, expensive furniture, gorgeous plate . . . with the use of which they are only imperfectly acquainted . . . such persons are often painfully reminded that wealth alone is insufficient to protect them from the mortifications which a limited acquaintance with society entails upon the ambitious."

However, even Day was faced with limitations as to the amount of "inside" ritual he could unravel for his eager readers. This was particularly true at the dining table, where "Fashions are continually changing, even at the best tables; and what is considered the height of good taste one year, is declared vulgar the next; besides which, certain *sets* have certain customs, peculiar to their own clique, and all who do not conform *exactly* to their methods are looked upon as vulgar persons, ignorant of good-breeding." Exactly what Jonathan Swift had objected to in the 18th century! If admission to a "set" was sought, the best advice Day could offer was the sentiment expressed by the *Spectator* a century earlier: take it easy; don't attempt to be "too fine."

Day could tell his merchants and manufacturers to keep their knives out of their mouths, and to use napkins instead of pocket handkerchiefs at table—"Nothing indicates a well-bred man more than a proper mode of eating his dinner"—he could tell their wives in what order to seat guests at table and how to reply to an invitation to a ball. But unfortunately he could not secure them the guests, nor the invitations to the desirable balls.

In Victorian England class distinctions were more sharply drawn than ever as the newest wave of affluence crested and showed every sign of becoming tidal. And the highest barriers were erected at the balls—the public balls, which were similar to today's charity balls, and held for the same reasons: to raise money for philanthropies and to give society an opportunity to preen itself publicly.

The quadrille requiring groups of four couples was danced at the balls, but heaven forfend that nonmixable classes should be stirred together in these formations. The democratic mixing that Beau Nash had insisted on at Bath was long forgotten. At country balls, where the danger of such accidental mixing was greatest, ball stewards stood guard. *Manners and Tone of Good Society,* whose anonymous author called himself "a member of the aristocracy,"

"Places for a country dance."
John Leech drawing for *Handley Cross* by Robert Surtees, 1851.

explained, "The stewards of these balls are, as a rule, the representatives of the various classes attending the ball." Apparently they were like shepherds, herding the classes together.

> Nowhere is "class" more brought into prominence than at a "Country Ball" [warned the book]. There is a recognized though unwritten law which everyone obeys, to infringe would be a breach of etiquette . . . each class has its own set, and a member of one set would be foolish . . . to attempt to invade another or higher set. Thus, a couple belonging to say the professional set, would not take their places in a quadrille at the top of the ballroom—which is always appropriated by the aristocratic element—under the risk of being mortified.

Few dared to run such risks, though some may have done it out of ignorance, not having read an etiquette book beforehand. The offending couple would either be cut dead and left standing partnerless, or would be coldly told, "We have a vis-a-vis, thank you."

In either case it was an experience to provoke the shivers. Etiquette books strove to spare the ignorant such a catastrophe. However, sterner measures were needed against the daring.

> At some public balls a cord is drawn across the ball-room to render the upper end unassailable, but this extreme exclusiveness is not often resorted to, "clique" and "class" being thoroughly maintained without its aid.

Social segregation began right at the palace gates. Only the correct people could gain admission to the presence of the queen. But fortunately for those armed with more ambition than birthright, the circumference of this charmed circle grew larger each year. *Manners and Tone of Good Society* found no cause for rejoicing in this, and complained, "Of late years everyone with the slightest pretension to fashion or wealth . . . endeavors to obtain a presentation to her Majesty . . . deeming [it] places them at once within fashionable society, thus giving them a position in the social scale otherwise unattainable."

In the list of "Persons entitled to attend drawing-rooms and levees" were included, in addition to the blooded aristocracy and the gentry, members of the military, clergy and bar; families of merchants, bankers and Stock Exchange members; and "persons engaged in commerce on a large scale." Retailers were the pariahs. "At trade known as retail trade, however extensive its operation, the line is drawn, and very strictly so,"* stated *Manners and Tone*. Darkly it warned all reckless retailers, "Were a person actually engaged in trade to obtain a presentation, his presentation would be cancelled as soon as the Lord Chamberlain were made aware of the nature of his occupation."

In contrast to English etiquette books, French manuals were comparatively free of class feeling and adopted a much less patronizing attitude to their readers. *Du Ton et Des Manières Actuel Dans le Monde* (1854) declared itself honored to be consulted and welcomed all readers to its pages. French society was undoubtedly as selective as English society, but French etiquette books

* My husband is a retailer!—E.B.A.

avoided the brusque language and exhortations to respect class that overflowed English books.

On many points the etiquette rules of England and the continent differed greatly and these had to be learned beforehand if social dialogue was to be attempted. For example, in England a gentleman meeting a lady of slight acquaintance on a promenade would not greet her unless she gave the first sign of recognition. In France the reverse was true and it would be rude for a gentleman to wait for the lady to make the first advance. He would greet *her.* Notable differences prevailed in table conduct as well.

Where in former years the English had looked upon French manners as the standard of refinement, a leadership they had grudgingly granted despite their refusal to take French lessons to heart, it was now the English who were the more refined—in *fact,* as well as in their own opinion. French etiquette manuals did not find a market in England.

French etiquette was essentially that of a bourgeois nation and had developed for the benefit and use of the middle class. English etiquette was grooved in the chilly format of precedence, for a nation that had retained an almost uninterrupted monarchy and venerated its aristocracy. In England, as Adam Badeau put it in *Aristocracy in England,* "Everybody looks up."

"Mrs. and Miss Dotherington!"
John Leech drawing for *Ask Mama* by Robert Surtees, 1858.

21 · THE CARDBOARD BARRIER

ONCE ETIQUETTE BOOKS APPEARED in England, they proved to be fine guides. But in order to form more than a reading acquaintance with the ways of society it was necessary to make human contact with some of its members. The accomplishment of this goal or, inversely, its prevention, was mainly the basis of 19th-century English etiquette. One of the first rules was: "Never introduce people to each other without a previous understanding that it will be agreeable to both." This applied even when out walking with a friend and encountering another.

Chance social contacts were not to be pursued, even if made at the home of a mutual friend. The fleeting nature of such acquaintances, already noted at Bath, finally crystallized into the following rule of etiquette: "Neither ladies or gentlemen, in making calls, are introduced to others whom they may meet in the parlors of those on whom their calls are made. They are at liberty to converse as freely as if they had met before, the fact that they are friends of the hostess being presumptive evidence of their social equality, but the acquaintance thus made must not extend beyond the drawing room."

Newcomers to a city might be armed with a letter of introduction to a desirable social leader, but the best way to succeed was to *send* the letter by messenger, accompanied by a calling card. If the social leader later presented herself in person at the aspirant's home, the newcomer could return the call and the acquaintance was under way. If only a card was left, acknowledging receipt of the letter, the door had been slammed shut.

The most formidable battles to enter society were fought with calling cards. The warriors were mainly women. For centuries they had played a passive background role while men had been the center pole of social life, but the coming of the Industrial Revolution had reversed these roles. Now, too busy with business affairs to spend their days in leisurely social activities, men left such matters to wives. Women quickly outdistanced men in their social ambition.

This drive in women drew Thomas Morton's attention in his play, *Speed the Plough* (1800), in which he created the offstage character of Mrs. Grundy, the target of Mrs. Ashfield's efforts to be noticed and accepted. How Mrs. Grundy came to symbolize censorship puzzles me; this was not her role in Morton's play. The constant references to her by Mrs. Ashfield were made not out of fear of committing improprieties, but as yearning to impress and outdo the Grundy family, "genteel as they think themselves." Farmer Ashfield, annoyed by his wife's striving to impress Mrs. Grundy, complained, "Always ding, dinging Dame Grundy in my ears. What will Mrs. Grundy say? What will Mrs. Grundy think? Can't thee be quiet?"

Mrs. Ashfield was the emerging *snob*, a word that was originally slang for cobbler, later was applied to non-academic residents of Cambridge, and around 1827 came to mean a vulgar, ostentatious striver impressed by wealth and position. Thackeray created a series of satirical pieces for *Punch* in 1846 and focused attention on the word. Later he brought together a series of his tart word-pictures of the various snob types in *A Book of Snobs*.

Ambitious snobs wanted to be seen as callers in the homes of important people, the initial step toward social success. To be called on in return by important people sealed the striver's success. Almost any ambitious climber could find a suitable pretext to leave a card at a desirable home—once. The trick was to receive a personal call in return and thus advance to the position of a regular caller at the sought-after home.

The whole system of calls and card leaving was as rigidly prescribed as any hierarchical procedure of medieval times, and it was a foregone conclusion that Mrs. Ashfield failed to make social contact with Mrs. Grundy. Either Mrs. Grundy had never returned Mrs. Ashfield's initial call or, just as bad, had returned it with a card. Country society was the hardest to breach because of its limited size; in the country, calling was "very much confined to individual status in society and class," proclaimed one etiquette authority.

In the city the crush was greater but the chances of success increased proportionately. The hope of winning in this social sweepstake was the compelling urge that drove ambitious women, pasteboards in hand, on a daily round of social visits. *Manners and Tone of Good Society* explained why the pace must never slacken: "Leaving cards . . . is one of the most important social observances . . . the first step towards forming or enlarging a circle of acquaintances." Having made clear the reason why, the author warned, "Neglect of this social duty, or the improper performance of it, or the non-fulfillment of its prescribed rules, would be a sure step in the opposite direction. The following is the . . . card leaving . . . etiquette observed in good society by both ladies and gentlemen, and may be fearlessly followed."

Armed with the forty-two pages of detailed instructions that followed, even an inexperienced Diana was ready to buckle on her card-filled quiver and fearlessly stalk Mrs. Higher-Up through the forest of Good Society.

Calls fell into two broad categories: those made on intimate friends and not bound by rules or protocol, and ceremonious calls, which were as heavily draped in protocol as a bandstand is in bunting. In addition to being formal repayment of a previous call, ceremonious calls were made to offer congratulations, condolences, or thanks for recent entertainment.

Hostesses received formally in the late afternoon; morning visits were as a rule reserved for intimate friends. If, for any reason—and it had better be a good one—a matinal encounter took place between casual acquaintances, it could prove a perilous adventure for the socially inexperienced. "A morning call is usually a tete-a-tete," said *Manners and Tone of Good Society*. Such an encounter "requires a considerable amount of tact and *savoir faire* to be gracefully sustained," and like strange dogs sniffing each other, each lady would be on the alert, "to discover the merits, or demerits, of the other." In such an hour it was social suicide for the hostess "to amuse her visitor by the production of albums, books, portfolios of drawings, or the artistic efforts of members of the family." Such gaucherie betrayed that the hostess "was not much accustomed to society."

"Madame, your cousin Betty wishes to know if you can receive her."
"Impossible! Tell her that today I receive."
Les Tribulations de la Vie Elégante, 1870.

The easiest way to avoid such unfortunate disclosure was, of course, to avoid tête-à-têtes.

Another error that betrayed the inexperienced hostess was failure to have the street door opened for a departing guest. "Never allow a person above the rank of a shopman to leave the room without your ringing the bell for the street door to be opened," warned *Etiquette and the Usages of Society*. "Thousands have been irremediably offended by having to 'let themselves out.' This deserves particular notice, as it is a very common omission with persons, who, having amassed a little wealth, set up for 'somebodies.'"

Refreshments were not necessary during calling hours, but if a caller arrived at teatime and found the hostess having tea, she would naturally be offered some, "neither persuasively nor coldly," said *Manners and Tone of Good Society*.

The use of "plates and d'oyleys at afternoon tea would be considered bad style." As for a "tea cozy," such an article "should never be seen in a lady's drawing room." And if the hostess preferred to have tea handed around by a servant, only a manservant would do, "not a parlourmaid," said *Manners and Tone* sternly.

These were city rules. For those who lived in the country, the course was played by "country" rules. Callers who had come a long distance were entitled to stay longer and to receive some kind of refreshment—tea for the ladies, a glass of sherry for the gentlemen. If the guests stayed for several hours, their horses, too, were treated like callers and given a bag of oats for refreshment. And if the horses had drawn a carriage to the premises, they were unhitched and allowed to relax for a few hours.

While it was an accepted convention that a city hostess could send word to the front door that she was "not at home," *i.e.*, "not receiving" if visitors arrived unexpectedly, the country hostess was sternly commanded never to do this.

As a general rule ladies greatly outnumbered men during calling hours. Most men now found these visits a nuisance, and a married man correctly expected his wife to assume this duty. A bachelor, especially a newcomer to the city, might find such circulation profitable but *Social Ethics and the Courtesies of Society*, warned that a gentleman *never* calls on a lady "without the knowledge and permission of her husband." Unmarried professional men such as doctors and lawyers were excused from the obligation of making calls to say thanks to a hostess who had entertained them, because their time was "more usefully occupied."

All of this calling back and forth required considerable record keeping in order to keep the social ledger balanced—and also to reveal any slights. "Keep a strict account of your ceremonial visits," said *Social Ethics and the Courtesies of Society*, "and take note how soon your calls are returned. You will thus be able, in most cases, to form an opinion whether or not your frequent visits are desired."

A hostess with a house guest under her roof would place a sitting room at the guest's disposal during calling hours, where the guest could receive *her* acquaintances and friends without any intrusion from the hostess. Lacking such premises, the hostess would nevertheless expect the guest to absent herself during calling hours unless the callers expected were friends of both.

Toward the end of the century some grumbling, even scoffing, could be heard about all the ceremony of calling and leaving cards, but *Etiquette for Women* urged its readers to ignore such complaints. Calling was serious, the author cautioned, and every aspect of its performance added a plus or minus to one's social career. It was even important to *handle* the cards properly and to offer them with aplomb to the servant who answered the door. "It is wise to place one or two cards in an easily get-atable position, for the eye of the servant is often critical and merciless, and you may be sure that she has no opinion of the bungling, flustered card-leaver." Who knows, she might even tell her mistress.

Calling was the most impersonal routine imaginable, with a technique of calculated slights and numerous subtle inhospitalities. But its elaborate development suited the chilly amenities of a period when women called their husbands "Mister" and seldom used a first name with a friend.

22 · THE FOOT IN THE MOUTH

"Vulgar" was the word that could send seismic tremors through the English middle class. If an etiquette writer wished to command his reader's instant attention, he had only to use that word.

There were dozens of ways in which the socially unskilled could betray their lack of experience, but the most direct route to total downfall was invariably through the mouth: when it opened to receive food, or to send our words.

To begin with the conventions of eating properly:

The fork was the keystone of polite eating. But in 1840, when Charles Day in *Etiquette and the Usages of Society* told the middle classes that eating with a knife was "glaringly vulgar," the fork was not yet in universal use among the English middle classes.

The English had always displayed strong resistance to the fork and had adopted it gingerly only in the 17th century. Long after, many country gentlemen had continued to reject it as too dainty. When they were finally won over, lesser folk in their shires still clung to the old habit of eating with knives. As rural families achieved industrial success and transferred to more urban surroundings, the knife in the mouth was often as much a tag of origin as a Yorkshire accent.

By the 19th century most of the upper class had added forks to the various emblems of their superior status—so much so that the German Prince Puckler-Muskau, in the journal of his English travels (1823), described knives in the mouth as "one of the greatest offences against English manners a man can commit." In Germany, even a prince could still put his knife in his mouth without causing an eyebrow to rise.

Until etiquette books began to enlighten the middle classes, they had little opportunity to learn of the knife's changed status, since they did not move in society. However, etiquette books had made their point so thoroughly by the second half of the 19th century that the subject was deemed closed by most authorities.

Apparently Europeans were as right-handed with forks as Americans until around the 1840s; then the fashionable upper class stopped shifting their forks back and forth. It is possible that as more and more middle-class eaters learned to shovel food into their mouths with tines instead of blades, the upper class hit upon this as a new class identification. It became fashionable first in England, but in 1853 a French etiquette book, *Manuel du Bon Ton et de la Politesse,* confided, "If you wish to eat in the latest mode favored by fashionable people, you will not change your fork to your right hand after you have cut your meat, but raise it to your mouth in your left hand."

A long list of elementary do's and dont's in this same French etiquette book—"Don't blow in your soup; don't drink from your saucer; don't throw bones on the table, but leave them at the edge of your plate; eat with your fork, not your fingers"—may indicate that the author consulted a long outdated book for his text, or that he appealed to a broader base of readers. French etiquette books were essentially more democratic than the English. There were marked differences, however, in what passed for good manners at the tables of each nation. French diners still rinsed their mouths at table in medieval fashion, using the *rince-doigt,* or finger bowl, for this, while English diners were warned not to use their "finger glasses" in this way. "Some think that *because* it is a foreign habit, the filthy custom of gargling your mouth at table can not be disgusting," said *Etiquette and the Usages of Society* sternly, in the 1850s.

By the end of the 19th century the French had grown so dainty and so averse to touching *any* food with the fingers that even the *rince-doigt* was eliminated from French tables. Conversely, napkins were considered essential by the French, but had disappeared from upper-class English tables in the 18th century and had not yet returned in the 1850s. *Etiquette and the Usages of Society* sadly and enviously commented, "It is a matter of regret that table napkins are not considered indispensable in England. With all our boasted re-finements, they are far from being general." But, if no napkins were provided, "A man has no alternative but to use the table-cloth . . . or his pocket handkerchief." Napkins were still not general in the late 1860s. *Habits of Good Society* warned its readers: "If host and hostess dine without napkins, it would be bad taste to call for one. It is always better to waive a refinement than to hurt feelings."

Napkins might be absent from tables, but fancy service was not, if the hosts aspired to be rated fashionable. Thackeray described "Dinner giving snobs," in "the middle rank of life, accustomed to mutton—roast on Tuesday, cold on Wednesday, hashed on Thursday"—who wasted their "small means on unnaturally costly enter-tainments," and attempted to impress their guests with such frills as footmen, who were really "green-grocers or carpet-beaters," earn-ing a few extra shillings on the side. At such dinners, the green-grocer-temporarily-turned-footman often served the soup with white-gloved hands. *Etiquette and the Usages of Society* sniffed at such adornments as just this side of vulgarity, not to be seen in "the mansions of people of distinction." A tea towel wrapped

"Dinner is sarved."
John Leech drawing for *Handley Cross* by Robert Surtees, 1851.

around the thumb was the more elegant way to keep it out of the soup.

All authorities agreed that dinner parties "ranked first among entertainments," and Thackeray gleefully exposed it all as so much "humbug . . . the dishes, the drink, the servants, the plate . . . and the hospitality." Here, too, an outsider's view of English efforts to keep up appearances was given by Prince Puckler-Muskau in one of his sprightly letters to his German sweetheart. "Custom here demands many luxuries," he wrote from England. "As much at the shopkeeper's house, as at the Duke's," because of the "aspiring and imitative manners of the country." Such luxuries included "servants in handsome liveries, a profusion of dishes and foreign wines, rare and expensive desserts, and in all things . . . 'plenty' as the English call it." But the prince saw what a Cinderella existence it was for many families: it went on "as long as there are visitors in the house; but many a family atones for it by meager fare when they are alone."

Nevertheless, newly affluent families continued to reveal their freshman status by serving lavish food and adorning their tables ostentatiously. One such adornment, the place card, was vetoed by *Manners of the Aristocracy* as "suggestive of a public dinner rather than a private entertainment." Those who would dine in the manner of the aristocracy were told, "They have never been adopted in the highest circles, where they are regarded as a rather vulgar and decidedly clumsy invention."

However, the widespread adoption of *Service à la Russe,* which meant that all the food to be served was no longer placed on the table at one time for all to behold, but was instead served in separate courses, or a dish at a time, brought menu cards into use around the 1870s. *Etiquette of Modern Society* declared them "indispensable," and indeed they were imperative if diners were to gauge their intake of each course realistically. "There should be one to every couple," said *Etiquette of Modern Society,* and every well-appointed table sported its profusion of menus, either written on porcelain menu slates or on cards which were perched in porcelain or silver menu holders.

The *quatorzième* was a less widely known and less frequently employed dinner adjunct of the 19th century, and perhaps as good an illustration as any of the artificiality of many entertainments. This professional dinner guest made a *fourteenth* if only thirteen were scheduled to sit down to dinner. Presumably the *quatorzième* was a replacement for a last-minute defector from the guest list. The profession was highly remunerative, to judge from the large estate left by one such professional dinner guest.

By the latter part of the 19th century most English etiquette books assumed that all but the lowest classes knew how to eat properly and did not downgrade their books by briefing readers on these points. An occasional bleat was heard against knives in the mouth by a book that did not hold its head—or audience—too high; but most Englishmen hoping to rise in the social scale knew better than to commit this solecism, to use the favorite warning word of etiquette books.

All those with reasonable social experience could see vulgarisms, but seemingly they were unable to *hear* them. The deafest of all was that particular example of bad taste under attack since Renaissance days: the name-dropper. Few 19th-century etiquette books let the errors of too much talk, or the wrong talk, go unremarked; but they tackled the name-dropper's case with fresh rancor as the hinges on the doors of society creaked and groaned under the strain of crowds pushing to get in.

"Nothing will more irretrievably stamp you as vulgar in really good society than the repeated introduction of . . . names of distinguished personages in reference to yourself," said *Habits of Good Society*. "It is absurd to suppose that you can reflect the light of these greater orbs," the author continued, comparing the name-dropper to the "pale pitiable moon when she quits her proper sphere and forces herself into broad daylight." Not that the author objected to pale moon people—he simply did not like to see them trying to shine like suns. "If a man is fit for good society, it can make very little difference whether his father was a chimney-sweep or a chancellor, at least to sensitive people. Indeed to insist on good birth in England would not only shut you out from enjoying the society of people of no ordinary stamp, but is now generally considered as a cowardly way of asserting your superiority."

Habits of Good Society wore blinders. Society as glimpsed in the pages of etiquette books was hardly composed of "sensitive people," and the son of a chimney sweep was not likely to get past the door of people high in society, despite an anecdote the author used to make his point. A society lady wondered at his friendship with a certain family whose mother had been a cook. "Well," said the democratic author (who may himself have been the son of a chimney sweep; he remains anonymous), "it is evident she did not bring them up in the kitchen."

A man's dimensions (a woman's too, for that matter) could be taken the moment a mouth opened and words poured out. Ecclesiasticus had said, "Praise no man before thou hearest him speak, for this is the trial of men." Judgment could be pronounced quickly on those who talked not wisely but too much. "People that want brains have always the most tongue, as if apprehensive their stupidity would not soon enough be perceived," said Jean Baptiste Bellegarde in the 18th century. The 19th century's Charles Day supplied specific examples of how too much tongue could disclose stupidity.

"Never talk largely of the Opera, on the strength of having been there once or twice," he warned. There was always the danger that some "frequenter" would be present who had "every opera, its casts and music, at his tongue's end." The same applied to a learned discourse on Titian and Rubens based on a superficial examination of "copies or engravings." "Remember that if you are quiet in society you will, at least, have credit for discretion," said Day.

The free use of vulgar language had completely vanished from polite conversation, and which words were taboo was by now too well known to require mention in etiquette books. Though much of the speech prudishness of the 19th century is often attributed to Queen Victoria, it began much earlier, as we have seen, and was already well established by the end of the 18th century. By 1818 Thomas Bowdler had cleaned up Shakespeare and Gibbon; Victoria was not born until 1819. However, with all the affectations of etiquette and the emphasis on ultra-refinement, more words continued to be thrown into the limbo of impolite talk.

The Society for the Reformation of Manners had succeeded in

The Society for the Reformation of Manners had succeeded in
stamping out oaths in polite conversation; in fact, they had succeeded so well that "bloody," formerly a popular expletive, could no
longer be used in a descriptive sense. *Beeton's Manners of Polite
Society* (c. 1876) cautioned hosts not to serve ladies meat "too
ensanguined." Evidently not only the word but the sight of "bloody"
was too much for the delicate sensibilities of the mid-19th century.

Well-bred English people never spoke of going to bed; they
retired. Even a bureau could not have "drawers." To refer to a
female as a woman" was insulting and a foreigner might cause a
fainting spell if he said "woman" to a lady's face. This finally
brought a blast from *Habits of Good Society,* frowning as it did on
many current pretensions. It declared that "woman" was just as
good as "lady," and delicacy was being carried too far when "Young
ladies faint—or try to—at the mention of a petticoat." Delicacy was,
in fact, being carried to such extremes that Lady Gough's *Etiquette*
ruled that even *books* by male and female authors should "be properly separated on bookshelves. Their proximity unless they happen
to be married should not be tolerated."

Words are as subject to the winds of change as sleeves, bonnets
and the cut of a lapel. When "petticoat" caused fainting spells,
"occupy" ranked with the reliable four-letter word for copulate as
equally impolite.

Important, from the point of social advancement, was knowing
how to *pronounce* words, proper ones, that is. *Manners and Tone
of Good Society,* which otherwise held its nose rather high in the
air, acknowledged that some of its readers might not know the
elegant elisions and this might "argue unfavourably as to the social
position of the offender." A list of some trickier blurrings included:
Cirencester, pronounced *Cisiter;* Belvoir—*Bever;* Pontrefact—*Prom-
fret;* Cockburn—*Coburn;* Strachan—*Strawn;* Mainwaring—*Man-
nering;* and apparently some readers still needed help with Chol-
mondeley, pronounced *Chumley.* But only the most elegant members of the Edwardian set knew to drop their g's. The man who
went dancin' or off for a weekend of shootin' spoke with the distinction of the aristocracy.

American visitors to England were given some speech first aid by

Good Form in England (1887), written by a fellow American. In the prevailing English fashion he omitted his name so I am forced to take his word as to his nationality; some doubts as to his reliability arose when he explained that all who dwelt in London were cockneys. Perhaps they were so-called in the 1880s, though "cockney" today is usually applied to the lower classes, and specifically those born "within sound of the Bow Bells." At any rate, in his day society no longer *lived* in London, but maintained houses there to use during the social season. At other times they lived on their country estates, "country" having lost its undesirable rustic connotation of the previous century.

While the society accent was immediately detectable and rang with the authenticity of Waterford crystal, the London cockney accent had many gradations. The nonaspirated *H* was the absolute bottom of the barrel. "For a person to drop an *h* is a sign that he is not a member of the upper classes. It is worse than bad form. It means utter social ruin," said *Good Form in England*. The reader could readily infer that the same ruin would befall those who associated with an *H*-dropper.

The book explained English "good form" from the size of tips to leave with servants when visiting an English home to "reversing" in the waltz. *That* was bad form. Perhaps, suggested the author, because the English could not master the difficult maneuver.

Anything ostentatious was sure to be tagged vulgar, and on this point the author quite literally choked at the thought of English reaction to diamonds or precious stones on a lady in the daytime. "Anything except, perhaps, the smallest-sized bonnet-string pin, would be—well, it is difficult to find words to express how bad the 'form' would be."

Fully one third of the book dealt with proper precedential treatment of the English aristocracy and upper class from royalty to gentlemen. "Gentleman," the American author assured his American reader, "is commonly thought to be an expansive term, almost without limits. In England it is not so . . . a gentleman must be one by *birth*. Conduct has nothing to do with it." That statement was open to argument from the English themselves.

23 · THE ENGLISH GENTLEMAN COMPLETED

THROUGH THE CENTURIES the ideal of the gentleman had occupied Englishmen's thoughts, but no tests had proved to be conclusive and all contained contradictions. The ideal had been embodied in the knight—who could be ruthless as well as brave; in the courtier—who could be conniving as well as courteous; and in the nobleman—who could be as boorish as the meanest villager in his shire. And since ungentlemanly behavior had never diminished the right of any of them to be called gentlemen it would seem that birth or position had the edge as a definitive gage.

There were outspoken and influential critics who thought it should be otherwise. Sir Richard Steele declared in the *Tatler,* "The appellation of gentleman is never affixed to a man's circumstances, but to his behaviour in them."

Not until the 19th century did the ideal of the gentleman become a figure of universal identification, and by his behavior and his bearing the world knew him. His mold was cast in the classrooms and on the playing fields of the English public schools when education, which had gradually become a respected attribute of a gentleman, became, in the 19th century, a necessary one. With the education went a total manner: like a hallmark on English silver, it labeled its bearer genuine.

The public schools, so-called, were, of course, about as public as a monastery, but they still retained the tag that had described them originally when they had been founded for common use. The comparison to a monastery is actually not inappropriate, for some of them grew out of early monastic schools founded to enlist and train future clerics, as well as to provide schooling for needy boys who would eventually perform some type of service for a livelihood.

Eton, Westminster, and the oldest of them all, Winchester, founded by William of Wykeham of "Manners makyth man" fame, were begun mainly for the church. Harrow and Rugby began humbly as local public grammar schools.

Young aristocrats received their education from private tutors and rarely attended such schools until the 18th century, when a change came about and the original and public purpose of the schools began to be lost sight of. Aristocratic families, especially those influential with the church, sought and obtained admission for their sons. This may have been due to a decrease in the number of tutors available, but more probably because the economic pinch on landed families caused them to reduce as many expenditures as they could. The reason is not altogether clear, but it is a fact that more of the gentry now attended the schools originally founded for needier boys.

Jonathan Swift disapproved of the trend. In an "Essay on Modern Education" he cautioned: "By mingling the sons of noblemen with those of the vulgar you engage the former in bad company." But being a churchman himself, perhaps his real reason was to reserve the schools for their original intent.

There was little about the schools to recommend them to either class at the time. In the 18th century, even the universities Oxford and Cambridge had lost much of the eminence they had gained during the English Renaissance. The public schools functioned mainly as disciplinary centers and offered their narrow curriculums more for strict training than for useful knowledge.

Severe punishments for the slightest infractions were the rule, and fagging, which made the younger boys servants and lackeys to the older students, recalled the medieval days when noble English youths were sent off to serve as pages at neighboring estates. Service had always been an English tradition in preparing a boy for manhood, and such training undoubtedly produced tough, disciplined lads, but did it produce *gentlemen*? Or, for that matter, did the narrow range of instruction prepare boys for the higher education befitting a gentleman as one educator pictured him? That educator, Dr. Thomas Arnold (father of Matthew Arnold), thought not.

Dr. Arnold was appointed headmaster of Rugby in 1828 and

there he went to work in earnest, the most "cunning gardener" of all. He did not change the emphasis on self-discipline. If anything, he intensified it. But he brought about a more friendly accord between masters and students and fostered the prefectorial system, developing a deep sense of honor and loyalty among his young charges. Under his guidance Rugby was among the first schools to offer a broader curriculum that included modern languages such as French and German, and to give the classical studies new vigor—especially Latin, which had continued to be taught by ancient standards as if solely for church use.

Dr. Arnold's efforts drew mixed reactions. But in large measure the educational and philosophical reforms that he introduced at Rugby influenced the reform of England's leading schools and created the new standard of measurement for a gentleman. The new standard, based as it was on education, would have pleased Henry VIII, his daughter Elizabeth, and the 16th-century educators Thomas Elyot and Roger Ascham.

Still another Thomas—Thomas Hughes, a pupil of Dr. Thomas Arnold at Rugby (Thomas seems to have been a magical name in English education)—was largely responsible for grafting onto the new model gentleman the old chivalric virtues of loyalty and courage, enhanced by fair play and good sportsmanship. These qualities he dramatized in *Tom Brown's School Days.*

Many other factors involving political and religious changes contributed to the reforms in England's schools, public and otherwise, but these are too complex to even touch upon in this book. That the schools did finally produce what has become the accepted prototype of the English gentleman, seems beyond doubt. It is well expressed in a report of a Public Schools Commission appointed in England in 1864 to study the operation of nine public schools, some of them already mentioned in preceding paragraphs. Though the report was not entirely favorable on all counts, it applauded the benefit to both students and the nation in:

> . . . a system of government and discipline for boys, the excellence of which has been universally recognized, and which is admitted to have been the most important in its effects on national character and social life . . . These schools have been the chief

"The conversation during the match."
Frontispiece, *Tom Brown's School Days*. American edition, c. 1860.

nurseries of our statesmen; in them, and in schools modeled after
them, men of all classes that make up English society, destined
for every profession and career, have been brought up on a footing of social equality, and have contracted the most enduring
friendships, and some of the ruling habits of their lives: and they
have perhaps the largest share in moulding the character of an
English Gentleman.

In the final analysis the English gentleman produced by the 19th
century was a little of all the types that had preceded him, retaining
all of their best qualities—the knight's courage, the patriot's loyalty,

the courtier's suavity and elegance. He represented the combined dream of Caxton, Castiglione, Henry Peacham, Thomas Arnold and Thomas Hughes.

Whether he was educated in the proper schools or acquired for himself through attention and application the qualities which the schools produced, the 19th-century gentleman was the product also of a whole new world—the commercial world of the Industrial Revolution. If he was a member of the constantly enlarging Ungentle gentle, the middle class as the Elizabethan *Institucion of a Gentleman* had described it: "Ungentle by his father, and not by lineage made noble, but by his own knowledge, labor, and industry," he had every right to call himself a *gentleman* if his actions suited the name. Dinah Craik spoke for him in *John Halifax, Gentleman* (1857). When Halifax's small son, overjoyed with their new house and carriage, exclaimed, "Father, we are gentlefolk now!" Halifax replied, "We always were, my son."

"Feet up."
A typical American rudeness, criticized at home and abroad.
From *Illustrated Manners.*

PART FOUR

The American Way

Fight in Congress between Lyon and Griswold, 1798.
Caricature and Comic Art by James Parton, 1877.

24 · THE INCORRIGIBLE AMERICANS

EUROPEAN ETIQUETTE was based on precedence and dominated by the doctrine of exclusivity. American manners were based on the bedrock of equality and freedom. On such a foundation, sound though it may be, it was not possible to speedily erect a structure of great refinement. Unlike Europe where class division had always been the accepted social architecture, and invisible retaining walls still separated the masses from the aristocracy and upper class, America was designed as one great auditorium of society.

As is usually the case when seats are not reserved and the best locations are open to all, those who were the quickest got the best choice. The competitive rush and bustle that typifies the United States followed naturally from such beginnings.

In the early 1800s Americans already bolted their food, pushed and shoved each other on stagecoaches and riverboats, winked at law and order and displayed lively impatience with any obstacles in their way. Charles Dickens in his *American Notes* saw the difference in the national characters of England and America symbolized by the signal Americans gave the stagecoach driver to start. "Where an Englishman would cry 'All right!' an American cries 'Go ahead!' "

Most Americans spurned English formalities as undemocratic affectations and in general viewed polished behavior as an assertion of superiority and therefore insulting in a land of equality. This attitude moved Mrs. Eliza Farrar, wife of a Harvard professor and an early writer on etiquette for women (*The Young Ladies Friend*, 1834), to complain, "Some persons have a great dread of ceremony, as if it implied a sacrifice of sincerity or simplicity." The *American*

Gentleman's Guide to Politeness and Fashion agreed and asserted that many Americans "regard Rudeness and Republicanism as synonymous terms."

As touchy as watch springs about their freedom to do as they pleased, Americans belligerently asserted their rights with no quarter asked or given if rights collided. Newspapers abounded with accounts of "fatal encounters" and "bloody affrays." Harriet Martineau, visiting America in the 1830s, reported in *Society in America* that Americans, though pleasant enough, were ready to kill one another at the drop of an eyelid, a predilection that gave New Orleans in the year 1834 more duels than days in the year.

Another English visitor, Thomas Hamilton, recording his impressions in *Men and Manners in America* (1833), saw America as a wide-open arsenal. Remarking about the ivory dagger hilt he saw protruding from beneath the waistcoat of a bystander he was told, "The whole population of the Southern and Western states are uniformly armed with daggers . . . even in the state of New York . . . many were armed with this unmanly and assassin-like weapon."

Not even the nation's capital was safe from the mayhem encouraged by such freedom with weapons and tempers. The New York *Sun* of December 20th, 1837, reported a fatal settlement with a bowie knife in the House of Representatives when the Speaker of the House slew a member of the Arkansas Legislature "on the floor of the house, while in session . . . in consequence of some offensive remark directed against him by the unfortunate member."

Similar episodes were recounted by James Buckingham, another English critic, who filled three volumes with his impressions of America, most of them uncomplimentary. "Members from the South and West, go habitually armed into the House of Representatives and Senate; concealed pistols and dirks being the usual instruments worn beneath their clothes," he reported.

Fighting courage was kept at forge heat with frequent gulps of whiskey or rum, and visitors to the young republic found the American capacity for alcohol a never-ending marvel. "Shocking" might more accurately describe the impact on English visitors, who seemed to have forgotten that excessive drinking among the lower classes was a problem in their own country as well.

Parallel social conduct to that in America of the early 19th century, even to the riotous drinking, can be seen in the Soviet Union today, where Russian shirtsleeve society in the name of equality has eliminated, or perhaps intimidated, any display of gracious manners. France did the same after the French Revolution. However, a cultivated aristocracy *had* existed in these countries. When the French destroyed polite and ceremonious behavior in a burst of social iconoclasm, the memory of what had once been reverenced at a distance lingered on. Eventually manners were re-called from exile. The same may happen in Russia. But American manners had no point of recall, having begun without a "parental" court and practically no aristocracy to establish an environmental pattern for emulation.

If anything, most colonial Americans were hampered by the memories and habits of their own rude or questionable beginnings. The great majority were English, many of them criminals and un-desirables conveniently dumped in the colonies. Some settlers came in willing bondage as indentured servants and field laborers, others came unwillingly, lured aboard ship to fill the hungry demand for workers in the colonies. Flight from religious persecution brought others from France and Germany.

From whatever lands and backgrounds they came, most early settlers were driven by brutal causes—persecution, hunger, fear, punishment. Desperation was a familiar emotion to most, and if any had ever known gentle conduct it was soon forgotten in the rigors of conquering the new land.

Though most early Americans came from undistinguished stock, a handful displayed a heritage of good breeding, either brought from the other side or acquired by virtue of their earlier arrival and success in the New World. The courtesy books of Peacham and Braithwaite had reposed in some colonial libraries and doubtless inspired and instructed the patrician gentlemen who helped to mold the social order of America into a democratic system. There had even been some who longed to maintain a semblance of royalty in

America, provoking a spirited argument in favor of a regal-sounding title for the Presidency among the framers of the Constitution. Thomas McKean, a signer of the Declaration of Independence and later a governor of Pennsylvania, proposed "His Serene Highness." General Muhlenberg liked the sound of "High Mightiness," used by the Stadholder of Holland, but he confided to Washington that he had finally decided against it because, though it would be suitable "if the office could always be held by men as large as yourself," if the future turned up a president of small stature "it would be ridiculous."

George Washington was not without a taste for the privileges of royalty, and he surrounded himself with considerable pomp (which Jefferson quickly eliminated when he became President). Martha Washington shared her husband's liking for ceremony and instituted the levee in the nation's capital. The levee was also favored in such social centers as Charleston. It was held at night with blithe disregard for the meaning of the word—a morning reception. One of Mrs. Washington's Friday-night levees was made memorable when the towering ostrich-feather headdress of a New York belle encountered the candles of a low-hanging chandelier and caught fire.

There were early signs that the aristocracy to flourish eventually in America would be based on financial success. The Marquis de Chastellux was struck by American reverence for wealth when he attended a Philadelphia Assembly in the 1780s and saw Mrs. Robert Morris treated with the deference usually reserved for royalty in Europe. "An honor pretty generally bestowed on her," observed Chastellux, "as she is the richest woman in the city, and all ranks here being equal, men follow their natural bent by giving preference to riches."

The wife of General Knox, returning to Boston at the end of the Revolutionary War, sneered at the new fortunes and commented, "The scum had all risen to the top."

Thomas Hamilton, scornful of "the estimation in which wealth is held in New York," described it as "a population wholly devoted to money-getting," where hosts invariably announced an inventory of a man's recently acquired wealth as they introduced him.

Numerous visitors flocked from European shores to survey the American scene and to express in print their opinions of American behavior. Frenchmen on the whole were warm in their praise, perhaps because they had recently shared a similar political convulsion. Those who criticized did so in subdued terms, displaying better manners than the English. The English were unanimous in their condemnation of American manners and followed the line of Isaac Weld, who came in 1795 looking for "a better place of abode," and returned to England convinced there were few worse places to abide in than America. Sourly he muttered, "Civility cannot be purchased from them on any terms; they seem to think that it is incompatible with freedom."

Of the French, the best remembered observer is de Tocqueville, who submitted by far the gentlest appraisal of American manners. One wonders if he even saw any of the sights that so horrified English visitors. At least, having been a guest here, he had the good taste not to gossip for pages and pages about the bad manners of his hosts. Instead, he threw a well-aimed dart at the English for doing just that.

> The English make game of the manners of the Americans, but it is singular that most of the writers who have drawn these ludicrous delineations belonged themselves to the middle classes in England, to whom the same delineations are exceedingly applicable . . . they do not perceive that they are deriding themselves.

Another Frenchman, Michel Chevalier, sent by his government in 1834 to inspect American public projects, remained for two years and inspected American citizenry as well. He found the Virginian "a worthy descendant of the English gentleman . . . gracious, accustomed to luxury and service from others . . . better able to command men than to conquer nature and subdue the soil." The Yankee he tagged as "reserved, cautious, distrustful . . . manners without grace . . . narrow in his idea, but practical." In the two he saw 17th century England transplanted. "They are the same men who cut each other's throats in England, under the name of

Roundheads and Cavaliers," he wrote in *Society, Manners and Politics in the United States*. He, too, criticized English derision of Americans. "The portrait they have drawn of the Americans is a caricature, which, like all good caricatures, has some resemblance to the original."

None of this restrained the English who reported, in gruesome detail, everything they saw, like a bevy of back-porch gossips staring into a neighbor's window.

Captain Basil Hall caused American tempers to flare in the late 1820s with his *Travels in North America*. He described Americans as cold and uncommunicative, especially during meals when their attention was focused, like animals, on their heaped-up food. But talk to an American about making money and he opened up like a steamed clam. It was one thing to make it, said Hall patronizingly, "but more difficult than the art of making money, is the art of spending it like a gentleman." Since many properly blooded Englishmen like Hall frequently made this same comment of the expanding English middle class, perhaps Americans should not have been so sensitive. Edwin Godkin, founder of *The Nation,* made the same criticism of his fellow Americans in 1866. "Plenty of people know how to get money; but not very many know what best to do with it. To be rich properly is indeed a fine art. It requires culture, imagination and character."

Andrew Jackson entered the White House just as Basil Hall completed his visit to America, and what may have been English exaggeration before now swelled into indisputable truth. Previous Presidents had been drawn from the small grass-roots aristocracy of America, but here at last was the incarnation of the American dream—the son of poor Irish immigrants, fatherless at two, without inheritance of any kind, self-made in every sense of the word.

American aspirations soared like balloons, and apparently manners hit new lows, descending to the level of the backwoods the Jacksons had emerged from. Mrs. Jackson, it seems, had begun an earnest effort to polish her manners a few years earlier, when Mrs. Edward Livingston, wife of one of Jackson's military aides, had taught her table deportment. But the conduct of Jackson's supporters, who thundered into the White House on the eve of the inauguration, ripped down curtains and tossed furniture about in a frenzy of lowbrow celebration, really set the tone of Jacksonian manners.

With the start of the Jacksonian period European criticism of American manners grew even more vehement and detailed. More English observers flocked across the Atlantic to see what was taking place in the land of the free and almost unanimously decided that freedom left something to be desired. Mrs. Frances Trollope expressed her opinion in *Domestic Manners of the Americans* (1832) and perhaps qualifies as the harshest critic of all. She filled two volumes almost exclusively with invective and complained, not illogically, that freedom for all meant that a slaughterhouse could be built next door to a mansion. She spoke from bruising experience, having acquired just such a neighbor during her brief residency in Cincinnati. When she remonstrated with the prospective builder that such an enterprise might be considered a nuisance in a fine residential area—and weren't there laws against it?—the entrepreneur replied, "That may do very well for your tyrannical country, where a rich man's nose is more thought of than a poor man's mouth; but hogs be profitable produce here, and we be too free men for such a law as that, I guess."

Thomas Hamilton agreed with Mrs. Trollope that there were areas where freedom needed boundaries, and stood ready to offer "willing testimony to the general fidelity of her descriptions." One place for such boundaries, he suggested, was the courtroom. "An American seems to look on a judge exactly as he does on a carpenter." He then described a scene in the New York State Supreme Court, where the jury sat eating bread and cheese while the foreman, similarly occupied, "announced the verdict with his mouth full, ejecting disjointed syllables during the intervals of mastication!"

Even Americans thought the courtroom deserved more respect than it was getting. *How to Behave . . . A Pocket Manual of Republican Etiquette* (1865) complained about the American habit of lolling, "carried even so far in America that it is not uncommon

"The solemnity of justice."
Domestic Manners of the Americans by Frances Trollope, 1832.

to see the attorneys lay their feet upon the council table; and the clerks and judges theirs also upon their desks in open court."

Hamilton's sharp eye and sharper tongue flicked everywhere. New Englanders he found crafty and cold. "Nature, in framing a Yankee, seems to have given him double brains and half a heart." Philadelphians pretended to the social superiority of America, but to him "Philadelphia is mediocrity personified in brick and mortar," and people too, he implied. Nowhere in the world was there food so bad as in the United States. The remarkable abundance of raw ingredients was to no purpose that he could see or taste, for once it was cooked—"If the devil sends cooks to any part of the world, it must be to the United States."

Some of his remarks were intensely personal, possibly libelous, but libel and plagiarism were as free as America itself in those days. Jefferson, he stated flatly, had not practiced what he professed. "Continually puling about liberty, equality, and the degrading curse of slavery, he brought his own children to the hammer and made money of his debaucheries. Even at his death, he did not manumit his numerous offspring, but left them, soul and body to degradation and the cart-whip. A daughter of Jefferson was sold some years ago, by public auction, in New Orleans, and purchased by a society of gentlemen, who wished to testify, by her liberation, to their admiration of the statesman, 'who dreamt of freedom in a slave's embrace.' "

Despite his sharp utterances, Hamilton's attitude to the United States was not entirely unfriendly. In some ways he liked the natural, unaffected ways of Americans and recognized that the formality of European conduct was "inseparable, perhaps, from the artificial distinctions of European society." However, his compliments were oblique, "The manners of the first-rate merchants of New York are not at all inferior to those of Liverpool or any other of our great commercial cities." And lest any reader think the essentially crude United States yielded many such medium-polite citizens, he quickly added, "First-rate merchants and lawyers compose a very small part of the population. Beyond that there is a sad change for the worse."

The hastily gobbled meal already symbolized Americans and was a target of British humor. When Dr. Abernethy, a celebrated English physician, attended a visiting American who complained of dyspepsia the patient asked, "Doctor, what shall I eat?" "Eat?" thundered the doctor, "the poker and tongs if you chew them well." Most Americans glimpsed at table by Hamilton did not chew at all, but "gulped and swallowed as if for a wager."

Evidently table manners sank completely out of sight on steamboats. Mrs. Trollope employed some memorable and vivid prose to describe the men at table with her on a Mississippi riverboat: "The frightful manner of feeding with their knives, till the whole blade seemed to enter the mouth, and the still more frightful manner of cleaning the teeth afterwards with a pocket knife."

Apparently Mrs. Trollope had not bothered to take a hard look at her side of the Atlantic, where the knife was still conveying food to many English mouths in the 1830s.

Thomas Hamilton saw similar performances on a steamer that plied between Albany and New York. Describing the scene at mealtime, he wrote, "It would be difficult to find a parallel beyond the limits of the Zoological Gardens. Men didn't eat—they *devoured,* under the uncontrollable impulse of some sudden hurricane of appetite."

American gobbling had at least one noted English advocate in William Cobbett. Though he found little to admire in American manners, he was not critical of American eating speed and thought Englishmen would be well advised to eat under a bigger head of steam. To spend more than thirty-five minutes total in the daily dispatch of three meals was time wasted, in his opinion. William Alcott, American etiquette-book writer, thought Cobbett's time allotment should be at least double. "Now *I* can swallow a meal at any time in five minutes," said Alcott. "But this is not *eating*. This swallowing down a meal in five or ten minutes, so common among the active, enterprising, and industrious people of this country, is neither healthy, decent, nor economical."

However, and beyond question, the chief cause of Europe's open disgust with American manners was the American male's addiction to tobacco chewing—and the consequent spitting. The crude habit seemed to prosper with the fortunes of the Democratic party, and once Andrew Jackson was firmly seated in the White House, the tobacco quid was firmly settled in American mouths. Charles Dickens in *American Notes* (1842) called Washington "The headquarters of tobacco-tinctured saliva," and spared no descriptions of the streams, stains, and miscalculated aims. "I was surprised to observe that even steady old chewers of great experience, are not always good marksmen," he chuckled. "Which has rather inclined me to doubt that general proficiency with the rifle, of which we have heard so much in England. Several gentlemen called on me who, in the course of conversation, frequently missed the spittoon at five paces; and one (but he was certainly short-sighted) mistook the closed sash for the open window at three."

Mrs. Trollope's descriptions of the chewing and spitting were graphic and nauseating. In justice to these two admittedly harsh critics of American manners, visitors seemed uniformly shocked by this rude and thoroughly American habit. The hazards of walking in the street or traveling in a coach with the windows open were recounted with malicious humor by male visitors. Women—foreign visitors and Americans alike—were sickened by it. Perhaps this was one reason they put their hands to the wheel in an attempt to steer American manners into more acceptable channels.

*Ladies racing madly for matinee seats, to the dismay of male beholders.
Appleton's Journal, 1872.*

25 · THE FORMIDABLE AMERICAN FEMALE

FOR THOSE OBSERVERS who saw America as a buzzing apiary nothing heightened the analogy more surely than the position of the American woman. She was a queen bee—and queen was a favorite term that both foreign and American writers applied to her. In keeping with her recognized sovereignty she extended her rule over American social behavior almost at once.

This was in great contrast to the European scene, where courtiers and noblemen had long been at the helm of social life and in many cases had written the books on courteous conduct. There, where the ghosts of Castiglione and Chesterfield still hovered, manners were dictated by men. Europe had always been the realm of the host, with women supplying a decorative but essentially passive background for male society. The *salonnières* and blue stockings were, after all, the exceptions rather than the rule.

America became the land of the hostess almost at once. American author Nathaniel Willis, writing in the first half of the 19th century, marveled at the position of American women and declared, "It is the women who regulate the style of living, dispense hospitalities, and exclusively manage society. . . ." In stronger terms he found America "the first country in the world in which the *female sex . . . is superior to the male.*"

De Tocqueville saw matters much the same way. "In no country has such constant care been taken . . . to make [the sexes] keep pace one with the other, but in two pathways that are always different." He saw European women as "seductive and imperfect beings . . . [who] almost consider it a privilege that they are entitled to show themselves futile, feeble and timid," while "the women of America claim no such privileges." However, De Tocqueville's comment that American women nevertheless sacrificed none of their feminine appeal, even when they "sometimes show they have the hearts and minds of men," could have applied with equal truth to the *salonnières,* mistresses, and female intellectuals of Europe.

Women were spun into their different molds on either side of the Atlantic by the potter's hand of the male. European men shaped their women into delicate porcelain. American males, it seems, preferred earthenware, which in the end was handled more carefully than the porcelain. There was, of course, the delicately bred Southern belle who would not "spread her hand by turning a door-knob, or touching tongs, or handling a heavy object," as contrasted with the sturdy pioneer type capable of seizing a musket and fending off Indians. But midway between these two extremes was the typical American woman whose equality with men had impressed De Tocqueville. It was she who ran the show, commanding the respectful protection of American men.

From the start American men had assumed a deferential attitude to women. Most social historians agree that initially this was due to the scarcity of women in colonial times. What sustained it in the 19th century when women were plentiful was probably ingrained habit. Whatever the reason, American men had become the managed while in Europe men were the managers. The American woman not only housebroke her husband into using a spittoon (not always successfully), but steered him into gainful social contacts, engineered the necessary social machinations to such an end, and often determined the goal of these machinations. In Europe it was deemed more appropriate to leave such matters to men.

As for American manners, few men—and those mostly publishers and clergymen—tried to improve them. Women led the determined assault via etiquette books. The number published in America from the 1830s on quickly exceeded anything in Europe or England, as if the defiant rudeness of Jacksonian America really masked an underlying wish and hope to behave better. At least sixty-seven different manuals of advice were published in the three decades before the Civil War, not counting the numerous editions and reprints of these works.

The female authors who dominated the field were led by Mrs. Eliza Farrar, Miss Eliza Leslie, Catherine Sedgwick, Lydia Child, and Sarah J. Hale of *Godey's Lady's Book,* and it is evident from the nature of the books that American women wanted to improve themselves as much as they wanted to improve their men. *The Young Ladies Friend, Etiquette for Ladies, The Young Woman's Guide, The Ladies Science of Etiquette, True Politeness; a Handbook of Etiquette for Ladies, The Behavior Book* by Eliza Leslie, and *The Lady's Guide to Perfect Gentility*—these books published in the middle third of the 19th century, give some idea of the etiquette wind in America.

Occasionally a female writer hid behind a pseudonym that suggested a beard, as in the case of Mrs. Margaret Conkling, who compiled *The Gentleman's Guide to Politeness and Fashion* (1857) and signed herself "Colonel Lunettes." Mrs. Conkling advised men against combing their beards in bizarre arrangements and urged them not to wear "flash stones" if they adopted the new fashion for sleeve-buttons (cuff links). "Few young men can consistently wear diamonds," she warned from behind her masculine disguise, a comment which could have helped to create the mistaken idea in many European minds that American streets were paved with gold.

Most female etiquette writers did not bother to conceal their identity but came right out into the open, telling men how to dress, eat, dance, talk, and help a lady onto a horse.

For the most part they struck off in their own independent American direction and urged their countrymen to have the courage of their own manners. Mrs. Farrar wrote the following, perhaps as a public rebuke to Mrs. Trollope for her unkind remarks about

American eating habits:

> If you wish to imitate the French or English, you will put every mouthful into your mouth with your fork; but if you think, as I do, that Americans have as good a right to their own fashions as the inhabitants of any other country, you may choose the convenience of feeding yourself with your right hand, armed with a steel blade; and provided you do it neatly, and do not put in large mouthfuls, or close your lips tight over the blade, you ought not to be considered as eating ungenteelly.

Americans ate with their knives for a longer time than did the English and French. When Americans finally abandoned knife-feeding, the English and French had gone another step and were now retaining their forks in the left hand. Stubborn to the last, Americans still clung to right-handed eating.

Americans revised other European rules of etiquette to suit their own needs and attitudes. Whereas the English strictly forbade a gentleman to greet a lady unless she had first given him a sign of recognition, American etiquette books airily dismissed such formalities and allowed either sex to make the first move.

If occasionally the text of an English etiquette book was adapted for American use it was revised to suit American tastes, and the scissors was applied to such class-conscious warnings as: "Shopkeepers and retailers of various goods will do well to remember that people are respectable in their own sphere only . . . when they step out of it, *they cease to be so.*"

That kind of talk would not do in America where the stratosphere was the limit, as Andrew Jackson had but recently proved. An American author would as soon order a New York storekeeper to sing "God Save the King," as tell him to stay in his own sphere.

Catherine Sedgwick in *Morals and Manners* (1846) told her readers to forget about such European nonsense as traditional birthright and silver or pewter spoons according to station. In America men were born spoonless. "You may all handle silver spoons if you will," said she. "That is, you may all rise to places of respectability." Mechanics, farmers, peddlers, shoemakers—all could follow their trade with pride knowing that if they fared well at it they were as much gentlemen as an Adams, a Monroe, or banker Bingham of Philadelphia.

The same applied to ladies, said Mrs. Farrar. "In this privileged land we acknowledge no distinctions but what are founded on character and morals." American women, however, preferred the distinctions that came with success and getting ahead of the next one. Few American women were without their own Mrs. Grundy to impress.

Their social competitiveness—far more vigorous than among English women—moved Frances McDougall in *The Housekeepers Book* (1837), to speak out against "the rage for vieing with our neighbors." Such rivalry induced "reckless spending" and filled households with ugly and superfluous possessions, she complained. And what good was all of this if the possessions and premises went unused by the family and the shuttered parlor was thrown open only for company? "Upon such occasions, children are seen to stare and look about them as if they had never beheld the place before," fumed Mrs. McDougall. "The master of the house fidgets from one seat to another as if he were anywhere but at home." Unable to contain herself, she exclaimed, "And this is being refined!"

Mrs. Farrar concurred, exhorting Americans to set aside company pretensions and enjoy their possessions themselves. "There is in some houses such a difference between things used every day, and those which are kept for company, that . . . an unexpected ring at the doorbell produces the greatest consternation." American households matched the English middle class in putting Spode or Meissen on the table for company, and dining Cinderellalike on chipped crockery when alone. "Now would it not be more refined and dignified, as well as more honest and comfortable, to live a little better every day and make less parade before company?" Mrs. Farrar demanded.

Responsible etiquette writers pushed the basic rules of courtesy rather than studied refinements. But socially inexperienced Americans were just as eager as their English counterparts to act "nice," and all over the land little fingers rose stiffly over the handles of teacups in the mistaken belief that this was elegant behavior. No

Addison and Steele were around to set such misguided notions straight, but "Aunt Magwire," a feature in *Godey's Lady's Book,* spoke for the magazine and its remarkable and energetic editor, Sarah J. Hale, in a series that satirized Americans who "had got their idees raised a good deal, and had some wonderful curus notions about ginteelity."

"Making herself at home."
Illustrated Manners, 1855.

To many Americans the finger glass (finger bowl) was a curious notion and caused confusion at some tables where gentility was zealously practiced, though etiquette writers tried to alert readers to its proper use. Miss Leslie gave, as a horrible example, a man misled by the slice of lemon floating in the glass, who took it up, drank from it, and exclaimed, "Well! If this ain't the poorest lemonade I ever tasted!"

Often those who strove hardest to be "nice" committed classic discourtesies in other ways. Miss Leslie, drawing on one of the most ancient precepts of courtesy from Ptahhotep, explained that it was contrary to good manners to "remind anyone of the time when their situation was less genteel, or less affluent than at present, or tell them that you remember their living in a small house or in a remote street."

To boast of one's own modest beginnings "when invited to a fashionable house among fashionable company," could be equally rude, especially to the host. "If you are not proud, it is most likely that your entertainers may be, and they will not be pleased at your lowering yourself before their aristocratic guests," warned Miss Leslie.

The Illustrated Manners Book (1855) advocated a kind of In-Rome-do-as-the-Romans-do approach for those who had arrived at the top of the social hill but occasionally found themselves in the company of the less elevated. Under such circumstances true courtesy demanded that impeccable manners be checked at the door like a wet umbrella. By way of example the author cited a lady who refused to take off her gloves at a rural ball and was called "stuck up." "If I sing with other persons, I must sing the same tune, in the same pitch, or I am a nuisance," said the author. "In such a case you have two things to choose between. Conform to your company, pour your tea into your saucer and take off your gloves, or go elsewhere."

The fluidity of American society, both economic and social, made for many such situations of disparate social experience. "A man may go to bed at night with less than nothing, and pull off his nightcap in the morning with some hundred thousand dollars waiting his acceptance," Thomas Hamilton told his English readers in 1833. With such feverish surges of good fortune, a wife accustomed to doing her own washing might suddenly find herself in the company of ladies who only saw a tub on those infrequent occasions when they stepped into it. In her presence *genuine* ladies would courteously avoid talk of housekeeping. "Women who have begun the world in humble life . . . are generally very shy in talking of housewifery after their husbands have become rich, and they are living in style, as it is called," explained Miss Leslie. "Therefore, do not annoy them by questions on domestic economy, but converse as if they had been ladies always."

Housework was *not* inconsistent with being a lady, declared Mrs. Farrar, exasperated by too many would-be ladies who thought that by wielding a mop they automatically forfeited such status. Why should they conceal their knowledge of housekeeping "as if it were a disgrace rather than a merit." "Their moral sense is clouded by some false notions of gentility," said Mrs. Farrar, "or their false pride makes them fancy certain occupations to be degrading, as if it were possible that persons would be degraded by doing that which they ought to do."

Lady had widespread and general application in America in

those days, and few there were who were not treated as ladies by American men. The responsibility for keeping this respectful male attitude in working order began in girlhood, and the same rules held that had been offered in medieval times. Emily Thornwell's advice in *The Lady's Guide to Perfect Gentility* to adopt "a modest and measured gait" with never a look around, since "this bad habit seems an invitation to the impertinent," could have been lifted from the advice the Knight of LaTour-Landry gave his daughters in the 14th century.

Museums and libraries were out of bounds for a proper lady to visit alone, said Miss Thornwell, "unless she goes there to study or to work as an artist." And if a young lady walked out alone after twilight, "she would not be conducting herself in a becoming manner."

The basic rule was never to play the coquette. Mrs. Farrar told her readers if a hand reached out to admire a breast pin, "Draw back and take it off for inspection." If the wandering hand, undeterred, tried to squeeze the lady's hand, "Show that it displeases you by instantly withdrawing it." And all of this shrinking and pulling back could be avoided in the first place if the young lady merely heeded Mrs. Farrar's opening sentence on the subject: "Never join in any rude plays that will subject you to be kissed or handled in any way by gentlemen." *The Pocket Manual of Republican Etiquette* agreed and entered "an earnest protest against the promiscuous kissing which sometimes forms a part of the performance in some of these games. No true gentleman will *abuse* the freedom which the laws of the game allows," declared the author. However, "if required," a gentleman would oblige with a "delicate kiss on the hand, the forehead, or at most, the cheek of the lady."

Kissing games aside, there were other opportunities to embrace a young lady. Hands could grasp a slender waist and perhaps accidentally graze a curve if a gentleman could afford to hire horses for a pleasant canter. Getting a belle into the saddle, "with her left foot on his shoulder" as a mounting block might be a bit strenuous, but when she dismounted, she was "received in the gentleman's arms." Apparently young ladies liked the opportunity for such embraces as much as did the gentlemen. A lady was "not to profess a passion for equestrian exercises" unless she had a horse of her own.

From *Our Deportment*, 1882.

"Young gentlemen are frequently drawn into expenses they can ill afford," said Miss Thornwell, critical of inconsiderate females who dwelt "excessively on the delights of horse-back excursions." Though it was an accepted practice for young couples to go Dutch treat, and both Mrs. Farrar and Miss Leslie urged it, apparently when it came to the expensive hiring of a horse, young ladies were willing to waive their right to share the check.

"Walking out" with a young man was a popular way of carrying on a courtship in privacy. Solitary walks might take the young couple over an occasional stile, and *The Gentleman's Book of Etiquette* described how to avoid offending maidenly modesty. "If she refuses your assistance in crossing it, walk forward, and do not look back until she joins you again," was the first rule. If assistance was sought, the gentleman could, from the top of the stile, help her up, "but let her go down on the other side first, and follow her when she is safe on the ground." Ankles were hardly exposed in such maneuvers. Ladies were never to show them even when they raised the hem of a dress dragging on the pavement. *The Lady's Guide to Perfect Gentility* told them how to do it discreetly with the folds of the dress gathered in one hand and held to one side. To use *both* hands would show too much ankle and was "vulgar, only to be tolerated for a moment when the mud is very deep."

It was well for American women to know and to appreciate "the courtesy shown to women in America," said Mrs. Farrar, calling it "something far better than the treacherous spirit of modern gallantry which prevails in the old world." That had "more of the lover in it." Safer by far was the American version which resembled a "father's or brother's protecting care." Furthermore, American men were courteous to "women of all conditions . . . rich or poor, old or young, ugly or pretty." For that reason American women could, and did, travel alone in safety. Such protection and courtesy was not to be expected in England where "An Englishman in a public conveyance is apt to have neither eyes nor ears for any woman beneath him in rank, unless she happens to be pretty, and then his attentions are of doubtful character."

What went on in the private thoughts of American men, one can only guess at. If some shared the widespread European attitude that the heads of most women were packed with feathers, American men were careful not to say so, certainly not in books that undertook to shape a man's viewpoint or behavior toward the opposite sex.

William Alcott in *The Young Man's Guide* (1832) spoke for American males in words that would have brought a snort from Lord Chesterfield. "Nothing will give more offense than to treat ladies as mere playthings or children. . . . A young man who would profit from the society of young ladies . . . must seek . . . their good will by quiet and unostentatious attentions."

Though Englishmen publicly professed similar admiration for "the purity and ignorance of evil, which is the characteristic of well-educated young ladies," upper-class Englishmen had their minds on the same gallantries as in Chesterfield's day, but now conducted them with utmost secrecy. Americans lagged far behind in such sophistication as mistresses and extramarital affairs. No "fast set" or dissolute nobility had set an example of fashionable lowered morality in the past. In America "mistress" conjured up a kitchen rather than a boudoir. Perforce, American men had little time for the idleness that begets mischief. They were too busy bringing honey to the hive.

From *Rules of Etiquette and Home Culture*, 1884.

26 · REPUBLICAN BRATS

When adult Americans gained their independence in the Revolutionary War, it seems they passed along the newly acquired freedom to their children. At least, from that time on, the conduct of American youth was noticeably more liberated. They demanded and received freedoms unthinkable in Europe and their conduct produced as many startled and negative reactions among foreign visitors as did American gobbling and expectorating. Visitors looked upon American children as little monsters, saucy to their elders, demanding the best food at the table only to waste it prodigiously, and terrorizing their helpless parents with the threat of tantrums at the first sound of "don't."

This is not to say that *all* young Americans were given their heads, or even that the overindulged and insolent predominated. Most children were probably normally well-behaved, attended Sunday school, did their chores and obeyed their parents to a reasonable point. But there were enough of the unruly especially in the cities to create the impression among visitors that most American children were disobedient brats. Their shocked disapproval is well-documented. And we have the word of America's etiquette writers as well.

It had been otherwise in colonial America. Parents then ruled

with the firm hand remembered from the Old World and demanded unquestioning respect and obedience. In keeping with
those times, the first manners book to be published in America,
Eleazer Moody's *School of Good Manners* (c. 1715) offered "One
hundred and sixty-three rules for children's behaviour," including
such basics as "Never speak to thy parents without some title of respect as Sir, Madame, etc. . . ."

Francis Hawkins' *Youth's Behaviour* guided such young colo-
nials as George Washington, who copied down his own set of rules
for polite behavior from its pages, possibly at the direction of his
father.

Daughters were not excepted. Thomas Jefferson, writing to his
eldest daughter, Martha, at school in Philadelphia in 1783, asked
for a list of books she was reading and outlined a program that
would occupy her safely from eight in the morning to bedtime and
would assuredly produce a polished and, hopefully, an accomplished young woman. "With respect to the distribution of time,
the following is what I should approve: From eight to ten, practise
music; from ten to one dance one day and draw another; from one
to two, draw on the day you dance, and write a letter next day;
from three to four, read French; from four to five exercise yourself
in music; from five till bedtime, read English and write." Jefferson
expected no less from Martha than Chesterfield had from his son.

Fifty years later parental control had diminished to such an extent that Mrs. Farrar expressed alarm over the decline in filial respect and sadly recalled "two generations back," when "formality"
regulated the conduct of youth and "prevented young people from
opening their lips unnecessarily, in the presence of their parents,
and made [young ladies] rise and courtesy every time their fathers
entered the room." Such deportment, while still the rule for young
people on the other side of the Atlantic, had apparently departed
from America along with the troops of Cornwallis and Howe.
European youth knew better than to seize the most comfortable
chairs in the room before their elders had been seated, but American youth now had to be reminded "never to lounge on a sofa or
rocking-chair whilst there are those in the room whose years give
them a better claim to that sort of indulgence."

To most European visitors American youth was as disobedient and uncontrollable as the colonists had been. Visitors usually spoke from the firsthand experience of sharing boardinghouse facilities where they could observe Americans dining and children whining in the communal quarters that were a way of life for many American town dwellers. Boardinghouse life made great copy and few visitors omitted it from their accounts or failed to point it out as a major defect in rearing American children.

James Silk Buckingham in his account of his American travels expressed the widely held English view: "The habit of living in public hotels and boardinghouses . . . is highly detrimental to the formation of character in the young. . . . This mode of life introduces the young of both sexes much too early into public life, and under circumstances of the greatest disadvantage."

Buckingham was shocked by the children he saw at the resort hotels of Saratoga and Virginia Springs. "Young children of six and seven . . . seen at concerts, balls, and 'hops' at hours when they should be in bed; and passing the day in the most frivolous amusements, playing at chequers or backgammon, coquetting and flirting in the gardens, eating and drinking everything at the table . . . without a single restraint on the indulgence of their wills, and with no useful or instructive occupation or pursuit for weeks in succession."

Harriet Martineau apparently saw less appalling behavior, and while she found American children "spoiled, pert and selfish," she saw some benefit in the freedom they enjoyed. She saw them as happier, more alert and inquisitive than the more rigidly disciplined youngsters of Europe. "The American child had the advantage of the best possible discipline—that of activity and self-dependence."

For some unfathomable reason Mrs. Trollope chose to omit American boardinghouse life and children's behavior from her two-volume tirade. But her son, Anthony, gave ample coverage to the spoiled brats he saw demanding beefsteak, cakes and pickles for breakfast and defying their elders. His reports were evidently not exaggerated and were born out by such American authorities as Miss Leslie. "There is no place in which children appear to greater disadvantage or are less governable than at hotels and boarding houses," she agreed, covering childhood behavior as completely as she did all other phases of conduct in *The Behaviour Book*. Such upbringing had to have "an unfavourable effect," and she symphathized with parents whose "circumstances . . . oblige them permanently to live in public with their young families."

Don't do it, implored *Rules of Etiquette and Home Culture*. "Do not board if you can help it." But little choice was available to many young couples seeking their fortune in the cities and unable to afford or to find a home to themselves. The boarding-house was often the only answer, and their children grew up in a public atmosphere that bred bad manners as bacteria breeds disease.

Children behaved their absolute worst in the public "drawing room." Here, complained Miss Leslie, they were "permitted by their mothers to spend much of their time . . . regardless of the annoyance which their noise and romping never fails to inflict upon the legitimate occupants of that apartment." How could parents be deaf to this noise? she wondered. Perhaps fear restrained them: "Conscious of their own inability to control them, they are afraid to check the children lest they should turn restive, rebel, or break into a tantrum."

As custodians of national behavior, most etiquette writers joined Miss Leslie in reviewing children's behavior and poured out cascades of verbiage from the 1830s on, calling youth to order and caviling at parents for letting them get out of hand in the first place.

"Is it compatible with filial reverence to contradict a father?" demanded Mrs. Farrar. "Or to leave the room whilst [the parents] are still addressing you?"

"Obedience to parents is the basis of all order and government," cried the *Young Lady's Book*. "Youth should bear in mind that every comfort they enjoy . . . they owe to their parents."

Ah! There was the crux of the whole trouble, cried numerous etiquette writers. Parents gave their children too much and denied them nothing. "Every wish of the child is studiously gratified," said Catharine E. Beecher, aghast that children were not taught

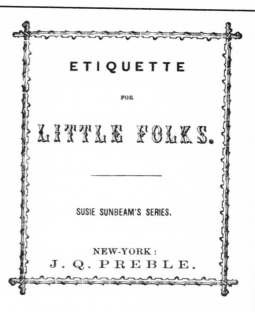

ETIQUETTE

FOR

LITTLE FOLKS.

SUSIE SUNBEAM'S SERIES.

NEW-YORK:
J. Q. PREBLE.

Frontispiece and title page, *Etiquette for Little Folks*, 1856.

some self-denial. Even such denials as safety demanded were replaced by "some compensating pleasure."

Too often, parents who overindulged their children and provided them with educational advantages were repaid with the sharp bite of a thankless child; ingrates, said Mrs. Farrar, who "think themselves excused from the duty of filial reverence because they are more highly educated than their parents . . . turning against [them] the weapons which their kindness has put in your hands."

Abolitionist Lydia Child thought children had entirely too much time for play and leisure. "In this country we are apt to let children romp away their existence till they get to be thirteen or fourteen." An end to that kind of nonsense, and they would grow up to be better-disciplined adults, said the high priestess of Calvinist belief in the virtue of work.

Sarah Josepha Hale, of *Godey's Lady's Book* fame, thought there were enough restraints on children, if anything, too many—though she was, admittedly, a lone voice. Why did parents seek to "repress [the] natural joyousness," of their children and make them feel "that to be active is to be very naughty? Lambs skip and bound, kittens and puppies seem wild with the joy of life; and little children naturally run, leap, dance and shout in . . . exuberance" said patient Mrs. Hale, displaying far more fortitude than most etiquette writers. In her etiquette book *Manners: or, Happy Homes and Good Society All the Year Round* (1868) she took the opposite position to Mrs. Child and devoted much space to games and recreations for children, heading one entire chapter, "Happy Sundays for Children." Her most famous words for youngsters are in the poem "Mary's Lamb."

Some etiquette writers took up the cudgels for children in the matter of conspicuous names. These had been acceptable at an earlier time in American life, but due for banishment by the 1870s. "Parents have no right, socially, to disqualify their offspring by affixing to them either inappropriate or unseemly appellations," scolded the *Bazar Book of Decorum.*

The *Manual of Etiquette* supplied a list of undesirable names that included a few not considered so today—Nancy, Betsey, and Patience. But certainly there was justification to cry out, "Do not disfigure your sweet little girls with names of Mehitabel, Jerusha, Arzina, Experience, and Resignation; nor your bright boys with those of Obadiah, Jehiel, Zerubbabel, Jedediah, Abiram, Jeguran, or Chedorlamer, when you can substitute others which are far more preferable."

There was no sign of improvement in the behavior of America's youth as the century progressed. *Manual of Etiquette* made the same complaint in the 1880s that had been heard in the 1830s: "The want of respect so prevalent in our midst, in the manners of children to parents; of the young to the aged." *Manners That Win* noted unhappily that most of "Young America" had the idea that "It is evidence of manly independence to speak or act disrespectfully to a parent or teacher"—which may have led the schools in the 1880s to take a hand in teaching manners in the classroom.

Etiquette books continued to offer advice on rearing children. *Manners That Win* summarized it in much the same way as had Ptahhotep in 2700 B.C., urging parents to instill good character in their children as the best legacy for the child's future welfare. "The child that is respectful, obedient, kind and truthful, has half learned the secret of success."

Everybody benefited if parents did their job well, said *Social Customs*. "Parents who bring up their children well and carefully . . . deserve the gratitude of the State, as well as that of their offspring."

However, signs of more serious problems developing now called for stronger lectures on the parents' roles. "What has caused such a terrible epidemic of crime in our midst?" demanded *Manual of Etiquette*, supplying its own answer. Parents were to blame, concentrating on "riches and the pursuits of fashion" while their children were left to "hirelings."

Social Customs concurred in this indictment of parents and pointed to the evidence: "Defaulting bank cashiers . . . and an army of embezzlers," most of whom had proved to be young people gone astray for want of proper training in their youth.

Fathers had their share of guilt in this, said *Manual of Etiquette*. They allowed their young sons the free run of their business premises (perhaps to get them out of mother's way?). "Many a boy has been ruined . . . from being allowed to associate with vulgar, unrefined, and vicious men employed about his father's premises and warehouses."

But the chief onus lay on mothers, and many had been poorly prepared for their future responsibilities by *their* parents. Even gentle poetess Margaret Sangster saw America's little girls as spoiled, pampered darlings, "A rosebud set with little wilful thorns." Rosebuds bloomed into mothers with little interest in bringing up their children. "If a mother allows her children to associate chiefly with those of low origin and manners, she cannot think that they will not be influenced by them," said *Manual of Etiquette*. The trouble with America's children was clear to that book—too many hired hands held the leading strings.

27 · HELP WANTED

In no area was American independence more decisively asserted than in domestic service. Though American etiquette books dealt extensively with relationships between employers and their hired domestics, following the example of European courtesy and etiquette books, the word "servant" almost never appeared in their pages before the Civil War. It had an unpleasant sound to American ears in the early days of the Republic.

Any American seeking domestic assistance knew enough to seek *help*. Help he might, but a free American served no one!

The fact that America was a slave-owning country and slaves were called "servants" contributed to the abhorrence for the word. Almost all etiquette books were published and sold in the industrial, urban North where slavery was opposed. Other reasons had conditioned American dislike for the word "servant." The French constitution of 1791 declared for equality and the brotherhood of man, but denied suffrage to "those in a menial capacity, *viz*, that of a servant receiving wages." Similar disqualifications appeared in the next two drafts of the French constitution in 1795 and 1799. One theory holds that these restrictions were imposed to discourage, and even punish, men who might be persuaded to serve the wealthy. In the first heat of *Egalité* and *Fraternité* the attitude was overwhelmingly: Serve yourself.

Housewives in America's industrial antislave North had little choice but to "serve themselves." In the rising economy of the 1830s with employment for all, Mrs. Farrar warned young wives not to expect a maid in their new lives, and if fortune favored them with one to treat her with courtesy. Somehow, many ladies refused to recognize the realities of the times: "Though it is a long time since domestics were numerous in the northern and eastern states of America . . . ladies often talk as if they were living in olden times and had a right to govern with absolute sway those whom they hire." Mrs. Farrar enlightened them on how matters really stood: "The unexampled prosperity of this great republic makes it so easy for young women to find lucrative employment in . . . trades and manufacture, that the service of private families is less sought than formerly. Hence arises the scarcity of domestics, and the numerous complaints which we hear from the mistresses of families, whose burdens are much increased by this state of things."

Most foreign visitors corroborated this state of affairs. Mrs. Trollope described as her "greatest difficulty in organizing a family establishment in Ohio . . . getting servants, or as it is there called, 'getting help,' for it is more than petty treason to the Republic to call a free citizen a servant. The whole class of young women,

Ladies attending a cookery school and proudly serving the results.
America Revisited by George A. Sala, 1882.

whose bread depends upon their labor, are taught to believe that the most abject poverty is preferable to domestic service."

To Europeans, who looked upon service as honorable work and those who performed it as no less respected than other members of the working class, the American attitude to service was incomprehensible, as well as inconveniencing. Even "working class" was a poor choice of words in America, said Fredrika Bremer, 19th-century Swedish writer. "One could not properly speak of a working class where almost every person works for his living."

Thomas Hamilton reminded Americans that "Young English noblemen [were] sent to Westminster or Winchester to brush coats and wash tea-cups." It was irritating that "the meanest American storekeeper holds the issue of his loins . . . above the discharge of such functions."

The Prince of Saxony, perhaps mindful of a fellow German noble who had married a waitress (and had her immortalized in the Liotard painting *La Belle Chocolatière*), twitted Washington Irving when he was presented at court: "With a republic so liberal, you can have no servants in America." "Yes, sire, we have servants, such as they are," replied Irving, "but we do not call them servants, we call them help."

When free Americans did "help" they held the whip hand and intimidated their employers, wrote Michel Chevalier in 1839, shocked to report that "On Sunday an American would not venture to receive his friends; his servants would not consent to it and he can hardly secure their services for himself."

The absence of livery on American servants surprised some visitors. William Cobbett, reporting his American travels in 1828, told English readers that a male servant in America would as soon wear "livery . . . as a halter around his neck."

Harriet Martineau admired the independent attitude of domestics but held this spirit responsible for the semipublic mode of life many American families were forced to adopt. "The boarding house life that prevails in America has been rendered compulsory by the scarcity of labour."

Many a needy young woman who would rather go hungry than wear an apron as a fellow American's servant, became a "day worker." In the early 19th century this meant a dressmaker or seamstress who came in by the day. Mrs. Farrar called for the greatest consideration for this "class of females," often "refined persons in reduced circumstances." From the concern Mrs. Farrar expressed over their pallor and thinness, most were on the verge of tuberculosis from lack of exercise and long hours spent "plying their needles from morn till night, day after day, week after week."

Mrs. Farrar requested "great delicacy" in dealing with them, and "if not convenient to admit them to your table, see, yourself, that they have their meals sent to them in good order. Never trust your domestics to wait properly on a dressmaker or seamstress, for there is often an unfriendly feeling produced in the former by the latter's not choosing to eat in the kitchen."

Miss Leslie, whose *Behaviour Book* was published in Philadelphia, assumed her audience to include Southern readers as well, and was one of the very few who used the word "servant" in her text. She, too, called for considerate treatment of employees. It was rude to talk of "Negroes" or "darkies" within the hearing of colored domestics. "And when the domestics are Irish, and you have occasion to reprove them for their negligence . . . or blunder, do so without reference to their country."

When help became more available as immigrants flocked in, especially colleens from Ireland, mistresses forgot earlier help shortages and imposed more demands. Catharine Beecher declared that there was "no subject in which American women need more wisdom, patience, principle and self-control."

The *Bazar Book of Decorum* took a particularly irate stand. "Servants are ordinarily regarded by their employers as so many pieces of mechanism . . . should they by any chance show any tendency to rest from work . . . the ever watchful superintendent infers that the machinery is imperfect and rejects it." The "machinery" was also subject to rejection or condemnation if it dared to reveal such human drives as falling in love and wanting to marry. Only the mistress, "may coquet, love and marry, and complacently regard herself as fulfilling her vocation."

At the end of the century, matters were right back to where they had been at its beginning. In the 1890s Paul Blouët reported,

"Americans, free though they may be politically, are at the mercy of their servants, whether in public or private life." Household help would only consent to stay on condition of "heavy wages and light duties." And a hotel keeper had "no choice but to submit to his servants or to close his hotel."

To Blouët, who came from freedom-loving France, "To throw off the yoke of the superior classes is very well," but, said he, "I am not aware that the yoke of the common people is at all preferable." The most desirable was the French way, which seemed to lie somewhere between: "The Englishman commands all his paid servants. The American obeys his."

The proud and independent American attitude extended also to tips, which Americans considered demeaning, though gratuities were expected from visitors by domestics (usually female) in private homes. However, men in public employment would as soon accept a tip as wear the halter William Cobbett had mentioned. Mrs. Sherwood, in 1884, contrasted respectful English waiters and porters with the rude ones at home. Pride, not servility, made the difference: "The American in a similar position would not show the politeness, but he would disdain a shilling."

This proud disdain of a tip had vanished as if it had never been by 1904, when Marion Harland described the parade of extended palms that figured in hotel life, beginning with two porters and concluding with the headwaiter who required two tips (at start and finish of her stay).

In some places, however, there was an attempt to maintain the old proud disdain, even if it had to be put into law. In 1919 Iowa still had a statute prohibiting tips.

> Every employe of any hotel, restaurant, barber shop, or other public places . . . or of any public service corporation engaged in the transportation of passengers in this state, who shall accept or solicit any gratuity, tip, or other thing of value . . . from any guest or patron, shall be guilty of a misdemeanor, and upon conviction thereof shall be fined not less than five dollars, or more than twenty-five dollars, or be imprisoned in the county jail for a period not exceeding thirty days.

From *Illustrated Manners*, 1855.

28 · THE WELL-GROOMED AMERICANS

AMERICAN ETIQUETTE BOOKS strove to lead their readers to that goal of perfection where they would not only behave according to the rules of politeness but would meet with equal success the standards of personal cleanliness and personal appearance. For example, if a lady did not know enough to pull a cap over her "curl papers" before answering the door or greeting her husband, Mrs. Farrar told her: "There is no more frightful appendage to a woman than they are." A lady was never to be seen by anyone while wearing them. Those who have noted with distaste the number of heads in hair curlers that parade the streets these days can only murmur a heartfelt Amen.

Teased hair and oversize coiffures also provoked complaints among the etiquette writers. "Female ingenuity seems exhaustless of device in twisting, plaiting, frizzing, knotting, heaping up, scattering, and torturing into every possible form and direction the flexible material which naturally covers the head, grumbled the *Bazar Book of Decorum,* published in 1870 by durable *Harper's Bazaar.* Hairpieces were so much in demand that former sources of supply—"peasants of Germany and the dead in hospitals and prisons"—could no longer meet "the present demand of fashion." As a result, revealed the *Bazar Book,* much of the false hair adorn-

"Proposed new style of whisk-ar."
Harper's Weekly, 1861.

ing heads was "the Hottentot product from Caffreland."

The hairy vagaries of men provoked loud opposition in etiquette books; this opposition brings to mind the 17th-century courtesy book protests against Cavalier hair styles—styles which apparently were being revived in the 1860s and 1870s. *The American Gentleman's Guide* (1876) cried out against long hair straggling in "uncombed and unkempt masses over the coat-collar." Such masculine hair styles were "A miserable imitation . . . of the flowing hair that in days of yore fell naturally and gracefully upon the broad lace collar . . . of the cavaliers." "The close-cropped hair" of the "thorough Englishman" was just as undesirable and reminded the author of "preparation for a strait-jacket." His advice was to choose a good barber and leave the task of styling to him, for one man's hair style could be another man's downfall.

The author also called for moderation in beard styles, as did *The Gentleman's Guide to Politeness and Fashion* (1857), firmly vetoing such bizarre beard and moustache arrangements as "Ram's horns or roped curls." Etiquette writers were not in agreement on the subject of beards. *Illustrated Manners* was all for beards and downgraded the smooth-shaven face. "Who would think of a close-shaven Jupiter or Hercules?" demanded the author. "The gods and heroes wear beards." It had taken time, though. He ruefully recalled, "Ten years ago [1845] a full beard in New York was stared and sneered at as a mark of the most ultra-radicalism, or the most pretentious exclusiveism."

Bathing, a 19th century health bugaboo, along with fresh air at night, also aroused mixed views among etiquette writers. In 1873 Catharine Beecher observed, "It has been supposed that large bathtubs for immersing the whole person are indispensable to the proper cleaning of the skin." This was not so, she flatly stated. But how then? one asks. "A wet towel applied every morning to the skin, followed by friction in pure air, is all that is absolutely needed," declared Miss Beecher, though she grudgingly admitted that "a full bath is a great luxury." Sarah Josepha Hale, editor of *Godey's Lady's Book* and author of *Manners, or Happy Homes* disagreed with Miss Beecher and ardently supported the bathtub as the basis of all personal cleanliness. At least once a week, she pleaded and her vigorous campaigning helped to establish the Saturday night bath ritual. Or perhaps to reestablish it? As long ago as the 15th century, English king Edward IV—who encouraged the spread of both culture and industry in England—made a regular Saturday night ritual of bathing his feet and his hair. When, if ever, he washed the rest of his person, is not clear.

Emily Thornwell, author of *The Lady's Guide to Perfect Gentility,* shared Mrs. Hale's enthusiasm for baths and urged her readers into them, leaving the frequency to their discretion. How infrequently they complied one surmises when Miss Thornwell exclaimed, "What must we think of those genteel people who never use the bath, or only once or twice a year wash themselves all over, though they change their linen daily?" Miss Thornwell grimly supplied her own answer. "In plain English, they are filthy gentry."

If a lady did not choose to bathe for the delicious feeling of personal cleanliness, she needed to be warned that some ladies gave off personal fumes, and she might be one of them. "Those who have enough of this odor about them to be perceptible to others . . . are often unconscious of it themselves." Therefore, if out of fear or laziness (and it was an effort in those days) she refused to bathe totally, she was at least to wash armpits and feet regularly, and to change stockings every few days. Miss Thornwell gave her a regular schedule for hose changing.

Total immersion was not recommended for gentlemen. *The Gentleman's Book of Etiquette* advised, "The best bath for general purposes . . . is a sponge bath." Aware that men were as reluctant as women to risk their health by opening their pores, the author assured them that a sponge bath "can do little harm and almost always some good." Armed with a large, coarse, water-logged sponge, they were to take careful aim, "and the part of the body which should first be attacked is the stomach."

With epidermis clean and underclothes fresh, the next step was the outer appearance, and here the competitive spirit took over completely. Americans, eager to outdo each other, tended to overdress. Etiquette writers blasted away on this point. One of the earliest to speak out was Mrs. Farrar, bent on improving the conduct of America's ladies in all matters, including dress. If she had her way, American ladies would don "a fixed costume" for church to discourage them from staring at each other appraisingly. This might, however, result in a drop in church attendance and if the opportunity to evaluate each other's costume brought ladies to church—well, let them wear their finery. Still, Mrs. Farrar hoped for "the time not distant when it will be considered ungenteel to be gayly dressed in walking the streets of the cities."

It was still distant thirty years later, when *Martine's Handbook of Etiquette* (which enjoyed a long life right into the 20th century) made a stronger complaint. "Most American ladies in our cities wear too rich and expensive dresses in the street . . . costly stuffs only fit for a drawing room or a carriage. This is in bad taste." They were overdressing more than ever in church, grumbled *Bazar Decorum:* "A well-bred French or English woman always chooses her most sober and unnoticeable dress in which to say her prayers in public, while an American puts on her newest robe and gayest bonnet to perform her genuflections before an admiring congregation of fellow-worshippers." But nothing deterred American ladies from wearing their finery to promenade along streets that were frequently muddy or from staring at each other's costumes in church.

Most tasteless of all was to dazzle one's guests in an obvious attempt to outshine them. Here *Bazar Decorum* called for some self-sacrifice in the name of good manners. "The polite hostess takes care to mark her conduct for the night by a total abnegation of self."

Shopping for finery to outdo each other was a favorite daytime pastime of many city ladies, apparently more prevalent in America than in Europe, for nowhere else did etiquette writers make such a point of the courtesies to be observed while shopping. Miss Leslie devoted several pages to the do's and dont's. It was fair to graze in the shopping pasture before buying, provided the shopkeeper was given fair notice that this was "merely looking around," and an immediate purchase was not intended. With this aboveboard ap-

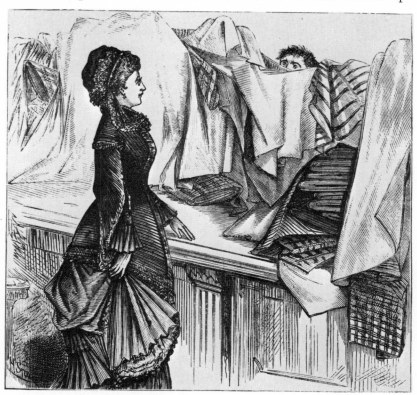

Undecided shopper: "You might cut me off a sample of each of these goods, as I may require something before the season is over." Harper's Weekly, 1877.

proach the shopkeeper would doubtless extend himself in the hope that the customer would return. But "to have such things brought to you as you have no intention of buying at all," was bad manners. It was equally bad manners to haggle with a storekeeper over a price. "The practice that is called cheapening, or beating down the price, is now nearly obsolete," said Miss Leslie, warning her readers that tradesmen would no longer "abate."

Miss Leslie reserved her most waspish remarks for those ladies who spent reluctantly. Though she recognized that it was always more pleasant to go shopping with a companion, and actually, from the point of propriety, more desirable, since ladies were not supposed to go about alone, still it was a great fatigue to both body and mind to go shopping with "a close economist." "Particularly if you know that she can afford a sufficiently liberal expenditure," Miss Leslie added. Even more fatiguing was the shopper who lacked the power of decision. Her time-consuming and embarrassing vacillations were vividly described, and Miss Leslie predicted, "The immense trouble she gives to persons behind the counter . . . will induce you to forswear . . . a second time."

Gentlemen concerned about proper attire could consult any number of etiquette books written especially for them. *True Politeness for Gentlemen,* a tiny 3-by-4½-inch volume containing all the information a proper gentleman needed to meet American requirements for civility in 1848 dwelt extensively on his wardrobe.

"Let your clothes be well made, fit you well, and be of the best materials," said the author. Cost should be no object, it would seem. However, circumstances might force the impoverished gentleman—"decayed" was the way the author put it—to wear "a bad coat, hat, or boots," but if he wore dirty linen, "it would remove him from his order." The state of the linen established the estate of the gentleman; only snow-white linen, crisply laundered, was fit attire for a gentleman, and the need to have it always in this state and of the finest quality was stressed by nearly all etiquette writers.

There were men who toyed with the idea of affecting the "ruffian" style of dress. Such attire could only be brought off by one who had "great elegance of manner and decision of conduct," warned *True Politeness for Gentlemen. Martine's Handbook of Etiquette* described the "ruffian" style as "the nonchalant and slouching appearance of a half-buttoned vest or supenderless [*sic*] pantaloons," and outlawed it categorically as worse than the "elaborate frippery of the dandy."

William Alcott's Calvinist orientation was evident in *The Young Man's Guide* (1850); he was exclusively for thrift. He saw male dress as filling four needs, and he listed them in what he conceived to be the order of their importance: covering, warmth, defense, and to improve appearance. Dress that combined all four functions was obviously the most desirable. But his credo was, essentially: "Let your dress be as cheap as may be without shabbiness. Think more about the cleanliness, than the gloss or texture of your clothes."

In the long run, said Alcott, a man's appearance would profit most if he learned to shave with cold water. Slavery to hot water meant the constant risk of slovenly appearance when no hot water was available. A mirror held a man in similar bondage; he should learn to shave without mirror or hot water and thus be free to pick up his razor any place, any time; especially as shaving was "a piece of work that must be done every day."

Alcott was so obsessed with the value of cold-water shaving that he devoted six pages to making his point—almost as many as he gave to another of his favorite tirades, the evils of "solitary gratification."

Gentlemen should be seen and not smelled, said *The Gentlemen's Book of Etiquette* (1860). "Use but very little perfume, much of it is in bad taste." A gentleman should also limit his jewelry—a snuffbox, watch, watch chain, studs, sleeve buttons and one ring was the full quota allowed a well-dressed man.

Young men could "follow the fashion farther than a middle-aged or elderly man," but if they followed it to its farthest perimeter they could be "taken for an empty headed fop." "A dandy . . . is the clothes on a man, not a man in clothes," warned *The Gentlemen's Book of Etiquette*. Fortunately, an American was not tied to dress proprieties as slavishly as an Englishman, who could use six different types of gloves in one day, if he started the day by driving his wagon to the hunt and ended it at a ball. Between the reindeer gloves for the wagon and the white kids for the ball were strung, like Aves between matins and vespers, gloves of chamois, beaver skin and kidskin that shaded from dark to light as the hours advanced.

Illustrated Manners did not agree that American men were free of fashion's demands. They might not require as many glove changes as an Englishman, but male fashions (women's, too) were subject to "sudden and extraordinary changes." Trousers changed "from meal bags to candle molds . . . hats from bell-crowned to steeple . . . boots from pointed to square-toes." The most quixotic and constant changes occurred in men's coats. "Tight and loose sleeves, large and small collars, short and long waists, and finally the tail, so short one year as scarcely to reach the thighs, next season jumps down to the calves." *Illustrated Manners* half expected it "to drag after the wearer the following year." As for gloves, American men required a few types: "Dark gloves in the morning, lighter gloves for half toilette; white gloves of absolute purity and newness for all full dress occasions." And mindful that some Americans frowned on white kid gloves as an undemocratic affectation, *Illustrated Manners* added, "And you will do well not to wear them obtrusively where it is not the custom."

If Americans were not properly bathed, garbed, toileted, barbered, shod and gloved, it was surely through no fault of the etiquette writers.

29 · THE VISITING AMERICANS

ETIQUETTE RULES to govern visiting were a matter of sheer survival for the visited. Miss Leslie deemed the subject important enough to begin her *Behaviour Book* with it, plus a declaration that "visit" was an inadequate term. Surely there was need to differentiate between a fifteen-minute perfunctory call and a fifteen-day stay as a house guest, she protested. "Visit" should apply to a social evening, or even a stay of a few nights; a brief call should be dismissed as a *vis;* but when a guest remained underfoot for more than a week, the stay could only be termed a "visitation."

Unfortunately, "visitations" were a necessary fact of life in the days before planes, trains and automobiles. The same spirit that moved wagonloads of pioneers over the jutting spines of mountain ranges to seek new homes beyond also moved them on purely social expeditions from Cleveland to New York, or from Charleston to Philadelphia. Young ladies living in rural areas visited city relatives in hopes of meeting beaux. City dwellers living in boardinghouses gathered up their children and hied off to the country for a breath of fresh air and relief from the confinement of their communal quarters. Few unwilling hosts dared to display the courage of one Harvard professor who refused to allow a visit from his sister-in-law, informing her, "Madam, I can't have you here; I am sick, my wife is sick; I have no hay or corn for your horse; I have no servants; and I had rather be chained to a galley-oar than wait on you myself."

Mrs. Farrar declared, "In no country in the world is the proportion of travellers to the population so great as in ours." The burden imposed upon hosts was enormous, and the guests too often ignored *their* responsibilities. Rules were needed to govern these "visitations" and the etiquette books pronounced them.

Departing house guest.
Rules of Etiquette and Home Culture, 1884.

Rule one was to make known upon your arrival "how long you intend to stay, that your hostess may plan her arrangements accordingly." Because beds were rarely allowed to cool off between visits and other guests were undoubtedly scheduled to arrive, polite persuasion should not induce the visitor to stay. Only "earnest and obviously sincere persuasion" counted.

Young ladies were generally "inconvenient visitors . . . expecially those abounding in beaux." Their visits should be confined to "gay idle families [living in] spacious homes."

All complaints about the lodgings were to be addressed to the chambermaid, *never* to the mistress: "The worst breach of manners is to let the mistress know that you have found or felt insects in your bed." However, not even the chambermaid was to be approached until "you have proof positive that your bed is not free from these intolerable nuisances." For quick action it was best to "promise her a reward in case of complete success." But at all costs, such an emergency was to be concealed from the hostess, who "may become your enemy for life" upon learning that such a complaint has been registered "in *her* house."

Another sure way to earn the hostess's displeasure was to visit "any person with whom your hostess is at enmity." Even one's most intimate friends were included, if they were "foes" of the hostess.

House guests were expected to attend to their own laundry, whether this meant taking it to a professional or doing it on the family premises. Writing paper, stamps, even ink, were the responsibility of the guest; to request these necessities of the hostess was bad manners. In any case the chances were good that the guest would find them in her room, as Miss Leslie also included them in the list of supplies she enumerated for the hostess.

These included a fire blazing comfortably in the guest's room upon arrival if the day was damp and chilly; "*two* pitchers full of fresh water on the stand"; towels, "both fine and coarse"; a slop jar, a foot-bath, extra blankets, and "at least one vacant bureau." If any of these comforts could not be provided, the hostess was not to make "the foolish apology that you consider her 'one of the family' . . ." A guest was to be treated as a guest.

When the guest departed, she was personally to leave a "parting gratuity" with each domestic, regardless of service rendered—or not rendered. But the most important injunction, by far, to the departing guest was the ancient one: not to abuse hospitality by gossiping about her hostess afterwards. *The Young Ladies Friend* called it a "painful and disgusting" breach of courtesy "to hear guests ridiculing the entertainments of those who had been doing their best to treat them with hospitality." Miss Leslie indignantly scolded "ladies so lost to shame" who for weeks afterward regaled their friends with "invidious anecdotes" about the family they had visited.

For the guest en route to her destination, travel etiquette covered deportment on stagecoaches, riverboats and, later on, trains. Mrs. Farrar sternly reminded stagecoach passengers of republican principles: "Never exclaim because a ninth passenger has been added at the last moment. Although his room would be preferable to his company, his right is as good as yours, and it is unkind to say or look anything that will make him feel an intruder." Happily, while travel facilities were frequently crowded and "used by persons of every description and condition . . . it very rarely happens that anything unpleasant occurs."

By 1853, Miss Leslie found it necessary to deal at length with proper behavior on trains, including some alarming emergency instructions on how to remove cinders from eyes. Surely more than a few cases of eye infection resulted from her instructions to "procure a bristle-hair from a sweeping-brush, tie it in a loop with a bit of thread, and let some one insert it beneath your eye-lid, and move it slowly all around, so as to catch in it the offending particle of coal and bring it out."

While women could and did travel alone in America without fear, reasonable precaution was at times advisable. Miss Leslie warned against making "acquaintance with any strangers, unless you are certain of their respectability." This applied to female strangers as well as male, and particularly any woman with "a profusion of long curls about her neck," whose eyes had a "meretricious expression." "Avoid saying anything to women in showy attire, with painted faces and white kid gloves," she ordered. "Respectable" women would never wear such formal accessories while traveling.

The deplorable lack of courtesy displayed by American travelers using public washrooms was already causing shocked criticism in the 19th century. In 1833 Thomas Hamilton described the filthy washroom facilities on a steamboat and the "public comb and brush suspended by a string from the ceiling . . . used by the whole body of passengers." It was beyond his powers to picture "a condition the pen of Swift alone could describe."

Similar charges were later leveled at train travelers, with charges of greediness added to the lack of fastidiousness. *A Manual of Etiquette* (1873) reported "Mr. Pullman of *Palace Sleeping Car Fame* . . . did not provide locks or bolts on ladies' dressing rooms" for good and sufficient reasons. "Were he to furnish these, but two or three ladies (?) in a sleeping car would be able to avail themselves of the conveniences, for they would lock themselves in, and prevent all others from sharing them."

The same book tartly rendered judgment on the traveler "who deposits luggage upon three seats in a car . . . takes possession of the fourth, and persistently reads either book or newspaper while others look in vain for a seat." Male or female, that traveler was

No place to sit down on the train.
Rules of Etiquette and Home Culture, 1884

"far more ill-bred than those who laugh and talk noisily, and scatter shells of nuts and rinds of fruit upon the floor."

In stagecoach, riverboat or train, and doubtless in many guest rooms, Americans displayed little instinctive civility. The reams of printed criticism poured upon them by etiquette writers was undeniably justified. Modern hostesses ruefully surveying the rumpled bedspread and lipsticked towels left in the wake of some guests, and travelers using a washroom in a modern train, may well ask if the lessons have been learned yet.

From *Illustrated Manners*, 1855.

30 · THE TALKATIVE AMERICANS

EUROPEANS LOOKED UPON AMERICANS as mere talkers, not conversationalists. One English visitor, asked to compare American abilities with those of his countrymen, replied, "Your fluency rather exceeds that of the Old World, but conversation here is not cultivated as an art."

By "fluency" he surely meant volubility, for never before had there been such an outpouring of criticism about the use of the human larynx as in American etiquette books of the 19th century. Scarcely an author passed the topic by.

"Conversation, is not to talk continually, as some imagine," said *The Lady and Gentleman's Book of Etiquette* (1852). "It is to listen and speak in our turn." Oh, when would Americans learn that "It is no less important to listen well than to talk well." *Martine's Handbook of Etiquette* recommended that they undertake the study soon; "Silence requires great genius—perhaps more than speaking—and few are gifted with the talent . . . I must recommend its study to all who are desirous to take a share in conversation, and beg they will learn to be silent, before they attempt to speak."

The usual deference paid to women in American etiquette books was abandoned when the subject turned to conversation. Though Ralph Waldo Emerson lauded American women as "queens" and "law-givers" in conversation—and perhaps the female tongues in his circle were brilliantly endowed—most etiquette writers proceeded from the premise that women merely talked too much. Unkindest cut of all—some of the severest critics were themselves women.

One of the gentler critics, Emily Thornwell, in *The Lady's Guide to Perfect Gentility,* warned her readers not to overflow the boundaries of conversation to become a monologist. "Even if you are gifted with the best powers, it will be wise for you to guard against excessive loquacity," she cautioned.

Miss Leslie was more outspoken. An ardent proponent of preserving women's femininity, she frowned on the female drive for equality and "women's rights" and criticized women for overestimating their skill as conversationalists in mixed company—particularly on subjects usually thought to be in the masculine purview. "Generally speaking, it is injudicious for ladies to attempt arguing with gentlemen on political or financial topics," she said flatly. "In comparison with the knowledge of men, the discussion will not elevate them in the opinion of masculine minds." If women sincerely sought "enlightenment" in these areas, they were best advised to listen attentively.

Female rivalry offered etiquette writers an opportunity for some particularly waspish comments. "Never praise absent ladies in the company of other ladies," snapped *Martine's Handbook of Etiquette.* "It is the way to bring envy and hatred upon those whom you wish well to." Avoid that hazard, said *Illustrated Manners:* "It is decidedly imprudent to be extravagant in your encomiums on the beauty of any lady's most particular friend."

While etiquette authorities were unanimous that too much talk was undesirable in either sex, almost all recognized the need to keep conversation afloat. Between the treacherous currents of volubility and the reefs of awkward silence lay the calm waters of small talk, but let no one underestimate the skill required to negotiate them successfully. Castiglione had stressed the importance of small talk; Chesterfield had urged his son to master it; American etiquette books now did the same.

"It is no easy matter to talk well . . . about nothing, or of everyday occurrences," said *The Manual of Politeness* (1837). Personal warmth and a genuine interest in other people went a long way toward accomplishing this, said the author. Unfortunately, these qualities, while "invaluable and unpurchasable," were usually "unlearnable" as well.

A few etiquette books that took up such elementary matters as not littering the tablecloth with bones were paradoxically highbrow about small talk, and obviously had picked up their material from English etiquette books. But where England's Charles Day had warned against "talking largely on the opera," unless the talk was grounded on real expertise, the American reader was told, "It will be decidedly condemnatory if you are ignorant of who composed *Fidelio,* and in what opera occur such common pieces as 'Ciascun lo Dici' or 'Il Segret.' " True, opera recently had come to America—the Astor Opera House, the first in America, opened in

Box in a New York Theater.
Domestic Manners of the Americans by Frances Trollope, 1832.

New York in 1847; but nevertheless arias were large talk for men who spat tobacco juice in the aisles of the opera house and hurled the dead carcass of a sheep onto a theater stage to show displeasure at a performance.

The Gentleman's Book of Etiquette and Fashion, by Cecil Hartley (1860), whose wife provided a similar volume for ladies, offered some practical suggestions for topics to avoid. As an example he cited, "the vulgar but popular proverb, 'Never talk of ropes to a man whose father has been hanged.'" But the most important abstention was from name-dropping. As all authorities before them had done, American etiquette writers unanimously condemned boasting of rich and important acquaintances. "A disgusting form of vanity very common in the United States," complained *Self-Culture,* warning that such boasting provided "an excellent standard for ascertaining the real social position and culture of many who are well guarded against detection in other respects."

If British visitors occasionally sought to lord it over democratic Americans by virtue of their British accent, Miss Leslie told her readers how to pigeonhole them correctly if they were merely pretentious upstarts. "However an Englishman or an Englishwoman may boast of their intimacy with the 'nobility and gentry,' there is one infallible rule by which the falsehood of these pretensions may be detected . . . the misuse of the letter *H,* putting it where it should not be, and omitting it where it should be. . . . It is never found but among the middle and lower classes." Phony gentry visited "ouses," had "hovens" in their kitchens, and their servants used an "arth" brush to sweep up the "hashes." Miss Leslie saw no reason for any democratic American to be impressed by *that* sort.

She was possibly the first American writer to warn Americans against the telltale *H,* and in this instance seems—to me, at least—as class-conscious as any English etiquette writer.

Outspokenness was labeled churlish by all etiquette books, and Miss Leslie also spoke to that point, advising her readers to back away promptly from anyone who began, "I'm a plain-spoken woman." What she spoke plainly to you, warned Miss Leslie, she would in turn repeat elsewhere *about* you.

The outspoken were social hazards said Henry Tomes in *The*

Bazar Book of Decorum. "Politeness is never recognized as an obligation by them." As an example he cited "a plain-spoken person of the plainest kind," who refused "to utter the compliment appropriate to the occasion" when asked to admire his hostess's first-born, and said instead, "Your baby, madam, reminds me of a Flat-headed Indian." A comparison not inappropriate, Tomes admitted, but in the name of politeness better left unsaid.

However, *some* plain speaking was badly needed. "Spades should be called spades," said Tomes, agreeing with similar sentiments appearing now in English etiquette books. Proscribed words differed in the two nations, and in some words Americans displayed even more prudishness than the English. Tomes was annoyed that Americans refused to say "cock" when most English visitors did not know what was meant by "rooster," and hearing American ladies ask for a slice of "bosom" when fowl was served made Englishmen smile. No less amusing was calling a rump steak a "seat fixing."

"Leg" was considered so indecent by some Americans that even animals could not have them. In June 1858, the Pittsburgh *Chronicle* reported that a circus horse had been destroyed because a fall in the ring had "fractured his limb." American chairs and tables stood on "limbs," and the underpinnings of pianos were modestly draped in cretonne, bringing more smiles to English faces.

Words dealing with the anatomy were nearly totally taboo. *Stomach* should only be uttered "to your physician, or in private conversation with a female friend interested in your health," said Miss Leslie. Words dealing with stomach function—dyspepsia, indigestion, or any disorders of the stomach—"are vulgar and disgusting." And especially if said at the dining table.

Country folk were the most prudish of all, said Tomes, but fortunately he saw signs of improvement even among them. "We are gradually getting over, in this country, this false modesty of speech, and it is now perhaps possible to discover within a hundred miles of a metropolis an occasional pair of female lips capable of pronouncing 'leg,' 'shirt,' 'body' or even 'trowsers.'"

The spreading use of superlatives was another American word malady that aroused etiquette writers. Mrs. Farrar expressed her

Jones: "*I am never at a loss for conversation.*"
Hostess: "*There must be some subjects you don't understand.*"
Jones: "*Then I say nothing, and look intelligent.*"
Drawing by Phil May

disapproval in 1838, complaining that young women misapplied "glorious" with equal disregard and inaccuracy to a picnic, a horse, his canter, and the basket of provisions on the horse's back. "Splendid" was equally irritating.

Henry Tomes recited the same peeves forty years later and objected even more to the high-pitched voices that shrieked them. "Loudness is peculiarly an attribute of American talk," he complained, tabulating some phrases that particularly affected his nerves and his hearing. "The 'most beautiful' ice cream; 'delicious' boots; 'magnificent' trowsers; 'awfulest' whiskers." "Awful," said he, was "the most abused word in the English language at the moment."

Bartlett's dictionary of Americanisms posted warnings in 1848 that "dreadful" was not a substitute for "very." Neither were "awful," "terrible," "desperate" or "monstrous." Uneducated people used such expressions for the purpose of emphasis, Bartlett's warned.

Miss Leslie, also in the fray, objected to some remarkably durable Yankeeisms. "Beat out" was an undesirable substitute for "fatigued," she said. "Floored" was no way to say "disconcerted." And no lady should say "slump," she warned. Why not is a mystery to me. The entire subject of slang was a mystery to Miss Leslie. "Where do they get it?" she asked. "How do they pick it up? From low newspapers, or from vulgar books?"

Common Politeness, another small volume, dealt with illiterate speech habits along with numerous other shortcomings in conduct. "A person of refined manners is never guilty of using expressions like hain't, his'n, tain't, and hadn't ought," said the book, warning also that it was impolite to laugh at one's own jokes, monopolize conversation or interrupt another speaker to finish his story for him.

Of all the etiquette books that attempted to polish Americans, this one, no thicker than a matchpack, was about the right size and spirit to deal with republican conduct. Its dicta, each beginning with "It is not polite," ranged from not spitting on the carpet or through an open window, combing one's hair at the dining table or seizing the largest portions of food, to not keeping a church congregation waiting in order to display one's virtuoso talents at the organ.

It was more a compendium of pet peeves than an etiquette primer, complaining of repaying debts with ragged currency when crisp bills had been borrowed, and criticizing sharp merchandising practices: raising prices in order to be "beaten down" and, for merchandise not in stock, a lower price quoted than the article was available for next door.

However, in its commands not to pay unsolicited visits with a noisy brood of children in tow, not to sport unbrushed shoes, uncombed hair and dirty fingernails, and not to talk like an ignoramus, *Common Politeness* reiterated every point made by etiquette writers in their efforts to improve American behavior, from guest room to discussion group. It provides a vivid picture of American bad manners for much of the 19th century.

A quiet flirtation.
America Revisited by George A. Sala, 1882.

31 · THE ROMANTIC AMERICANS

GETTING MARRIED absorbed the interests and energies of 19th-century America to such an extent that *Illustrated Manners Book* (1856) was moved to remark, "Getting married, please observe, is not the sole object of society, however important." Despite this admonishment, *Illustrated Manners* gave the subject forty-two pages, and most etiquette books supplied equally generous coverage. How to choose, how to woo, how to survive jilting, how to avoid seduction, how to ask her, how to ask "papa," were covered in minute detail, receiving far more space than how to conduct the actual ceremony. The offhand treatment given the wedding ceremony in etiquette books indicates that it was conducted along more modest lines than it is today.

Romantic marriage was as much a part of the American dream as every boy's chance to become rich or President. While American wives were subordinate legally to much the same extent as their European sisters—"the husband and wife are one and that one is the husband"—there was a world of difference in the American husband's attitude to his wife. Where a European husband might view her as a possession, often acquired in negotiations that had all the elements of horse trading, the American husband's attitude approached reverence. He saw her as the fulfillment of a romantic dream, in a gauzy mist of idealism that was meant to befog him to the grave. With few exceptions, this attitude was fostered by every etiquette book. In their way, they helped to set the pattern for some of the unrealistic, overly romantic expectations of young brides. Consider this passage from *How to Behave* (1856):

> The husband should never cease to be a lover, or fail in any of those delicate attentions and tender expressions of affectionate solicitude that won him his "heart's queen." It is not enough that you honor, respect, and love your wife. You must put this honor, respect and love into the forms of speech and action.

Or this excerpt from *American Family Keepsake* (1849), under "How to Treat a Wife," which imposed the role of soothing angel, usually assigned by European etiquette books to the wife, squarely on the shoulders of the American husband.

> You may have great trials and perplexities in your business . . . but do not therefore carry to your home a clouded brow. Your wife may have had trials which, though of less magnitude, may have been as hard to bear. A kind, consoling, and tender look, will do wonders in chasing from her brow all clouds of gloom.

There were, of course, other sentiments. *Etiquette for Ladies* (1843), which sounds suspiciously like an unaltered English etiquette book despite its Philadelphia imprint, dared to dissent and urged American ladies to step to the beat that English ladies marched to, but few American men dared to hope for a wife who would "Never act contrary to his inclinations," or who would "Receive his wishes with attention, and execute them as quickly as possible." Some wives might be willing to "Apologize promptly, and in an affectionate manner, if you have allowed yourself to run into an ill-humour," but in the main, *Etiquette for Ladies* was beating the wrong tempo for American ladies.

Even William Alcott, whose stern Calvinistic beliefs prodded the blue-collar readers of his *Young Men's Guide* into less romantic expectations, did not look for outright obedience from a wife. In fact he disliked "the idea of a woman's conforming to her husband's views merely to please him, without considering whether they are correct or not."

However, Alcott had his own ideas about wifely conduct. No young "farmer or mechanic" should choose a wife who couldn't put together a darned good meal by herself; a husband should accept nothing less. "And never fear the toil to her," he said. "Exercise is good for the health. Thousands of ladies who idle away the day, would give half their fortunes for that sound sleep which the stirring housewife seldom fails to enjoy." It was folly to seek such a wife among overindulged girls who had been educated "to play music . . . waste paper and ink in writing long half-romantic letters, or read novels." With all this fancy education girls were becoming unfit for domestic cares, and the more demanding ones would be asking for servants before long. "Servants!" Alcott snorted, "For what! To help them [the young married couple] eat, drink, and sleep?"

The safest choice was a girl of simple tastes with a quick step. The key to her total personality might be seen in a young lady's feet, and a prospective swain was advised not to throw himself there until he had inspected her *shoes* carefully. "Look at her shoes!" Alcott shouted. "If they are trodden on one side, loose on the foot, or run down at the heels, it is a sign of the slipshod." And how would a man like to face a slipshod wife each morning? he demanded. If the young man refused this counsel and persisted in making an unwise choice, well, then, *caveat emptor*.

The best place for Alcott's readers to look for a mate was in the country. City girls had other ideas. And everything that Alcott criticized they hungered for, from pianos to servants. Even country girls needed an occasional lecture, which Jane Swisshelm gave them in a series of essays on deportment, *Letters to Country Girls* (c. 1840). She told her readers not to emulate the ways of city girls, but probably stirred up longings with her disparagement of "hundreds of girls in every large city, who parade the streets in feathers, flowers, silks, and laces, whose hands are soft and white as idleness can make them." Surely most girls in ambitious, soaring America would willingly swap milk pails for the chance to "lounge around reading novels, lisping about fashion . . . thumping some poor hired piano until it groans, and putting on airs to catch husbands, while their mothers are toiling and boiling in the kitchen."

American girls seemed to want the best of everything, and that best slightly better than their neighbor's, even if it meant reaching beyond their means. This total disregard of financial limits moved William Alcott to devote several pages of *The Young Man's Guide* to damning credit buying in America.

Mothers were to blame for much of this, reasoned etiquette writers. Mothers did little to train their daughters to a more realistic attitude and, in fact, fostered extravagant ideas.

Lydia Child complained in 1838 in *The Frugal Housewife* that, as a result of improper training, girls saw marriage as a "delightful dream" composed of expensive household furnishings, "white gloves and pearl earrings . . . jumbled up with a lover's looks and promises." If anything, mothers gave daughters too much training in the art of snaring a husband and taught them little else, sniffed Mrs. Child. The fruits of such training were evident in the too rich and expensive dresses worn in the streets. This was unequivocally labeled "bad taste," by etiquette writers. But female pulses only beat faster at the thought of "sweeping the sidewalks in costly stuffs only fit for a drawing room." Bad taste or not, it was one good reason for the intense husband hunt.

If, despite the training received from their mothers, daughters lacked initiative in pursuing a mate, mothers often took a hand themselves. And how the etiquette books wished they would desist! "There are thousands of men who have a horror of match-makers— of mammas who spread their nets, like unto so many spiders—of daughters whose sole object and only thought is to catch a husband, and who are ready to accept any good match that offers," said *Illustrated Manners.*

In Europe men assumed the initiative in courtship. But in America, where all young people mingled freely in the manner of Europe's lower classes, unhampered by strict chaperonage, which was not introduced into America until well after the Civil War, the initiative often originated with the girl.

In Europe men sought to improve their fortunes through marriage. In America this was more frequently true of women, who were categorically judged to be "More ambitious than men. . . . For one woman who marries below her station as it is called, a hundred marry above." And if a husband's station were not high enough at the outset, an American wife could, and probably would, push him to the level at which she wished to live.

Alarm over the aggressiveness of American girls was expressed by Mrs. Farrar. "Policy and propriety both cry aloud to the fair ladies of this favored country, to let matrimony alone, until properly presented to their consideration, by those whose right it is to make the first advance." Such forwardness was not necessary in America, she asserted, "where there is a fair chance of every woman's being married who wishes it."

Lydia Child agreed. She was aghast at the "undue anxiety" and the "foolish excitement" displayed by maidens yearning to be otherwise. "This leads them to contract engagements . . . merely for the sake of being married as soon as their companions," she warned, calling on mothers to teach their daughters not "to exaggerate the importance of getting married." Too many hearts were being recklessly exposed.

Well, there was no harm in letting a man know that his attentions were welcome, said *How to Behave*. Naturally, women should not propose, but "they 'make love' to the man none the less." If it could be managed in "some way entirely consistent with maiden modesty," the author saw no reason why a maiden should not let a man know that he pleased her—especially if he was the man of her dreams. "Maiden modesty," however, seemed in short supply.

Illustrated Manners bowed to America's courtship revolution and admitted that in these matters "We no longer accept the English, German, or French school of manners. We have come to our own. The American belle of good society, in nine cases in ten, looks over the field, makes her choice from the circle of her admirers, gives the needed encouragement, and decides for herself her life's destiny." She might even do the proposing, for all the author knew; it was not an unreasonable conjecture, he thought.

Since the choice seemed very much up to the girl, *Martine's Handbook of Etiquette* advised her, "Do not marry a weak man. He is often intractable or capricious, and seldom listens to the voice of reason, and most painful must it be to any sensible woman to have to blush for her husband, and feel uneasy every time he opens his lips." Worst of all, *Martine's* pointed out, such a husband could not be held up as a guiding example to the children. No self-respecting European etiquette book would have dared to plant such seditious ideas in a woman's mind.

Dislike for masculine authority—or perhaps the urge to assert their own—stirred in American women. As girls, they did not think it necessary to "ask Pa" when they chose a mate (more often they consulted "Ma"), though some etiquette authorities held out for at least a perfunctory request for parental approval. *How to Behave* pooh-poohed this formality back in 1856. "Asking the consent of parents and guardians is, in this country where women claim a right to choose for themselves, a mere form and may often be dispensed with." However, if "Pa" *was* consulted and threatened to kick over the traces by objecting, there was only one "remedy"— and it was recommended, with *How to Behave's* blessing, to a freedom-loving bride. "If she is of age she has a legal as well as moral right to bestow her love and her hand upon whom she pleases."

The trapping instinct ran deep in young ladies, and with the hunting season wide open and constant, the wary male was well advised to obtain a copy of *Illustrated Manners* and carefully study the forty-two pages it devoted to matrimony. There he would find detailed instructions on how to tack, dodge and evade, and a particularly vivid description of how the quarry was run down.

> Many a man has foolishly entered upon a flirtation—been drawn into an engagement, and compelled to marry against the strongest repulsion. . . . Whole circles of relatives sometimes join to surround a victim, and drive him into the trap set for him . . . if

"Ringing him in."
Illustrated Manners, 1855.

you make a mistake, the moment you suspect it . . . stop. . . .
Have no nonsense about it. Apologize . . . express your regrets,
make any amends in your power . . . be sued, fight, do anything
but marry.

For a man, flirting was just plain hazardous. He could almost
bank on "one of two results: Having engaged the affections and
excited the hopes of the lady, you will feel compelled to marry
her; or you will be disgraced, possibly cowhided, or shot."

Young ladies were not under the same obligation and could flirt
with no more than a reprimand from the etiquette books. Often
they deliberately led men into a proposal for the sheer thrill of it,
and numerous etiquette books thundered protests against such un-
sporting conduct. Nevertheless, many pretty girls took careful aim,
and many luckless men landed uncomfortably on their knees only
to be rejected. "Since a refusal is, to most men, not only a disappointment, but a mortification, it should always be prevented, if
possible," said Mrs. Farrar. A more succinct statement on the subject was made by *Rules of Etiquette and Home Culture.* "Some
young ladies think it smart to encourage a proposal and then refuse
it. This is not a sign of good breeding."

There was also the confusing convention of "a Lady's first refusal," a common ploy to judge from its frequent mention in
etiquette books. "It is not always necessary to take a lady's first
refusal as absolute," the suitor was advised. "Diffidence or uncertainty . . . may sometimes influence a lady to reply in the negative . . . to her later regret." Unless it was an absolutely firm
refusal, "A gentleman may repeat his suit with propriety after
having once been repulsed." However, if he repeated it too often
it could easily "degenerate into importuning," and for that reason
the lady who meant "No!" should say it firmly. The hesitant "No"
could then be translated as "Maybe."

One can only presume that men read the etiquette books as
avidly as did the women and therefore knew these rules. Otherwise
confusion and error could easily result and the lady who was being
coy (or who wanted to delay in the hope of landing a better choice)
could end empty-handed.

Simplex Munditis, an etiquette book for men, objected to the bent knee and requested suitors to propose standing up, "as it lends dignity to the occasion and allows of more freedom in expressing feelings."

The man who couldn't use his tongue was obliged to use a pen. *The Lover's Casket,* an etiquette book that dealt exclusively with courting techniques, called such suitors "faint-hearted lovers" and while it recognized the timid nervousness that might cause some men to "adopt the expedient of proposing by letter," it flatly declared, "This is always objectionable where a personal interview is to be had . . . either too-impassioned or too matter-of-fact." However, if a man could not bring himself to *say* the words, he simply had to write them and stake his chances on his epistolary skill.

Illustrated Manners faulted the written proposal for even more valid reasons: "It is to be remembered that the written word remains." Still there were many who lacked the courage to bend the knee and say the words, and for them, one of the innumerable manuals on correct letter writing supplied the answer. *The Lovers Letter Writer,* a popular 19th-century English manual, enjoyed wide circulation in America and covered every exigency from "To a Lady he has seen but once," to "Disclosing a passion he has long felt, but hitherto concealed."

Examples were also provided for the young lady's reply, affirmative or negative; letters for the young man to address to the parents; and their replies. In all, there were sixty-six examples, and those who could not find the letter for their particular need had better speak up.

Of particular interest is a letter in *The Lady's Guide to Perfect Gentility,* to be used by "a lady in answer to a letter in which her suitor intimates his wish to discontinue acquaintance." A *lady* should permit a suitor to withdraw, but not without having the last word.

Sir:

I acknowledge the receipt of your last letter, which now lies before me, and in which you convey the intimation, that the position which, for some time past we have regarded each other, must henceforth be abandoned.

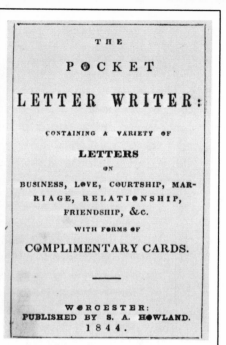

Frontispiece and title page, *The Pocket Letter Writer,* 1844.

Until the receipt of this letter, I had regarded you in the light of my future husband; you were, therefore, as you have reason to know, so completely the possessor of my affections, that I looked with indifference upon every other suitor. The remembrance of you never failed to give a fresh zest to the pleasures of life, and you were in my thoughts at the very moment in which I received your letter.

But deem me not so devoid of proper pride as to wish you to revoke your determination, from which I will not attempt to dissuade you, whether you may have made it in cool deliberation, or in precipitate haste. Sir, I shall endeavor to banish you from my affections, as readily and completely as you have banished me; and all that I shall now require from you is this, that you will return to me whatever letters you may have of mine, and which I may have written under a foolish confidence in your attachment, and when you were accredited as the future husband of,

Sir,

Yours as may be,

HENRIETTA ALLSTON

The Pocket Letter Writer (1844), took love letters in stride along with sample letters for those who would borrow money, or refuse to lend it, or, having lent it, dun for it. The samples covered every conceivable social need, invitations issued, accepted and declined, condolences, and a handy formula for a cryptogram meant to be read between the lines. This one was headed "Female Ingenuity" and was used, said the author, by a newly married young lady, who was obliged to show her husband all the letters she wrote.

> I cannot be satisfied, my dearest friend;
> blest as I am in the matrimonial state,
> unless I pour into your friendly bosom,
> which has ever been in unison with mine,
> the various sensations which swell
> with the liveliest emotions of pleasure,
> my almost bursting heart. I tell you my dear
> husband is the most amiable of men.
> I have now been married seven weeks, and
> have never found the least reason to
> repent the day that joined us.
> My husband is
> in person and manners far from resembling
> ugly, cross, old, disagreeable and jealous
> monsters, who think by confining to secure a wife;
> it is his maxim to treat,
> as a bosom friend and confidant, and not
> as a plaything or menial slave, the woman
> chosen to be his companion. Neither party,
> he says, should always obey implicitly;
> but each yield to the other by turns.

For the reader who may be baffled, the letter's message was:

> I cannot be satisfied, my dearest friend,
> unless I pour into your friendly bosom,
> the various sensations which swell
> my almost bursting heart. I tell you my dear
> I have now been married seven weeks, and
> repent the day that joined us.
> My husband is
> ugly, cross, old, disagreeable and jealous.
> It is his maxim to treat

as a plaything or menial slave; the woman
he says, should always obey implicitly.

While it is true that young people were encouraged to follow
their own inclinations in choosing a mate and not to feel con-
strained to consult parents beforehand, once a girl had her suitor
firmly by the hand, good conduct dictated that he make a formal
request for hers. This was a harmless gesture when no resistance was
anticipated; indeed, in the case of a father who might lavish cash
or property on his daughter, it was advisable.

At such a confrontation flowery protestations of undying love
were meaningless, and the situation was better served by a concise
summary of financial standing and future prospects.

With the marriage agreed to, it was time for the bride's parents
to take over the wedding arrangements and provide her with a
trousseau: "All the habiliments necessary for a lady's use for the
first two or three years of her married life."

In contrast to the many pages in today's etiquette books devoted
to arranging a wedding, 19th-century etiquette books dismissed the
mechanics of getting married with a few paragraphs. Wedding
ceremonies were not yet staged with the splendor and theatrical
effect of the third act of *Lohengrin*. Wagner's famed wedding
march was composed in 1848 and Mendelssohn's in 1842, and not
until some years later did they become the staples they are today.

Illustrated Manners remarked primly on the bawdy jokes and
tasteless customs that had attended wedding celebrations in earlier
centuries and were now happily at an end in the 19th. "At the
very best, there is enough in the wedding ceremony, and its attend-
ant circumstances, that is repulsive to the pure instincts of the
modest pair; and we cannot help thinking that the less so strictly
personal and private and delicate a matter is intruded on public
observation, the better." Hopefully the author added, "The time
may come, when our present marriage customs may seem as barbarous as those of our ancestors do to us."

Disapproval of public display extended even to a kiss bestowed
by the groom on the bride at the end of the ceremony. "Never
followed in the best society" was the ruling in etiquette books that
could bear to discuss it at all.

The practice, or more accurately the nonpractice, originated in England, where, according to one English authority, Queen Victoria "was kissed by the Duke of Sussex, but *not* by Prince Albert."

However, the essential purpose of marriage rites seems always to have been, as Westermarck put it in *A History of Human Marriage,* "to give publicity to the union." And even in the decorous 19th century there were those who wanted the nuptials to be celebrated as publicly as possible.

Illustrated Manners had no real quarrel with those who could afford the tariff and helpfully referred its New York readers to "Mr. Brown (Isaac Hull Brown, sexton of Grace Church) undertaker of weddings, funerals, and other fashionable occasions." Brown was the social organizer of his day, anticipating the influence later wielded by such social maypoles as Ward McAllister, Harry Lehr and Elsa Maxwell. In *Queens of American Society,* Mrs. Ellet caroled of him, "Where Brown is found, to Fashion's eye is hallowed ground."

Brown combined the services of a professional host, party planner, caterer and bridal secretary. The last was by far his most important function. *Illustrated Manners* explained how he operated.

> All you have to say is, "Mr. Brown, my daughter is to be married Tuesday week—Grace Church—two hundred dollars." "Mr. Brown, a little wedding party at my house on the 17th—about, say, two hundred people, and cost, well, six hundred dollars." It will be done; and if your visiting list is short of the requisite number, Mr. Brown will furnish you guests of the most exceptionable style and deportment—dancing gentlemen, supper men, literary, artistic; he has a list of all and will arrange invitations.

Mr. Brown's counterpart existed in other cities. However, in smaller towns "where these higher demands of civilization are as yet unprovided," families were obliged to organize their own wedding parties. In ten slight paragraphs (as contrasted with the sixty-two to sixty-seven *pages* devoted to weddings in today's leading etiquette books) *Illustrated Manners* outlined all that needed to be done for a fashionable wedding: the number of attendants, suitable hour for the ceremony, proper dress for the entire wedding party, and how and what to serve at the wedding feast.

From the 1850s on, America, taking its cue from English weddings, considered an elaborate procession to the altar in bad taste. "The less procession the better," was the rule. The bride on her father's arm was one way to approach the altar, but many etiquette books favored: "The bride and groom walk arm in arm behind the first bridesmaid and groomsman."

The bride's white gown could be topped by a bonnet instead of a veil if she chose. Her choice of headgear regulated the attire of the groom—a dress coat and black trousers if she wore a veil; a frock coat and light trousers if she wore a bonnet.

As a general rule, and regardless of whether the ceremony was held in a church or at home, and at whatever hour, it was usually followed by a reception for family and friends and invariably called a "breakfast," even if it was late afternoon.

Apparently simplicity was giving way to more competitive display by 1873, when *Manual of Etiquette* pleaded that wedding entertainments be kept "within the limits of the entertainer's means; it is exceedingly foolish . . . to make a grand display at a daughter's wedding, and run in debt for it, or else scrimp for the rest of the year."

Wedding gifts were getting out of hand even earlier. Miss Leslie took up the matter as a fast-developing nuisance in 1856. "We know not why when a young lady of fortune is going to be married, her friends should all be expected to present her with bridal gifts," she complained. "It is a custom that sometimes bears heavily on those with little to spend."

Worse still, "Now that it is fashionable to display all wedding gifts arranged in due form on tables, and labelled with the names of the donors, the seeming necessity of giving something expensive, or at least elegant, has become more onerous than ever." The whole system seemed a crying shame to her: "Gifts lavished on one who is really in no need of such things; and whose marriage confers no benefit on anyone but herself." In a final burst of indignation Miss Leslie demanded, "Why should she be rewarded for gratifying her own inclination in marrying the man of her choice?"

Other etiquette writers followed Miss Leslie's lead and tried to halt the spread of nuptial tribute but failed completely. Gifts were expected from an ever-widening circle and grew more expensive each year. By 1873 *Manual of Etiquette* (by Mrs. Sara Orne Johnson, who called herself "Daisy Eyebright") looked back nostalgically. "Thirty or forty years ago one heard comparatively little concerning wedding-presents. Fond friends would gladly offer some little memento which would serve as a pleasant reminder . . . now such trifling gifts are hardly considered respectable by fashionable people."

Ah—but "Daisy" saw a change dawning, a "new fashion, which is rapidly gaining ground among the aristocratic circles of society in the United States. The words *No presents received* are engraved upon the cards of invitations." Optimistically she predicted, "This new fashion will, undoubtedly, find many followers and ere long only those will offer wedding-gifts to bride and groom, who are bound to them by ties of relationship, or the warm sentiment of affection."

"Daisy" was all for this new system. "Young people should not expect friends to furnish their house with various luxurious appurtenances." Furthermore, gifts received would eventually need to be reciprocated "in similar form," and when that day of reckoning occurred, "Many a husband has been forced to deeply regret the reception of the very wedding-gifts he had deemed so very delightful to receive; and in his secret heart has bitterly condemned the custom."

Bazar Decorum commented testily, "The quantity and value . . . have become of late . . . excessive . . . and burdensome." But what aroused the author most was the "marvelous inappropriateness" of so many of the gifts—"a silver tureen sent to a young couple whose prospects in life hardly indicate the probability of . . . a simple pot of soup."

The hope that *No presents received* would catch on seems to have died aborning. Moans and groans about wedding presents continued in etiquette books as the 20th century began, and the grumbling in *The Standard Book of Etiquette* (1901) was typical of the by now routine protests. "The custom of presenting gifts to the bride and groom has grown until it has become much of a burden and something of a farce, from the absolute uselessness of many of the articles sent and the annoying duplication." *The Lover's Casket* (1902) also felt obliged to file a protest, deeming such words consistent with its thorough coverage of all matters relating to courtship and marriage. "The ostentatious parade of gifts is one of the vulgar evils of the day," *Casket* charged. "Many a person is invited to a wedding because it is suspected or expected that he or she will send a nice present."

The etiquette writers fought a game but losing battle. In the end the American way with wedding gifts won out and attics filled with unwanted statuary and tasteless gimcracks. And eventually the newlyweds dug themselves out of the gift wrappings and faced the realities of marriage.

Possibly the most succinct statement on this moment of truth was made by *Bazar Decorum* at the conclusion of its concise discussion of wedding etiquette, from the ceremony to the departure of the young couple on their honeymoon trip. "On their return they expect visits from all those to whom bridal cards (announcements) have been sent, and the usual succession of dinner and evening parties, after which they lose their distinctive character, and become incorporated into the vast mass of ordinary people."

From *Social Etiquette* by Maude C. Cooke, 1896

32 · NEW INFLUENCES

IN THE SAME WAY that English manners underwent a gradual transformation in the 18th century as a result of economic and social changes, so American manners showed the effect of similar influences in the 19th century. However, in America, the changes came with the speed suitable to a country where everything was being done in a hurry.

In 1870 *The Bazar Book of Decorum* had still complained, "It is not an essential principle of democracy to be rude and dirty. Just because a man tips his hat to a lady and has his shoes blacked does not make him an aristocrat."

By 1884 it was a different story. "There is no country where there are so many genuinely anxious to do the proper thing as in the vast conglomerate which we call the United States of America," wrote Mrs. John Sherwood in *Manners and Social Usages,* preparing to lead Americans where they obviously wanted to go: into society—*any* society, as long as it was a rung above their present footing. The forty new manuals published in the 1880s emphasized the change that had taken place with such titles as *The Correct Thing in Good Society, Success in Society, The Usages of the Best Society, Manners, Culture and Dress of the Best American Society,* and *The Ceremonials of Good Society.*

The cause of this redirection of American manners lay primarily in the affluence that followed the Civil War, an era that Mark Twain (with fellow author Dudley Warner) named suitably and described vividly in *The Gilded Age*. The sudden visibility of American society also had bearing. Lively reporting in New York newspapers, particularly in the New York *Herald,* originator of the society page in American newspapers, made society attractively conspicuous. The plainest Americans were now aware of a moneyed aristocracy in their midst, living in turreted mansions as vast as palaces, where society queens commanded wigged footmen (probably imported from England) and enough retainers to do justice to a minor Napoleonic empress. All this was made doubly alluring by its attainability. Any American who could amass a suitable fortune could live in the same fashion. No rules of precedence or lack of armorial bearings stood in the way; the passkey to American society was money.

However, a little tooling was necessary before the key would slide in easily, and the best locksmith was the wife. Maude Howe, in an article for *Harper's Bazar,* told her how to go about it: "Give liberally to charity, go on committees and meet there the educated and well-bred. Keep your eyes open to the way they do things, and soon you are able to play the game."

These efforts evoked the same lamentations among early settlers in America's upper social stratum that were to be heard in England. "Changes not for the better have taken place during the last few years in American social life in every quarter of the Union . . . most perceptible in New York, Saratoga, and Newport," mourned Mrs. Elizabeth F. Ellet in *Queens of Society* (1868). Her alarm over the "fast set" in society was fed by "the wildest stories in current gossip," not the least of which was the use of marijuana by some socialites. One woman, building a splendid house near Central Park, "is said to get herself up with hasheesh," confided the horrified Mrs. Ellet.

Leaving aside Mrs. Ellet's dark allegations about its behavior, society's extravagance was beyond doubt, and was aped by all moneyed folk who had not yet achieved acceptance in its ranks. Wealthy hostesses staged splendid balls at which impoverished dukes and lesser nobility cavorted, eager to graft their impecunious titles onto American fortunes. Public balls were nearly as lavish, providing backgrounds for opulent gowns and jewels. Mrs. Ellet, aghast at it all, reported that six hundred balls had been given during the season of 1865–66 with "an estimated seven million spent by ball-goers, the average cost of a suitable dress being a thousand dollars, without jewelry."

Mrs. Sherwood was casual about a forty-dollars-per-head luncheon in the 1880s. "A thousand dollars is not an unusual price for a luncheon, including flowers and favors, for eighteen to twenty-four guests." Describing the vogue for elaborate favors and souvenirs in *Manners and Social Usages,* she blandly declared, "Fifty dollars for a satin box filled with candy is not an uncommon price." And a French journalist reported with astonishment, "Mr. C. Vanderbilt pays his chief cook ten thousand dollars!"

Without doubt the hosts who staged lavish entertainments took the most direct route to social prominence. "In New York, Mrs. Auguste [*sic*] Belmont has obtained a celebrity for magnificent parties," reported Mrs. Ellet. "The same may be said of many ladies who have as yet no history," she tartly added. "It is very easy to create a sensation in New York or any large city. . . . To rise and reign among the money-worshiping idiots of this kind . . . it is only necessary to possess millions and scatter money lavishly for show."

Most new-rich Americans were undaunted by such chilling disapproval. The very rich aped the extravagant entertainments of the Astors, the Vanderbilts and Mrs. Stuyvesant Fish. The less rich had to be satisfied with smaller-scale efforts but made them nevertheless.

At lower levels, the goad to improved behavior was the influx of new immigrants with whom those moving upward in the economic scale did not wish to be identified. The immigrants, in turn, were helped along or shamed into better manners by their children, who now received etiquette instructions in the classroom. *How to Teach Manners in the School Room,* by Julia M. Dewey (1888), a thorough textbook for teachers and pupils, gave specific examples for classroom participation so that children could learn the principles of polite behavior through actual demonstration. The teachers were made aware of *their* responsibility in Mrs. Dewey's stern warning: "The manners of the pupil are usually similar to those of the teacher."

The urge to improve manners was epidemic. As new money sought to imitate the old and to wine, dine and dance alongside it, as Americanized newcomers sought not to be tagged by the behavior and mannerisms of immigrants, the most compelling urge in America, it seems, was to be able to look down on those just below. Socially mobile, upward-bound America could be observed taking on the characteristics of Jonathan Swift's fleas.

> So naturalists observe, a flea
> Hath smaller fleas that on him prey:
> And these have smaller fleas to bite 'em
> And so proceed *ad infinitum.*

In America the fleas were for the most part ladies. Unlike Englishmen, who were keenly aware of social position and reluctant to associate with a parvenu except for strictly business reasons, American men were for the most part indiscriminately democratic. American women were not.

Constance Fenimore Woolson (niece of James Fenimore Cooper) looked with distaste upon the disintegration of democratic ideals in American parlors, declared women responsible for it and prophesied "If our government were delivered wholly into the hands of women of fashion and society, we should have a monarchy and hereditary order of nobility established within a twelve-month."

Ambition and social drive were by now the outstanding characteristics of the American woman, and her position as queen of the realm was fully consolidated. French observers visiting America in the 1880s declared her supremacy undeniable, and her insatiable demands "her glory and distinction." "What this exigent household queen wants she must have and she *gets* it," wrote one. "That which sets her apart as upon a pedestal from all her kind in other lands is that she *makes her husband earn what she wishes to spend.*"

She wished to spend plenty—most of it for display and social competition, said Paul Blouët, caustic observer of America in the second half of the 19th century. American women were over-dressed, overjeweled and "always dressed for conquest." Exceptions to this general rule were only seen by him in Boston, where ladies seemed "more English in style and wore diamonds sparingly for evening." He also found the rustling silks and staggering bonnets worn at theater distracting and inconsiderate. American women, "even among the cultivated classes, have sovereign contempt for all that is not silk, satin, or velvet," he reported. As for the middle class, they naturally imitated the luxury of the millionaire's wife. "In a democratic country frogs try to swell into oxen," said Blouët, "and puff themselves out until they burst, or rather, until their husbands burst."

To John Graham Brooks, turn-of-the-century American historian who anthologized many such complaints, the conclusion seemed obvious: "Since the root of all our commercial greatness is her ambition, we thus get at the real origin of the much-noted American deference to women."

She earned that deference and her royal status, declared Mrs. Sherwood in a lengthy peroration equating manners with reigning. "The well mannered and well behaved American woman . . . is the queen of the man who loves her. To still the carpers, Mrs. Sherwood supplied a list of what the queen gave in return.

> She must be first servant-trainer, then housekeeper, wife, mother, conversationalist . . . keep up with the advancing spirit of the times . . . be beautifully dressed, play the piano . . . be charitable, thoughtful . . . a student of good taste and good manners, make a home luxurious, ornamental, cheerful, and restful . . . dress and entertain in perfect accord with her station, her means, and her husband's position . . . she must go to the cooking-lecture, come home and visit the kitchen . . . she must steer her ship through stormy seas, and she must also learn to enjoy Wagner's music.

In this list of activities and accomplishments the picture of the female paragon sought by American males emerges. However, minus the driving competition, it was also a picture of the perfect European wife.

33 · NEW ORACLES OF BEHAVIOR

AMERICAN SEEKERS after The Word in etiquette were rarely in doubt about the identity of their authorities. While English etiquette writers usually hid behind such enticing anonymities as "A member of the aristocracy," "An aristocrat," or "A member of the nobility," leaving it to the reader to guess if they were all they professed to be, Americans could read and follow with assurance; American etiquette writers blazoned their identity for all readers to see.

Among the best-qualified were the Howes: Florence Howe Hall, Maude Howe, and their mother, Julia Ward Howe. Julia, though best known for the "Battle Hymn of the Republic," frequently surveyed American manners. In a lecture, "Is Society Polite?" she took a critical view of society and decided it was not.

Maude Howe was a frequent contributor to magazines, and her advice on how to break into society has already been mentioned in the preceding chapter.

Florence Howe Hall was perhaps the most expert guide of the three, and put her advice into two successful books, *The Correct Thing in Good Society* and *Social Customs*. In the latter work, her warning to the overambitious to climb cautiously, if at all, sounded more English than American. But then, times *were* changing: "Where society is divided into certain cliques or sets, as is often the case in our cities, a lady belonging to the less fashionable clique should hesitate long before calling upon one of a more fashionable circle, even though she may have been introduced to the other lady."

But the star of all the etiquette writers who undertook to guide the manners of affluent hopefuls was Mary Elizabeth Wilson Sherwood. Her *Manners and Social Usages* (1884) was as authoritative, departmentalized and thoroughly detailed as Emily Post's *Etiquette* some fifty years later. Mrs. Post merely added to a structure already erected by Mrs. Sherwood.

Mrs. Sherwood first appeared in the firmament of American etiquette writers with a series of features for *Harper's Bazar* (founded in 1867 and spelled with one *a*, after the German *Der Bazar*, the leading European fashion periodical, whose fashions the American *Bazar* regularly presented to its readers).

Immediately Mrs. Sherwood glowed with the steady brilliance of Venus and soon outshone all other authorities, including Henry Tomes, her popular predecessor at *Harper's Bazar*, whose etiquette articles in that magazine had resulted in his *Bazar Book of Decorum*.

Mrs. Sherwood's experiences on the magazine convinced her that Tomes misjudged Americans in presuming they liked their manners bad. Letters from *her* readers indicated otherwise. Thousands wrote "in good faith to *Harper's Bazar*" asking such questions as "Should mashed potatoes be eaten with a knife or a fork?" or "Can napkins and finger bowls be used at breakfast?" Mrs. Sherwood rightly concluded that a great hunger for information was going unappeased. Not that books were lacking to give the answers. But unfortunately, "Many attempt to write who know nothing of good society by experience, and their books are full of ludicrous errors," said Mrs. Sherwood, dismissing most of the existing competition. Secure in the knowledge that *she* could indeed write from experience, she offered guidance to those who had literally dug up their money: "The miner's wife having become rich, asks how she shall arrange her house, call on her neighbors, write her letters." Among those who had grasped basic etiquette there were still many who wanted to know "How shall we give a dinner party?" "What is the etiquette of a wedding?" "When does one wear a dress coat?"

Mrs. Sherwood had learned the answers in her childhood, and after many years in Washington with her congressman father had mastered the art of protocol. She had never ceased to adore society and she described it with great skill, the ring of authority pealing

"The modern dinner-table."
Frontispiece, *Manners and Social Usages* by Mrs. John Sherwood, 1884.

from every paragraph as she conducted her readers behind the scenes into the homes of those who had absorbed etiquette along with mother's milk.

Flat descriptions would never do for Mrs. Sherwood. She fleshed out details. Water glasses were "elegantly engraved"; the champagne glass "flared"; "Bohemian green glass" held the hock; "ruby red glass" held the Burgundy; three "delicately cut and engraved glasses" held lesser wines. The reader might reel from the Dionysian jumble specified for the properly set table, but he undeniably had a picture of it. And a dinner guest fresh up from the mining camps would not be puzzled by a strange new addition to the table silver if he read her book: "A small, peculiarly shaped fork laid by each plate at the right hand is for the oysters," Mrs. Sherwood explained.

Where other authorities were satisfied merely to recite the rules, she sought to lead Americans far beyond the bare-bones dogma of etiquette to a taste for the gracious life. "Up the Hudson, out at Orange, all along the coast of Long Island, the garden party is almost imperatively necessary," she proclaimed. "In remote country places ladies should learn to give these parties, and, with very little trouble, make the most of our fine climate." Even a small patch of lawn would do to catch the festive spirit of a garden party at Newport.

With Delphic authority Mrs. Sherwood covered etiquette in every conceivable aspect, from correct golf attire for ladies—"The regular golf uniform is a red jacket and a short, tight skirt, which adds to the gaiety of the green, and has its obvious advantages"— to the touchy subject of introductions.

Some of the most diverting chapters deal with "The House With One Servant" and "The House With Many Servants." In between there was "The House With Two Servants," but that house presented the fewest problems of all. "Many large families in this country employ but one servant," confided Mrs. Sherwood. Her description of its management could instill confidence into any lady of limited means. Willingness to take on a few light duties was essential, and Mrs. Sherwood assured her that rinsing breakfast china and glassware on washday mornings was not a disagreeable task. Especially when "All gentlemen say they like to eat and drink from utensils that have been washed by a lady." With her usual attention to the minute details Mrs. Sherwood described "the neat wooden tub with a little cotton yarn mop and two clean towels," which the maid was to set before the mistress still seated at the breakfast table. With ladylike grace the mistress would then rinse the dainty pieces while the maid dispatched the heavy dishes and silver in the kitchen.

Other small tasks assumed during the week, such as preparing starch and stoning raisins, made it possible to stretch a maid's capacity, provided the maid was "young, strong, and willing." And above all, willing to get up at 5 A.M. to do "two hours good work before breakfast," on the Sunday she wanted off.

"The House With Many Servants" could present the most serious problems, especially if the mistress was newly rich and for the first time dealing with a staff of servants. Mrs. Sherwood's recommendation to her was an English housekeeper, "at least for a year." This experienced hand, dressed in *moiré antique* and lofty manners, a combination sure to subdue the most recalcitrant servants, would whip the staff into proper shape and save the inexperienced mistress much heartache.

The most difficult of all to contend with was the lady's maid, "who can be, and generally is, the most disagreeable of creatures." Unfortunately, this servant was also the most indispensable in "The House With Many Servants" if its mistress was to live like a lady. Her personal maid often accompanied her to a ball, attended to her cloak, captured any stray hairs that might have escaped from her coiffure and loosened corset stays if the dancing proved too strenuous.

American lady's maids were less pampered than the English or continental variety, and obliged "to make their own beds and eat with the other servants." But the same high European standard of performance was expected. "They must be first-rate hair-dressers, good packers of trunks, and understand dressmaking and fine starching." However, expect to pay for this, Mrs. Sherwood warned. "A woman who combines these qualifications commands very high wages, and expects, as her perquisite, her mistress's cast-off dresses." French maids were unquestionably the best, but "apt to be untruthful and treacherous."

Readers interested less in the management of a French maid and more in the correct way of conducting mashed potatoes to the mouth might rightly have snapped Mrs. Sherwood's book shut. But those uncertainly clutching their first gilt-engraved invitation to a ball knew they were in the presence of a master guide. With her help a successful assault on society seemed assured.

Proper attire for lady's maid [left] and parlor maid. Manners and Social Usages by Mrs. John Sherwood, 1900 edition.

34 · ADVANCED ETIQUETTE FOR AMERICANS
※心※

THANKS TO SUCH qualified guides as Mrs. Sherwood and the Howes, and numerous others less happily endowed with lustrous names and writing ability (this last lack was often solved by borrowing English texts verbatim), Americans could learn exactly what to do in all social situations. At least sixty new titles were published in the 1870s and 1880s, and most of the previously published volumes continued in popularity.

Upward-bound wives who had done their etiquette reading knew to wear formal attire when invited to dinner and slipped white kid gloves—the badge of the upper class in America as it was in England—on themselves and their husbands whenever possible, and certainly for all formal appearances. Men were advised to carry an extra pair at balls in case sweaty palms made the first pair clammy.

All etiquette books from the 1880s on coached their readers in ballroom etiquette as if life in America was spent exclusively in a whirl of cotillions and germans. Even *Our Deportment,* which recognized that all Americans were not necessarily emulating Mrs. Vanderbilt and which temporized on formal attire to the extent of saying "In some circles evening dress is considered an affectation, and it is well to do as others do," nevertheless devoted nineteen pages to ballroom etiquette.

It remained for Ward McAllister, fatuous self-appointed arbiter of New York society, to make the definitive statement on ballroom conduct: "There are only about four hundred people who are at ease in a ballroom," he said of New York society, initiating the phrase "the Four Hundred."

Illustrated Manners gave some helpful instructions on this score.

"A successful ball must have good music and plenty of people to dance."
Rules of Etiquette and Home Culture, 1884.

For one thing, married couples were to avoid dancing together. "A married man pays his court to other ladies, his wife accepts the attentions of other gentlemen; and the married couple who should be seen dancing or talking much with each other, would become subjects of general ridicule. Here in New York," the author added, "husbands and wives do not even go to the same parties unless they prefer to do so. It is presumed that they have enough of each other's society in private." A shudder from the ghost of Richard Allestree; in the 17th century he rebuked married couples for doing just that.

Masked balls, which received attention from numerous etiquette books, were a bit over the heads of most readers, who were unlikely to receive engraved invitations commanding them to appear "In character from *Waverly*," the example one authority quoted. The "Kettledrum" was more within the general scope. At these afternoon receptions a young lady dressed as a drummer was posted near the teatable. An occasional drum roll reminded guests that they were at a "Kettledrum."

Most afternoon social life was confined to making calls—"the simplest society duty," said *The Home Book,* but not one to be neglected, the author made clear, rehearsing the hostess to star in her role. "On these afternoons the hostess is in usual afternoon dress . . . always choice and delightful . . . her guests find her . . . busy with some elegant trifle of lace or wool-work, writing letters, or touching a sketch to be laid aside on the entrance of visitors." The self-conscious preparations typified calling itself—no longer a spontaneous neighborly gesture.

Calling cards, earlier rejected by Americans as affectations, became popular after the Civil War and now wielded the same cutting edge as in England, rebuffing would-be acquaintances by not being left in return. American ladies pursued their card-leaving rounds according to the rules in the etiquette books, and silver salvers, placed conspicuously in hallways, mounted with the disbursed pasteboards. The height of the card pile might be interpreted as a clue to the social standing of the hostess.

A card could mean "Thank you"; "I'm returning your call"; or "Come see me." But separated from its donor and mingled with a few dozen other cards, the exact meaning intended was uncertain. If the crush had been great that afternoon, the hostess could not be sure the caller had bothered to enter her parlor. Only the *pour prendre congé* card, initialed P.P.C. in a corner to indicate the caller was going away and had called "to take leave," conveyed a clear meaning. With no code for other meanings, uninscribed cards required guesswork.

To reduce some of the confusion presented by a heaped card

Calling cards. Our Deportment, 1882.

tray, a system of bending corners evolved in England and was quickly followed in America. Depending on which corner was bent, the card telegraphed, "I came in person but you were out"; "Hello to all the family"; "Hello only to the mistress of the house"; "Sorry your aunt passed away." Unfortunately for many who were newcomers to society's ways with calling cards, it was all too easy to turn the wrong corner—and this in spite of detailed explanations in most etiquette books. "Oh, what a tangled web we weave, when first we practise cards to leave!" exclaimed one American etiquette writer. Happily the custom of "cornering cards" ended with the 19th century, hailed with gratitude by etiquette writers and lady callers alike.

Cards and calling received pages of space in etiquette books from the 1880s on and the etiquette rules governing them became as cold and restrictive as in England, for the same reasons: entrance to a home as a caller might provide the opportunity for making social contacts; and there were those who did not welcome them.

Consequently the friendly American custom of introducing visitors to each other was abandoned, at least in the society in which Mrs. Sherwood moved. As she explained it, though callers were expected to converse freely under the hostess' roof, as in England, "They may cease to know each other when they go down the front steps." Nor was a hostess to flout this rule, said Mrs. Sherwood. "A lady in her own house can in these United States do pretty much as she pleases, but there is one thing in which our cultivated and exclusive fashionable city society seems agreed, and that is, that she must not introduce two ladies who reside in the same town."

Furthermore, ladies who were not acquainted were not to be brought together for the purpose of meeting until the would-be introducer had ascertained "how the new acquaintance would be received, whether or not it is the desire of both parties to know each other." This "good-natured desire of a sympathetic person that the people whom she knows well should know each other" could have disastrous sequels. "She strives to bring them together at lunch or dinner, but perhaps finds out afterwards that one of the ladies has particular objections to knowing the other. . . . The disaffected lady shows her displeasure by being impolite to the pushing lady, as she may consider her. Had no introduction taken place . . . she might have still enjoyed a reputation for politeness. Wary women of the world are therefore very shy of introducing two women to each other."

Though in her heart Mrs. Sherwood agreed that a friendly introduction hurt no one, she was obliged to point out that kindness was not under discussion. Etiquette was. Good etiquette forbade indiscriminate introductions and furthermore—here Mrs. Sherwood put her finger on the quivering nerve of the matter—a lady's position could only be maintained "by a certain loyalty to her own set." •

Our Deportment (1882), possibly because it was compiled by a man, John H. Young, took a lighter view of the mechanics of forming an acquaintance and declared that "two ladies . . . who are known to each other only by sight, should upon first opportunity, make themselves acquainted with one another." This was easier said than done, and Mr. Young did not explain how it was to be accomplished—only that an introduction was to be sought. Mrs. Sherwood had already shown how difficult *that* could be.

With etiquette grown so uncompromisingly pretentious it is not surprising that Nathan D. Urner, who signed himself "Mentor," took some Swiftian gibes in two psuedo-etiquette books, *Always* and *Never*. *Always* would guide "either sex into the enpurpled penetralia of Fashionable life." *Never* was a "Handbook for the uninitiated and inexperienced aspirants to society's giddy heights and glittering attainments!"

Occasionally there was a flash of the old American spirit, as when Florence Howe Hall objected because the English accent had become so fashionable with Americans, and with Americans who did not quite know how to mouth it, at that. Though she agreed that American speech could stand improvement, she did not approve of affectation. Speech needed attention among those ladies who said "kep" instead of "kept." No matter how richly they emblazoned their new china with a family crest, their true social status was as visible as a wart on the nose. Put "*ts*" where they belong and leave the English accent to the English, exhorted Mrs. Hall. "Imitation is a sign of weakness in nations and individuals."

Eating Indian corn.
America Revisited by George A. Sala, 1882.

Mrs. Hall defended the American custom of eating corn on the cob, though American etiquette writers were divided on it and some considered it barbarous. It aroused many comments and not a few rebukes both at home and abroad. One admiring outburst came from the English journalist George Augustus Sala, who thought it delightful to see a pretty young lady "dexterously twirl a corn-cob till she had nibbled off all the grains . . . without soiling her fingers or her symmetrical chin." Mrs. Hall, familiar with society's latest ways, recommended "two little silver-gilt spike-like arrangements, used by a lady who gives many elegant dinners at Newport."

The chaperon was a subject on which there was complete unanimity among etiquette writers and in society itself. "One of the first demands of a polished society," said Mrs. Sherwood; "Taking the position of an English or continental matron," said Florence Howe Hall; "Etiquette has made chaperonage an established and even rigid law," declared *Social Etiquette of New York*.

The chaperon arrived on the American etiquette scene in the latter half of the 19th century. A female Cerberus, she sat in the parlor when her charge received gentlemen, accompanied her to the skating rink, to balls, parties, dinners and theater, guarding her from, among other perils, "the danger of a bad marriage." Southern belles, considerably less restricted by chaperons, continued to enjoy much of the freedom of former years. But not girls of Eastern society. Even Agnes H. Morton's *Etiquette* (1892), which did not bother much with society's ways and instead declared itself for "Those who dwell within the broad zone of the average," stood absolutely firm on chaperonage. In the old democratic spirit absent from so many etiquette books of the 80s and 90s, Mrs. Morton declared that any American girl could qualify as a lady without be-

271

longing to the leisure class. "In our republican land, no one can draw such definite boundaries," said Mrs. Morton. The girl who worked for her living as "a teacher, stenographer or bookkeeper," belonged as much in society as "the banker's daughter." But when out in society "she must live by the same conventions" as the banker's daughter and observe "the absolute condition of chaperonage."

It does seem surprising that Mrs. Morton, who updated a 1911 edition of her book with many 20th-century modernizations, remained firm on this subject of chaperonage, though she welcomed modern innovations and countenanced the use of the telephone to extend and acknowledge invitations long before it had won clearance from other social authorities. "The new dynasty of wire and wireless is destined to dominate us," she wrote and, with remarkable prescience saw the hazy outlines of TV, predicting, "even telephotography."

However she failed to see developments that were much closer at hand with respect to chaperonage. The safety bike, first appearing in 1889, was to weaken the chaperon's hold almost at once. There was no room for her on a bicycle built for two, and few chaperons were willing or heedless enough to follow their charges on wheels. Soon the wheels of the automobile would hasten the end of the short-lived American chaperon. Wheels, plus athletics, were to change the conduct of America's ladies. And eventually change ladies everywhere.

from *Social Etiquette*, 1896

Farmer: *"Pull up you fool! The mare's bolting."*
Motorist: *"So's the car!"*
Punch, 1901.

PART FIVE

Twentieth Century Changes

Pharmacist (to battered female covered with scratches): "The cat, I suppose."
Battered female: "No. Another lady!"
Drawing by Phil May

35 · SIGNS OF ANOTHER REVOLUTION

ALTHOUGH AMERICAN ETIQUETTE—like American women—was to abandon much of its corseting in the 20th century, never in American history had there been so much printed preoccupation with etiquette as in the first decade of the 20th century. At least seventy-one etiquette books and twice that number of magazine articles were published between 1900 and 1910.

Significantly, most etiquette books now avoided "Society" in their titles—perhaps for a good reason. Society's reputation for vulgar spending and tasteless antics had gone from bad to shocking with millionaires staging dinner parties where guests in formal attire dined on horseback or drank toasts to a monkey as guest of honor. One wildly foolish dinner, staged by former champagne salesman Harry Lehr, protégé of Mrs. Stuyvesant Fish, feted the canine pets of friends. Mrs. W. E. D. Stokes, caught up in the animal fever, gave a genuine Renaissance touch to the prevailing Medicean spirit by concealing live bullfrogs in a table centerpiece. Vaulting into the champagne goblets of the startled guests, the frogs recalled the live-bird pies of 16th-century banquets.

The competition to outdo one another with lavish entertainments climaxed with two particularly extravagant balls, each costing several hundred thousand dollars. One, a costume affair hosted by the Bradley Martins, recent arrivals in high society, and the other presided over by James Hazen Hyde, a young playboy whose wealth bore the gloss of inheritance, so scandalized the public that shortly afterward both Hyde and the Bradley Martins went off into voluntary European exile. It was enough to drive society off the covers of etiquette books.

For its own part, society avoided "etiquette" as an unspeakable word. Anyone who found it necessary to inquire about etiquette did not belong in society. Only for such infrequent occasions as weddings, christenings and funerals could etiquette be referred to without arousing shudders among the well-bred. If newcomers to society had questions to ask about correct table settings, proper dress or the rites of social calls, they were well-advised not to call it "etiquette" and, better still, to address their questions anonymously to such popular journalists as Marion Harland, Dorothy Dix, and Gabrielle Rozière, whose articles in *Delineator* magazine were built around the E. T. Quette family.

The texts in etiquette books had changed little, but the market appeal had changed noticeably. Typical of the new crop were such down-to-earth titles as *Done Every Day, Practical Etiquette, Everybody's Book of Correct Conduct, Everyday Etiquette, Dont's for Everybody,* and *Etiquette for Americans.* Once again, as they had endeavored to in the mid-19th century, etiquette writers proposed to improve the manners of the great mass of Americans.

And high time! the magazine articles cried unanimously. "Are We Polite?" asked *Current Literature.* "Has the American Bad Manners?" asked the *Ladies Home Journal.* "Has Courtesy Declined?" demanded *Munsey.* Yes, positively! cried dozens of others screaming about "The Decay of Manners," and "Modern Manners and the Unmannerly Age." Other articles labeled the widespread behavior "Minor Crimes" and "Everyday Crime, Habitual Rudeness." *The Independent* thought it high time Americans became their brother's keeper and said so in an article, "Improving One's Neighbors."

Many thought the worst culprits of all were women. And, as in the past, some of the most severe critics were themselves women, annoyed with the way their sex was invading business and athletics, and in their rush for new liberties endangering the natural rights of women to be catered to and protected. Condemning women for being as pushy and aggressive as men, Amelia Mason, writing on "The Decadence of Manners," in *Century Magazine,* protested that one could no longer recognize a lady by her dress: "Well-dressed women push over one another."

"Lady" had deteriorated into an imprecise term, complained

Miss Mason bitterly; ladies now came in many varieties including "wash-ladies, scrub-ladies and foreladies." The meaning of "lady" was in the eye of the beholder, said Maude Howe, describing a drunken loafer's description of a hair-pulling match between two fishwives as "two ladies having a fight."

Furthermore, some ladies were beginning to dress like men. "The typical girl of the day," said Miss Mason, "puts on mannish airs with mannish clothes and spices her talk with slang." (She obviously objected to the vogue for tailored suits for women that began at about this time.) Also typical was this girl's disrespect "as she puts down her parents, her elders, and her superiors." Miss Mason saw it all as a woeful change from the good old days, seemingly unaware that Mrs. Farrar had made the same complaints—in almost the same words—in 1834.

The modern behavior of women was all of a piece with modern art, wrote another articulate but anonymous female in the *Atlantic Monthly* criticizing "futurist trends in art, music, architecture, literature, and young women's behavior." Changes were coming swiftly in all these areas, she agreed, but swiftness did not always characterize ascent, "The swiftest progress of all being down hill." Obviously annoyed with the Fauve-ish Armory art show of 1913 in which Marcel Duchamp's "Nude Descending a Staircase" caused such a furor, she declared thumbs down on futurist art and bold "futurist" maidens. For her part she would "rather go back to even the eighteenth-century conditions than to have my sex make up so large a part of the Rude descending a Staircase."

"Are Our Women Ruder than Our Men?" asked Marion Harland in *The Independent*, replying with many paragraphs of *Yes*. Women were destroying all the myths that had been concocted about them, from Milton, Dante and Swinburne's impassioned glorifications to the "Sugar and spice and everything nice" that little girls were made of. Now females were made of some peppery substance that strangled their tongues when a gentleman politely offered his seat in a crowded ferry or tram. "Not one in ten women thanks the man for his courtesy," said Miss Harland, implying that such conduct was causing American men to forget *their* traditional courtesy.

Many men *had* abandoned it, and the *Standard Book of Etiquette* supported their action, particularly in packed trams. Ladies were told: "It is an indication of ill-breeding to show signs of displeasure if, on entering a crowded car, no seat is offered." After all, said the author righteously, "It should be borne in mind that the gentleman has a right to his seat, and is under no obligation, except that of politeness, to give it up, and weariness or weakness may render it inadvisable for him to do so."

Even in 1872 Appleton's Journal criticized ladies who spread their skirts over two seats. Here three ladies occupy seats intended for six passengers, "ignoring the claims of a masculine intruder."

Of the etiquette books of the early 20th century, Marion Harland's *Everyday Etiquette* (1905) had the widest appeal. Any book with the name Marion Harland attached to it (psuedonym of Mrs. Albert Payson Terhune, wife of a prominent clergyman) commanded immediate attention among average American families.

As the well-established author of more than twenty-five books and numerous magazine articles and as a widely read authority on household and family management she had built up a large following that looked to her for the truth on everything domestic from Amenities to Zwieback. Mailbags of correspondence from readers who sought to learn "the by-laws of polite society" had prompted her etiquette book written with the collaboration of her daughter, Virginia Van de Water. She responded to public demand as Mrs. Sherwood had done some twenty years earlier.

But unlike Mrs. Sherwood, Miss Harland was not dazzled by society, nor did she move in it, except as an interested observer. Recognizing the bulk of her readers to be "people of rude upbringing . . . who have longings and taste for gentlehood," she set to her task of preparing them to move up. Particularly the woman "to whom changed circumstances or removal . . . to a fashionable neighborhood involved the necessity of altered habits."

Miss Harland understood that woman well, her "natural desire to mingle on equal terms with the better sort of rich people," and enshrined her in the key chapter: "Mrs. Newlyrich and her Social Duties." Since she was a "woman of worthy aspirations and innate refinement, raised by the whirl of fortune's wheel from decent poverty to actual wealth," Miss Harland proposed to make the transition as painless as possible and anticipated various situations that might confront her.

The first experience of being announced by an usher or footman at a party could be traumatic if she were not prepared for it. If hearing her name shouted out sounded like "the trump of doom," to her "unaccustomed ears," Miss Harland assured her that the assembled guests would be as unaware of her as of the carpet. "Stubborn conviction of your insignificance is the first step that counts in the acquisition of well-mannered composure among your fellows."

Butlers or plural household staff were not mentioned in *Everyday Etiquette*. Miss Harland's readers would manage with one in help, but even that one might pose problems for the inexperienced Mrs. Newlyrich. "Engage no servant who patronizes you," Miss Harland warned.

Perhaps the most serious stumbling block in the way of Mrs.

Newlyrich's social progress was her husband. "Men, as a whole, do not take polish readily," Miss Harland said, reiterating a fact already noted for decades by previous writers. "Unless John Newlyrich wore a dress-coat before he was twenty-one, he is not quite at ease in a 'swallow-tail' at forty. . . . He butters a whole slice of bread, using his knife trowel-wise. . . . He cuts up his salad. . . . He never gets over the habit of speaking of dinner as 'supper.'" Such antics could affect a wife "like gravel between the teeth," and there was little hope of improving such a husband.

Actually, Mrs. Newlyrich's best hope for success in society was herself. On that note Miss Harland concluded with a chapter on "Self-Help and Observation" urging careful study of those whose behavior it seemed desirable to emulate.

Similar advice was widely dispensed in other books and in magazine articles. Ruthless self-appraisal was urged on those who sought to improve themselves, encouraging numerous societies for "self-improvement" into being. One volume, *The Man Who Pleases and the Woman Who Charms,* told both sexes how to turn up their personal assets like the burners on a gas stove. Emily Holt, another popular etiquette writer, of whom more later, anticipated Dale Carnegie with *Secret of Popularity,* written, she declared, "for the especial benefit of those men and women who wish to be liked and admired and . . . do not make friends readily." Those who felt they lacked personal charm had only to look in her book to find the answer to self-improvement. It was a course in creating a good impression with the first handshake, appraising a social situation correctly and profitably, and making the most of "all little opportunities."

Children's manners received increased attention in the first decade of the 20th century and now were taught routinely in the public schools. The increase in adult etiquette books was paralleled by a similar increase in titles for the young. *Young Folks' Book of Etiquette, Polite Pupil, Little Book of Courtesies for Children* and *Boys' and Girls' Manners* were typical, but the most original, and possibly the most effective, to judge by their remarkable longevity, were the Goop books by Gelett Burgess. *Goops and How to Be Them* (1900) and *More Goops and How Not to Be Them* (1903), are still in print intimidating children into acceptable behavior.

The second decade saw a decline in both quality and quantity of etiquette books. Understandably, in the sobering climate of World War I, only eight were published during the years 1915–1919. However, certain changes in future conduct, and the liberation that would follow these changes, were clearly forecast during the war years. The Vernon Castles danced their way to fame with shocking modernity that included Irene's bobbed hair and shortened skirts, chaperons were edged aside, and such formalities as the ceremonious visit which had moored well-bred conduct for many decades now showed signs of slipping.

Prohibition delivered a *coup de grace* to the weakened restraints of the new generation and ushered in a period of defiant laxness. The old order was clearly changing, but it was not to die in one swift stroke. Changes would need to be phased out.

Vigorous support for the old order was still to be found in the new crop of war millionaires who wanted to live by the old gracious standards, with staffs complete from butler to second cook to do their bidding; and their wives hungered to "receive" ladies of social distinction. Many of the new rich had as little knowledge of what was considered correct by society as their counterparts had exhibited in the eighties and nineties. Pretentiousness marked their homes filled with ormolu-frosted French furniture. Ostentation prevailed at their tables, and their social conduct in general was charted from Mrs. Sherwood's newly republished (1919) *Manners and Social Usages,* for the moment the only reliable beacon to light the way for New Money.

The Twenties, which were to prove the most significant decade in American etiquette history so far, started off inauspiciously enough with the reissue of Mrs. Sherwood's book and reprintings of three others from the previous decade. Of particular significance was *Encyclopedia of Etiquette,* by Emily Holt, first published in 1901. It is important to our story because, in 1921, it became, quite by accident, the introduction to a new era in etiquette books.

Miss Holt's *Encyclopedia* was written in the language of the Gibson girl. America was entering the era of the John Held, Jr., flapper. Nevertheless, Nelson Doubleday, sensing the time as ripe for a hard-sell promotion of etiquette because of increased public outcry against deteriorating manners, decided to unload some unsold stock of the Holt book (possibly the 1914 edition), backing it up with an aggressive advertising campaign conceived by a bright young copywriter, Lillian Eichler (Mrs. T. M. Watson).

Miss Eichler's gimmick was a series of advertisements that depicted common etiquette errors and asked "What's Wrong in This Picture?" or "Has This Ever Happened to You?" A 1935 article in the magazine *Outlook,* about leaders in the advertising field, extolled Miss Eichler's undeniable talent for promotion and the success of the campaign, but reported that the Holt *Encyclopedia of Etiquette* "rolled back [to the publisher] just as quickly when readers found that the old etiquette book was illustrated with pictures of women in bustles." The illustrations were prewar, it is true (if the 1914 edition was the one), but devoid of bustles. Possibly the book promoted by Miss Eichler may have been *Everyman's Encyclopedia of Etiquette,* by Miss Holt, issued by Nelson Doubleday in 1920.

However, there is no doubt that Doubleday recognized the enormous potential for etiquette books (though when had this *not* existed in America?) and a new *Book of Etiquette* by Miss Eichler herself promptly appeared in 1921, backed by a similar advertising campaign.

Miss Eichler's book was nearly as old-fashioned as Miss Holt's. Her chapter on "Introductions" opened with the statement, "The days of gallant cavaliers and courteous knights who bowed profusely and doffed their feathered hats to the very ground when introduced to the ladies of the court are over." They were indeed— with Stutz Bearcats and raccoon-coated collegians making the scene in Miss Eichler's girlhood days.

A little farther along she gave the green light to "the warm, cordial handclasp," confiding that "The stiff formal bow is quickly losing all its prestige in the best social circles." Equally in the style of the nineties—if not actually picked up from one of the old books —was this statement: "It is important to remember that the first intimation of recognition after an introduction must always come from the lady. A gentleman does not offer his hand nor does he bow or nod to the lady he has met only once before until she has made the first movement."

Miss Eichler quickly prepared a "revised" edition in 1924, *The New Book of Etiquette,* in which she declared, "The ordinary book of etiquette still concerns itself with rules and regulations originated by ponderous gentlemen who lived in the Middle Ages or in the time of the Renaissance. But no power can crush the new simplicity and informality that have grown up in American society . . . we seem to be standing on the threshold of a new era, social and intellectual . . . we are cutting loose from the fads and fashions established by the pompous dandies of the 17th and 18th centuries." Just what these recently abolished "fads and fashions" were is not clear to me, unless Miss Eichler meant the curtsey, already dead for some time, or the low, sweeping bow, also long moribund by the 1920s. Some of Miss Eichler's passages belied her professed understanding of the changing order. "When a young man is asked to call by a young lady, he does not ask to see her alone but requests of the servant at the door that he be announced to *the ladies.* This is especially important for it infers [*sic*] that he expects to be presented to the young lady's mother or her chaperon."

Much of the chapter on "Calls and Calling Customs" in the first edition of Miss Eichler's *Book of Etiquette* is quoted almost verbatim from books that date well back into the 19th century. In her "New" edition she declared that books devoted too much space to "the now nearly obsolete custom of card leaving," but then devoted considerable space to it herself—thirty pages' worth—making it clear that her readers were expected to leave plenty of cards when *they* made a call.

No, for all her fine talk Miss Eichler did little to "modernize" etiquette. But her old-hat approach brought Emily Post out of her corner, fists clenched, ready to go the full fight to a decisive victory as the new etiquette champion.

36 · THE AGE OF EMILY POST

FEW OF THE HUNDREDS of etiquette books published in America since the time of Jackson left any more than a thumbprint on American behavior until Emily Post came along in 1922. Then, in the way that Victrola identified phonographs, Kodak cameras, Frigidaire refrigerators, and Kleenex cleansing tissues, "Emily Post" became a synonym for etiquette. Purchasers of her book rarely asked for it by title, let alone its full title, *Etiquette, the Blue Book of Social Usage.* To ask for "Emily Post" was sufficient.

She blessed etiquette with new respectability, said a quote in a 1922 issue of *The Literary Digest,* confirming society's former low opinion of the subject:

> Until quite recently, etiquette as such was barred from polite conversation. . . . To discuss etiquette, it was held, indicated the discusser's uncertainty as to its precepts. To allow an etiquette book to lie in open view on the sitting room table was unthinkable. Nothing would so clearly intimate to the visitor that the possessor was a parvenu still engaged in familiarizing himself with the elements of good breeding. But all of this is of the past . . . as definitely as the horse and buggy.

No one was ashamed to be caught with Emily Post's *Etiquette* on their popular new living-room accessory—the coffee table. At its first appearance the book zoomed to the top of the nonfiction bestseller list, crowding Papini's *Life of Christ* into second place and sharing the number one spot with Sinclair Lewis's *Babbitt,* a novel that, appropriately, highlighted social ineptitude. Everybody was reading Emily Post. "What would Emily Post say?" now replaced "What would Mrs. Grundy say?" the familiar challenge to social blunders for over a century. Emily Post became a byword almost overnight.

But why was Emily Post proclaimed the voice of authority? After all she had not—as some people seemed to think—*invented* etiquette. It had engrossed numerous Americans for nearly a hundred years. Other experts had, in the past, guided America's faltering steps to refined conduct: Mrs. Farrar, Miss Leslie, the authoritative Mrs. Sherwood, Marion Harland with her immense following of readers, and the more recent Lillian Eichler who had devised such clever advertising for etiquette books. Yet not one of them had come to *personify* etiquette.

Mrs. Post became a virtual synonym for etiquette because she spoke in a *new* voice filled with passion and conviction that promised salvation and solution to all who were adrift in uncertainty about correct behavior—at the precise moment when Americans longed for just such leadership.

"The country is gript, nay enthralled, by a rebirth of interest in etiquette," said *The Literary Digest*. "The recently recrudescent in-

"No place for a man of manners."
This is a London artist's interpretation of Mrs. Post's remark that even in a crowded elevator, "a gentleman can reveal his innate respect for women by not permitting himself to be crowded too near them." The editor asks, "Has Mrs. Post ever seen a crush in the Piccadilly tube lifts?"
London Opinion, 1923

terest in etiquette . . . seems to be sweeping the country," said best-selling novelist Gertrude Atherton. And looking back at the changing morals and manners of the twenties, it is understandable —this nationwide urge to shore up the old standards crumbling under the impact of the automobile, prohibition, postwar euphoria and the movies.

Exactly as opponents to their increased freedom had feared and predicted, women—at least young women—had forsaken their traditional responsibility for good deportment and now behaved and looked more like males all the time, with their corsets removed, their breasts flattened, their hair "shingled" and their bodies baked to a rugged outdoorman's brown, following the lead of gamine Coco Chanel, who had introduced the fashion for sun-tanning shortly after World War I.

Scantily dressed girls danced the Charleston, wriggled the Black Bottom, nipped from flasks filled with bathtub gin, waved long cigarette holders and gave the chief coloration to a generation that looked to the movies to set its standards and was called "Flaming Youth." "Females Afire" might have been more accurate. No wonder the older generation mourned the passing of the chaperoned party, now replaced by the petting party. In their frantic eagerness to restore some decorum, they turned more hopefully than ever to etiquette books.

Mrs. Post welcomed them with evangelical fervor, prepared to lead old and young, rich and poor, wherever they wished to be directed—a presentation at the Court of St. James, or a fraternity house party, or safely past revealing barbarisms. A few selections from her list of "Illiterate Pronunciations" conveys some idea of the type of reader Mrs. Post expected to find prowling through her pages: "gentleman," not gempmun; "family," not fambly; "picture," not pitcher; "film," not fillum; "girl," not goil. And she warned against such pretentious pronunciations as *"iss-you* instead of *ishue,"* and Paris "with trilled r's and hissing s's."

Timing, fervor and encyclopedic coverage contributed to Mrs. Post's instant success. But perhaps her greatest talent lay in her flair for dramatic presentation and the dramatis personae she mustered to make her etiquette points: Mrs. Cravin Praise, Mr. Stock-san Bonds, Mrs. Climber, Mr. and Mrs. Greathouse, Mr. and Mrs. Oneroom, Mrs. Oldworld, Mrs. Wellborn, Mrs. Oncewere, the Upstarts, the Richan Vulgars, Mrs. Greymouse—the list is endless and the characters immediately identifiable.

To be sure, Miss Harland had used Mrs. Newlyrich not too long before, and continental writers, particularly in earlier days, had used picturesque names to make their points—the 18th-century *Spectator* had drawn blood with Tom Tawdry and Mrs. Modish. But such an extensive cast as Mrs. Post employed had never before played the boards.

Mrs. Post dramatized with all the elements of pathos, comedy and suspense. In her chapter on "Formal Dinners," meant to demonstrate that such affairs were not for novice hostesses, she opened with a first act in which the reader saw Mrs. Worldly set her well-trained staff in motion for dinner "In a Great House." The cook was notified: "Twenty-four for dinner on the tenth." There, as far as Mrs. Worldly was concerned, the matter rested until shortly before the event, when a menu would be submitted to her, "which she will merely glance at."

What about china, silver, linens? "She never sees or thinks about her table, which is in the butler's province." Mrs. Worldly is the mistress of an experienced staff that can be entrusted with details. She has seen to that. Now she leaves matters to them.

The guest list is Mrs. Worldly's only responsibility, and she does attend to the sensitive matter of seating the guests. "The morning of the dinner her secretary brings her the place cards [Mrs. Post carefully explained, for the benefit of some who had never seen a place card. "The name of each person expected is written on a separate card"] "and she puts them in the order in which they are to be laid on the table, very much as though she were playing solitaire."

Surely any reader can imagine Mrs. Worldly performing this pleasant little social task just after breakfast in her Louis XV bed propped against a lacy hillock of ruffled pillows, her wicker breakfast tray with its Nymphenburg china pushed to one side on the Porthault coverlet.

Mrs. Post, invariably witty if the circumstances permitted, concluded her account of Mrs. Worldly's dinner preparations by send-ing her off to greet her guests "with nothing on her mind except possibly a jeweled diadem," secure in the knowledge "that her chauffeur is on the sidewalk; the footmen are in the hall; her own maid is in the ladies' dressing room, and the valet in that of the gentlemen, and that her butler is just outside the door."

Now, under the heading "How a Dinner Can Be Bungled," Mrs. Post presented the dramatic second act of "Formal Dinners."

Mrs. Newwed, with "quite a charming house" and wedding presents that "included everything necessary to set a well-appointed table," is tempted to try a formal dinner party and decides "it would be such fun to ask a few of the hostesses who have been most kind" —including, naturally—ah! that element of suspense—Mr. and Mrs. Worldly. Nora the cook, when told who the guests will be, "eagerly suggests the sort of menu that would appear on the table of the Worldlys." A staff consisting of Nora, aided by Sigrid, the maid, and Marie, the chambermaid, "who was engaged with the under-standing that she is to serve in the dining-room when there is company," seems adequate to manage dinner for Mrs. Newwed's twelve guests. But no—three in help, as yet untried and inexperi-enced, was not sufficient to produce a dinner for twelve that would proceed as smoothly as Mrs. Worldly's production for twenty-four. Disaster followed disaster. The living-room fireplace, untried as yet, smoked to the point of asphyxiating the guests, who waited and waited, their "eyes red from the smoke" while the dining-room door "might be that of a tomb for all the evidence of life behind it." Finally the door opened, but Sigrid, instead of bowing slightly and saying in a low tone of voice, "Dinner is served . . ." fairly shouted, "Dinner's all ready!"

In the next scene the guests were at the table, which had checked out all right for appearance earlier in the evening when Mrs. New-wed had inspected it—though, as Mrs. Post made clear, the poor young bride had not been sure of what details to check.

The oysters arrived and were satisfactory. But another inter-minable wait before the soup—a brew that looked, and unhappily tasted, like dishwater. Most guests stopped after the first spoonful but Mr. Kindhart choked down all of his. The soup plates were removed "by piling one on top of the other, and clashing them together, in the doing." Another long wait preceded the fish course "which was to have been a *mousse* with *Sauce Hollandaise. . . .* [It] is a huge granulated mound . . . with a narrow gutter of water around the edge and the center dabbed over with a curdled yellow mess." At this point Mrs. Post drops the culinary horrors and reveals only the horror curdling the young bride for whom "there is no way of dropping through the floor."

The guests returned to the living room, now fireless but also cold and cheerless as well, and soon Mrs. Newwed, attempting to apologize for the fiasco, burst into tears. Mr. Kindhart patted her hand with a gentle "Cheer up, little girl, it doesn't really matter!" But Mrs. Post is not so kind. Ah, but it *does* matter, she warns. The facts about Mrs. Newwed's dinner party will be broadcast by the other guests. Mrs. Post even predicts what they will say: "Whatever you do, don't dine with the Newweds unless you eat your dinner before you go, and wear black glasses so no sight can offend you." Not out of malice will they speak, but out of consideration for other friends who may, if not cautioned, also come away hungry from a dinner at the Newweds.

Mrs. Newwed must learn straightaway that to give a successful dinner *she* must be familiar with the mechanics. An experienced cook and waitress are not enough. "No dinner is ever really well done unless the hostess herself knows every smallest detail," declared Mrs. Post, as Pandolfini had told Florentine hostesses back in 1430. A successful hostess would appear to be unaware of details, but let there be "one dull button on a footman's livery, and her eyes see it at once!"

Mrs. Post wrote with lifelong familiarity of a world where a dull button on a footman's uniform approached social calamity. It was in every way the same world of wealthy society that Mrs. Sherwood had described and lived in. And it would seem that *The Literary Digest* had been correct in saying that not too long ago the residents of that world would no more admit to reading an etiquette book than they would butter a whole slice of a bread at one swoop. We have the word of Emily Post's son (and biographer) Edwin Post that the youthful Emily and her friends considered Mrs. Sherwood's *Manners and Social Usages* a "laughing stock," "etiquette" a word scorned by correct people, and Mrs. Sherwood a traitor to her class because her "avowed purpose in writing her work had been to help the socially ambitious squirm into the ranks of good society."

Mrs. Post still retained her girlhood loathing of etiquette when she was persuaded by her friend Frank Crowninshield, then editor of *Vanity Fair,* and Richard Duffy of Funk and Wagnalls to write a book on the subject. Her first response was an indignant No! but when Crowninshield sent Emily a copy of an etiquette book "by a writer whose name was unknown to Emily in any connection" (her son does not say who the writer was, but the evidence points to either Emily Holt or Lillian Eichler) the answer changed to a resounding Yes! It was not only the book but also the advertisements to promote its sale that brought Emily out of her corner ready to do battle.

The advertisements featured such dining errors as eating olives with a fork or oysters with a spoon. They were attuned to the trend in advertising, then beginning, to exploit embarrassment. Along with not knowing which piece of silver to use (or not to use) or how to manage an introduction, Americans were now seen to be suffering from halitosis, B.O. and, in general, total social insecurity.

Mrs. Post fumed at the thought of correcting manners as if they were armpit odor. A sensible book *was* needed that could answer such questions—if indeed there were so many who needed to ask them—but with straightforward answers. She nursed her resentment of the advertisements right into the pages of her book: "A favorite illustration depicts one person holding an olive on a fork while two others laugh mockingly at the blunder." Watch out! warned Mrs. Post. "The caption says something about the outcast who did not know better than to eat an olive with a fork. The real outcasts are of course the two who with inexcusable rudeness attract attention to the fault."

Interestingly enough, in 1670 Antoine de Courtin, in *The Rules of Civility,* warned his readers not to help themselves to olives with a fork, "Which mistake I have seen the occasion of very good laughter."

Along with the authority of her impeccable social background, Mrs. Post also had the skill of an experienced writer. Her career as a novelist and feature writer began shortly after her marriage to Edwin Post, but not because reduced finances forced her to earn a living, as has been said. Financial problems did develop later and Emily's income from writing proved welcome indeed, but initially her career began because her husband was happiest with his hand on the tiller, and Emily, prone to seasickness, was happiest on land. Unfortunately this disparity extended to all their tastes, and the young couple who had started out blissfully enough soon drifted into separate paths.

Edwin, a successful financier at thirty, was interested almost exclusively in sports and athletics. Emily was encouraged into artistic and intellectual pursuits by her father, Bruce Price, noted architect responsible for the Château Frontenac in Quebec, and a planner of Tuxedo Park, society's private preserve. She sketched, painted, did expert little mock-ups of interiors to amuse herself, supervised her two small sons and in general lived the leisurely life of New York and Tuxedo Park society.

Her writing career began when Francis Hopkinson Smith, noted novelist and close friend of the Price family, saw letters she had written while on a recent European trip. Through the novelist, Emily met the editor of *Ainslie's Magazine,* who encouraged her to write a novel, *Flight of the Moth,* for serialization. In 1904 it was published in book form. Emily remained a professional from that time on and in 1909 produced *The Title Market,* a prize-winning novel.

The Posts gradually grew even further apart and Edwin now frequently detoured from the boat deck to the boudoir of his show-girl mistress. If Emily knew about these side trips, the relationship —at least publicly—remained equable. However, when the scandal sheet *Town Topics* got wind of Edwin's affair and demanded the customary tribute of a $500 ad—the price of escaping mention in the paper—the situation boiled up. As a matter of principle, Edwin balked at submitting to blackmail. On the other hand, he was reluctant to expose Emily to public scandal. But when the Posts' family lawyer saw this as an opportunity to rid the society world of the nuisance of *Town Topics*—and Emily, when consulted, agreed that it should be done—Edwin helped to deliver *Town Topics* into the arms of the law. But soon afterward Emily removed herself from his legal embrace.

Some years later she wrote *Etiquette* and began a whole new career as America's official arbiter of manners. By 1945 (according to Alice P. Hackett's *Best Sellers of Fifty Years*) *Etiquette* had sold 666,000 copies. It is now in its 98th printing and has been revised eleven times. Sad to say, much of the fun and games has gone out of the later editions and the entertaining cast of characters has entirely disappeared except for a fleeting mention of Mrs. Worldly and Sally Stranger in the first few pages. Emily Post's *Etiquette* remains as authoritative as ever, but is now only one of several equally authoritative and encylcopedic works. Emily Post's wit has been removed, and I, for one, miss her tart warning against embellishing introductions in order to impress. To introduce "Mr. Dusting—he has just returned from Egypt, where he's been searching for buried Pharaohs," was acceptable to identify a special field of interest. "But this can be overdone," Emily warned, "and the hostess who habitually exploits her friends as though she were the barker at a side-show is a bore no less than a pest."

That delightful Mr. Dusting, to whom the sediment of centuries of Pharaohs seemed to cling, has been replaced by a crisp "Mr. Tennis. He has just won the tournament at Forest Hills." And the warning, "You may create the effect of trying to impress one acquaintance with the importance of another," is a dehydrated substitute for that circus barker of a hostess.

For her own part, Emily proved to be as flexible as a yogi. A few years after *Etiquette* was published and acclaimed a runaway success, she offered a revised edition noteworthy chiefly for her own revised attitudes. "Chaperons and Other Conventions" had been altered to "The Vanishing Chaperon and Other New Conventions," which a quote in *The Literary Digest* hailed as "Putting a Kick in Etiquette to Pacify Flaming Youth."

Mrs. Post, in an interview, explained her revisions. "In the last five years very radical changes have taken place. 'Bobbed manners' is no longer merely a phrase, it is a fact." Particularly she had faced up to "the trend of modernism in the younger set as it has to do with stalking the male by the young female. . . ." That new young female had substituted her own latchkey for the chaperon of other years, and would tolerate no nays if she chose to blow her own cigarette smoke rather than conform to the recent first efforts to make smoking acceptable for women: advertisments that showed a pretty young woman saying to her cigarette-puffing escort, "Blow some my way."

Mrs. Post faced it all philosophically. "The young girls of today do pretty much as they like, and if they insist on smoking, what can the old-fashioned people do about it? We must realize that the modern generation will not be thwarted. It does what it wants."

Novelist Gertrude Atherton praised the influence of Emily Post and declared that it was sorely needed because "As a nation, we are the most ill-mannered in the world. . . . Commonness is a national vice," she asserted. Describing the happy results that "a little polish" could achieve for most people, she suggested—and not entirely in jest—"That Emily Post take up a collection and start Schools in Manners in all the small cities and towns—and some of the larger ones. Her name would go down to posterity as a public benefactor." And if that did not prove feasible Mrs. Atherton suggested "that her book be included in the curriculum of every public school and that no pupil be allowed to graduate unless he or she can stand an exhaustive examination in it."

Mrs. Atherton's suggestion, made soon after the publication of *Etiquette,* did not go entirely unheeded. Julia Richman High School in New York City began a course in social training in 1925 "in an effort to raise the living standards of its students," the school placement bureau having learned that "otherwise able girls often fail because of such traits as lack of personal neatness or of good manners." The New York *Sun,* commenting in 1926 that "Throughout the country educators are talking about teaching character, manners and morals," called attention to one school that was actually doing it. "The John Adams High School of Cleveland provides for a regular class period of forty-five minutes a day for training girls in poise and good manners."

Mrs. Post did not personally attempt to spread her influence through the public schools. But almost at once she began a determined effort to convert Americans to the continental style of eating. In a 1929 article in *Collier's* magazine she criticized the American way of "zig-zagging of the fork from left to right and right to left again, with each mouthful that is cut."

Mrs. Post evidently was but one of a coterie bent on changing the American way of eating. A few years earlier, in a 1926 *Delineator* article, a Mrs. John Alexander King had also supported the continental style, but admitted that "the matter of eating in the so-called European way has been considered a foolish affectation by many exceedingly well-bred people in this country who say they will not be influenced by imported manners."

However, Mrs. King saw attitudes changing and hailed the augury for the future by titling her article, "America Changes Her Table Manners; Vogue of Eating in the European Way."

Mrs. Post noted no such improvement by 1929 and snapped that Americans apparently suffered from paralysis of the left hand, able to use it only "in the one position of holding a fork prongs down and securing a piece of meat while the right hand cuts."

Mrs. Post did not push her influence to the point of declaring "zig-zag" eating a breach of etiquette. However, she made it clear that in her world it *was,* testily declaring, "Who if anyone practices it I have no idea."

Mrs. Post's own world was a narrow one, on the verge of disappearing. Her thick volume of etiquette was composed mainly of regulations, for if one were to reduce manners to their essential substance it would hardly be necessary to write a book. The whole subject can be summed up in a three-word phrase: consideration for others.

Presumably today's rules of etiquette are designed with this thought in mind, though many earlier rules of etiquette would not have passed this test. Even today, in our concern for etiquette, do we sometimes lose sight of what manners really are? Is etiquette enough? Do we perhaps pride ourselves on knowing all the rules, measure others on this scale, and forget or overlook the true essence of gentle breeding, which is gentleness itself?

Those who fear that we are hearing the last whisper of an age that valued politeness should draw heart from a survey of the past. Concern over deteriorating behavior is nothing new. Social behavior has fluctuated from the restrained and disciplined to the unrestrained and permissive, depending on what influences were at work.

Change is constant. Even sexual mores have swung from open licentiousness to extreme prudishness and now back again, it seems, to the former. There are those who doubt that sexual conduct should be considered in terms of morality; is it not, after all, only a matter of custom? That subject is not for discussion here; it merely illustrates the point that the most hard-bound customs can be as alterable as the superficial rules of etiquette that decree the thickness of a slice of bread or how to take up an olive.

However, that significant three-word phrase that is the root of gentle manners has remained unchangeable and apparently as lasting as the pyramids, in whose land its concept first emerged. Perhaps it remains so—as yet beyond improvement as a personal code and the basis of life lived with others—because it is the cornerstone of all civilized behavior. Consideration for others separates the savage from the civilized man.

Consideration for others is not inborn. It is instilled. The task of instilling it has been the role of parents and teachers since Ptahhotep first undertook it. If the manners we see around us are bad, we must look to ourselves to see why. The rude behavior of youth is often the mirror of ourselves—or the sum of our failure as teachers.

Perhaps all of us need to pay more attention to the three-word phrase that gives meaning to our manners. Though polished behavior and etiquette add grace and flavor to our lives, the greatest personal enrichment lies in mastering the technique of genuine courtesy. The gracious deed, the gracious word, the considerate silence, the polite delay—in the end bring greater rewards and approval than the way we handle our forks.

ACKNOWLEDGMENTS

Each book that brings the past closer to the present owes a debt to libraries, the custodians of man's recorded knowledge. On that score this book is deeply obligated, and particularly to the libraries of Princeton University and the University of Pennsylvania. Grateful thanks is tendered them for the extensive use of their facilities and books, and for permission to reproduce illustrations from many of their rare books. (The author's own collection of courtesy and etiquette books is also represented.) Boundless gratitude is also due to the Trenton Public Library for the unrestricted use of its early books, and for the valuable aid rendered by its reference department.

I am especially grateful to my daughter, Jane, for starting it all by asking a question, and to my editor, Evelyn Gendel, who guided the answer.

BIBLIOGRAPHY

By no means does the following bibliography represent all the books that engaged my attention in writing *The Best Behavior,* but it does include the sources I have found most useful. It is hardly necessary to add that I am indebted to all who have tilled the field ahead of me.

John E. Mason's scholarly work on courtesy books up to the time of Lord Chesterfield, *Gentlefolk in the Making,* has been of particular value. Arthur M. Schlesinger's readable and entertaining *Learning How to Behave* is a penetrating study of the development of American manners. Both of these volumes, plus many others listed below, contain excellent bibliographies for further reading. A selected list of courtesy books is also given.

ARUSMONT, MME FRANCES WRIGHT D', *Views of Society and Manners in America 1818–20.* New York, 1821.

ASHTON, JOHN, *Old Times.* London, 1885.

BENJAMIN, LEWIS S. (pseud. Lewis Melville), *Bath Under Beau Nash.* London, 1907.

BERRY, MARY, *Social Life of England and France from 1660–1830.* London, 1844.

BLOCH, MARC L. B., *Feudal Society.* Chicago, U. of Chicago Press, 1961.

BLOUËT, PAUL (pseud. Max O'Rell), *A Frenchman in America.* New York, Cassell, 1891.

———, *John Bull and His Continent.* New York, Scribner's, 1884.

———, *Jonathan and His Continent.* New York, Cassell, 1889.

BOBBITT, MARY REED, *A Bibliography of Etiquette Books Published in America Before 1900. New York* Public Library, 1947.

BREASTED, JAMES HENRY, *The Dawn of Conscience.* New York, Scribner's, 1933.

BRENTANO, SISTER MARY THERESA, O.S.B., *Relationship of the Latin* Facetus *Literature to the Medieval English Courtesy Poems.* University of Kansas, 1935.

BROOKS, JOHN GRAHAM, *As Others See Us.* New York, Macmillan, 1908.

BRUGSCH-BEY, HEINRICH KARL, *Egypt Under the Pharaohs.* London, 1891.

CHESTERFIELD, EARL OF, *The letters of Philip Dormer Stanhope, Earl of Chesterfield* (3 vols.), edited by John Bradshaw, M.A. LL.D. London, 1892.

CHEVALIER, MICHEL, *Society, Manners and Politics in the United States.* Boston, 1839.

CLARK, G. KITSON, *The Making of Victorian England.* Cambridge, Harvard University Press, 1962.

CLIMENSON, EMILY, *Elizabeth Montagu, the Queen of the Blue Stockings.* New York, Dutton, 1906.

COBBETT, WILLIAM, *A Year's Residence in the United States.* London, 1819.

CRAIG, WILLIAM HENRY, *Life of Lord Chesterfield.* London and New York, 1907.

CRANE, THOMAS FREDERICK, *Italian Social Customs of the 16th Century.* New Haven, Yale University Press, 1920.

CUBBERLEY, ELLWOOD PATTERSON, *The History of Education.* Boston, Houghton Mifflin, 1922.

DEFOE, DANIEL, *The Compleat English Gentleman,* edited by Karl D. Bülbring. London, 1890.

————, *Works,* edited by Sir Walter Scott. Oxford, 1841.

DICKENS, CHARLES, *American Notes for General Circulation.* London, 1842.

DRAKE, NATHAN, *Shakespeare and His Times.* London, 1817.

EBY, FREDERICK, and ARROWOOD, C. F., *History and Philosophy of Education, Ancient and Medieval.* Englewood Cliffs, N.J., Prentice-Hall, 1940.

FINNEY, RUTH, *Lady of Godey's.* Philadelphia, Lippincott, 1931.

FURNIVALL, FREDERICK J., M.A., *Early English Meals and Manners.* Published for Early English Text Society, London, 1869.

GODKIN, EDWIN LAWRENCE, *Reflections and Comments.* New York, Scribner's, 1895.

GRANT, MRS. ANNE McV., *Memoirs of an American Lady.* New York, 1809.

GUNN, BATTISCOMBE (editor), *The Instruction of Ptah-hotep and the Instruction of Ke'Gemni,* 2nd edition. London, 1918.

HAMILTON, THOMAS, *Men and Manners in America.* Philadelphia, 1843.

HAZLITT, WILLIAM CAREW, inedited tracts, *Illustrating the Manners, Opinions, and Occupations of Englishmen During the 16th and 17th Centuries.* London, 1868.

HELTZEL, VIRGIL B., *A Check List of Courtesy Books in the Newberry Library.* Chicago, 1942.

HUIZINGA, JOHAN, *Waning of the Middle Ages.* London, 1924.

HUNT, GAILLARD, *Life in America 100 Years Ago.* New York, Harper and Row, 1914.

JAMESON, ANNA M., *Shakespeare's Heroines.* New York, 1889.

KELSO, RUTH, *Doctrine for the Lady of the Renaissance.* Urbana, Illinois, U. of Illinois Press, 1956.

————, *Doctrine of the English Gentleman in the 16th Century.* Urbana, Illinois, 1929.

————, *Institution of the Gentleman in English Literature.* Urbana, Illinois, n.d.

LARNED, JOSEPHUS NELSON, *A Multitude of Councellors.* Boston, Houghton Mifflin, 1901.

LECKY, WILLIAM EDWARD HARTPOLE, *A History of England in the 18th Century,* 4 vols. New York, Appleton, 1879–82.

————, *History of European Morals from Augustus to Charlemagne.* London, 1869.

————, *History of the Rise and Influence of the Spirit of Rationalism in Europe.* London, 1865.

MARTINEAU, HARRIET, *Society in America.* New York, 1837.

MASON, JOHN E., *Gentlefolk in the Making.* Philadelphia, U. of Pennsylvania Press, 1935.

MINNIGERODE, MEADE, *The Fabulous Forties.* New York, 1924.

MONROE, PAUL, editor, *A Cyclopedia of Education.* New York, 1911–13.

MONTAGU, LADY MARY WORTLEY, edited by her great-grandson, Lord Wharncliffe, *Letters,* 2 vols. Bohn Library edition, London, 1898.

MOORE, JOHN, M.D., *A View of Society and Manners in France, Switzerland, and Germany.* London, 1789.

NEVINS, ALLAN, *American Social History*. New York, Holt, 1923.

NOYES, GERTRUDE E., *Bibliography of Courtesy and Conduct Books in 17th Century England*. New Haven, 1937.

PALMER, ABRAHAM SMYTHE, *The Ideal of a Gentleman*. London, 1908.

PERRY, THOMAS SERGEANT, *Evolution of the Snob*. Boston, 1887.

POST, EDWIN, *Truly Emily Post*. New York, Funk and Wagnalls, 1961.

POWERS, DR. EILEEN, *The Goodman of Paris (from Menagier de Paris, c. 1393)*. London, 1928.

PRESTAGE, EDGAR, *Chivalry*. New York, Knopf, 1928.

PUCKLER-MUSKAU, PRINCE, *Tour in England, Ireland and France in the Years 1826, 1828 and 1829*. Philadelphia, 1833.

PUTNAM, MRS. EMILY JAMES, *The Lady*. New York, 1910.

REYNOLDS, MYRA, *The Learned Lady in England*. Boston and New York, Houghton Mifflin, 1920.

ROSSETTI, WILLIAM MICHAEL, *Queene Elizabethes Achademy . . . With Essays on Early Italian and German Books of Courtesy*. Early English Text Society, Extra Series, No. 8, London, 1869.

SITWELL, EDITH, *Bath*. London, 1932.

SALMON, LUCY MAYNARD, *Domestic Service*. New York, Macmillan, 1901.

SCHLESINGER, ARTHUR M., *Learning How to Behave*. New York, 1946.

SELDEN, JOHN, *Titles of Honor*. London, 1614.

SMITH, REGINALD, A. L., *Bath*. London, 1944.

STONE, MRS. ELIZABETH, *Chronicles of Fashion*. London, 1845.

SWIFT, JONATHAN, *Works*, edited by Sir Walter Scott. London, 1824.

————, *Works*, edited by Temple Scott. London, 1907.

TALMUD, *New edition of the Babylonian Talmud*, 20 vols. in 16. New Talmud Publishing Company, 1869–1903.

THACKERAY, WILLIAM MAKEPEACE, *Book of Snobs*. New York, Appleton, 1852.

THOMPSON, ELBERT N. S., *Literary Bypaths of the Renaissance*. New Haven, Yale University Press, 1924.

TOCQUEVILLE, ALEXIS DE, *Democracy in America*.

TRAILL, HENRY DUFF, editor, *Social England*. London, 1893–97.

TROLLOPE, MRS. FRANCES, *Domestic Manners of the Americans*. London, 1832.

VAIL, ROBERT W. G., *Moody's School of Good Manners: A Study in American Colonial Etiquette*. 1942.

WATSON, FOSTER, editor, with others, *The Encyclopaedia of Education . . .* London, 1921–22.

WATSON, FOSTER, *English Grammar Schools to 1660*. Cambridge University Press, 1908.

WECTER, DIXON, *Saga of American Society*. New York, Scribner's, 1937.

WHARTON, GRACE AND PHILLIP, *The Queens of Society*. London, c. 1860s (?).

WINGFIELD-STRATFORD, ESMÉ CECIL, *Those Earnest Victorians*. New York, Morrow, 1930.

WRIGHT, LOUIS B., *The Cultural Life of the American Colonies*. New York, Harper and Row, 1957.

WRIGHT, THOMAS, *History of Domestic Manners and Sentiments in England During the Middle Ages*. London, 1862.

————, *The Book of the Knight of La Tour-Landry*. Early English Text Society, London, 1868.

A SELECTED LIST OF COURTESY BOOKS
(c. 2500 B.C.–1800)

The titles have been arranged chronologically, and by the countries in which the books first appeared, to give the reader a view of the development of courtesy literature. In a few instances where the influence of the book was most directly felt in England, its English date marks its first appearance on this list.

For a more complete list of early courtesy books, the reader is referred to *A Check List of Courtesy Books in the Newberry Library*, Chicago, 1942; and *Gentlefolk in the Making*, by John E. Mason, Philadelphia, 1935. Unfortunately, both end with the year 1775. A bibliography of later European and English etiquette books does not exist as yet. However, American etiquette books have been covered well in *A Bibliography of Etiquette Books Published in America before 1900*, compiled by Mary Reed Bobbitt, New York, 1947.

c. 2500 B.C., Egyptian
The Instructions of Ptahhotep

c. 950 B.C., Hebrew
The writings of King Solomon and King David which provided the heart of the wisdom books of the Bible. Their completed form was arrived at between 400–200 B.C.

c. 200 B.C., Hebrew
Ecclesiasticus, the proverbs of Jesus, son of Sirach.

c. 350 A.D., Hebrew
The Talmud. Palestinian Talmud completed c. 350 A.D.; Babylonian Talmud, the version used today, completed c. 500 A.D.

c. 1000, Western Europe
Hebrew Household Books. The first writings on manners to appear in Western Europe. These were specifically for young people.

c. 1200, Western Europe
Disticha Catonis, followed by *Facetus* writings.

c. 1215, Western Europe
The Italian Guest, Thomasin von Zerklaere (or Tommasino di Circlaria).

c. 1260, Italy
The Tesoretto, Brunetto Latini.

c. 1290, Italy
Fifty Courtesies of the Table, Bonvicino da Riva.

c. 1300, Italy
Del Reggimento e dei Costumi delle Donne, Francesco da Barberino.

c. 1300, Spain
Le Libre del Ordre de Cavayleria, Ramon Lull.

c. 1371, France
Book of the Knight of La Tour-Landry.

c. 1380, France
Les Contenances de la Table.

c. 1380, France
Livre de trois vertus; and *The Book of Fayttes of Armes and Chyvalrye,* Christine de Pisan. The latter title is taken from the Caxton translation, c. 1490.

c. 1393, France
Le Menagier de Paris.

c. 1430, Italy
Governing of a Family, Agnolo Pandolfini.

c. 1430, Italy
Della Vita Civile, Matteo Palmieri.

c. 1430, England
Stans Puer ad Mensam (The Boy Standing at the Table).

c. 1430, England
How the Good Wife Taught Her Daughter. Adapted from earlier *Facetus* writings.

c. 1430, England
How the Wise Man Taught His Son. From earlier *Facetus* writings.

c. 1450, England
Urbanitatis (*The Booke of Urbanitie*). Used by young servitors, including the grandfather of Anne Boleyn, at the court of Edward IV. Edward, a patron of education, culture and the arts, prepared the way for the absolute monarchy of the Tudors.

c. 1460, England
The Boke of Nurture, John Russell.

c. 1460
The Boke of Curtasye.

c. 1460, England
The Babees' Book.

c. 1477, England
The Booke of Curtesye. The first *printed* courtesy book; earlier titles were manuscript books. Printed by William Caxton.

c. 1480, France
Le Livre de Bonnes Moeurs, Jacques LeGrand. Translated and printed in England by William Caxton, 1487.

1484, England
The Curial. The evils and machinations of court life. Translated and printed by William Caxton from the French work by Alain Chartier, c. 1440.

c. 1486, England
The Boke of St. Albans, attributed to Dame Juliana Berners. A book on hunting conduct, printed by Caxton but first compiled c. 1380. The alleged authoress was prioress of Sopwell nunnery.

c. 1500, England
The Young Children's Book.

c. 1510, Spain
Various works on court conduct by Antonio de Guevara, a Franciscan monk. Presented an idealized picture of the perfect prince. Translated into Italian, French and English.

1521, England
The Manner to Dance Bace Dances, Robert Coplande.

1526, England
De Civilitate Morum Puerilium, Erasmus.

1528, Italy
The Courtier, Baldassare Castiglione. Translated into English, 1588.

1529, England
Doctrynal of Good Servants.

1529, France
Le Traicté de la Vraye Noblesse.

1530, England
The Boke of Nurture, Hugh Rhodes.

1531, England
The Boke Named the Governour, Sir Thomas Elyot.

1532, Italy
The Prince, Niccolò Machiavelli. Translated into English, 1540.

1532, England
A Lytil Book of Good Manners for Children, Robert Whittyngton. An English translation of the Latin work of Erasmus.

1534, England
A Ryght Fruitful Monicion concernynge the Order of a good Christen Mannes Lyfe, etc., John Colet, "somtyme Deane of Paules." A fellow lecturer, with Erasmus, at Oxford.

1540, Italy
Libro dell' Arte della Guerra, Niccolò Machiavelli.

1544, Italy
Il Gentil' Huomo, Fausto da Longiano.

1549, Germany
Grobianus, Friedrich Dedekind. A satirical work that derived its name from Grobian, patron saint of *grobbe narren* or boors. Translated into English, 1604 and again in 1739.

1549, Italy
La Nobilitate delle donne, Lodovico Domenichi. Translated into English, 1559.

1551, Italy
Il Duello, Girolamo Muzio.

1553, England
The Arte of Rhetorique, Thomas Wilson. Advice on conversation and letter writing.

c. 1557, England
The Schoole of Vertue and Booke of Good Nourture for Chyldren and Youth to learne their dutie by, Francis Segar.

c. 1557, England
Instruction of a Christen Woman, translated from the Latin of Juan Luis Vives by Richard Hyrde. Vives was tutor to Mary Tudor.

c. 1557, England
The Office and Dutie of an Husband, translated by Thomas Paynell from Lodovicus (?) Vives. Probably Juan Luis Vives, as above.

1564, Italy
Il Galateo, Giovanni della Casa.

1568, England
The Enemie of Idlenesse; teaching the maner and stile how to endite, compose and write all sorts of epistles and letters; as well by answer as otherwise, William Fulwood.

1568, England
A Brief and Pleasant Discourse of Duties in Mariage, Edmund Tilney.

1570, England
The Scholemaster, Roger Ascham.

1570, England
The Mirrour of Good Manners, translated from the Latin of Dominicus Mancinus by Alexander Barclay.

1571, Italy
Il Gentilhuomo, Girolamo Muzio.

1577, France
L'Académie Française, Pierre de la Primaudaye.

1579, England
Cyvile and Uncyvile Life, for the English courtier and the countrey-gentleman . . . to make him a person fytte for the publique service of his prince and countrey. Published again in 1586 as *The English Courtier*.

1579, England
A General Rehearsal of Warres; . . . five hundred several services of land and seas, as sieges, battailes, skirmiches and encounters, a praise and true honour of soldiers; proof of perfite nobilitie, Thomas Churchyard.

1579, England
The Mirrhor of Modestie, A mirrhor mete for all mothers, matrones and maidens, Thomas Salter.

1579, England
"*A Treatise wherein dicing, dauncing, vaine plaies or enterludes with other idle pastimes, etc., commonly used on the Sabath day are reprooved*," John Northbrooke.

1580, Italy
La Civile Conversatione, Stefano Guazzo. Translated into English by George Petrie in 1581.

1585, Italy
The Courtiers Academie, Conte Annibal Romei. The title of the 1598 English translation is given.

1586, England
The Blazon of Gentrie, John Ferne. An early work on heraldry.

1586, England
The French Academie, wherein is discoursed the institution of manners. Translated by Thomas Bowes from part of a French series by Pierre de la Primaudaye, published in installments from 1577 to 1608.

1586, England
The English Myrror: a regard wherein all estates may behold the conquests of envy; a work safely and necessarie to be read of everie good subject, George Whetstone.

1589, France
Instruction pour tous Estats.

1590, England
The Booke of Honour and Armes. Translated from the Italian of Girolamo Muzio.

1590, England
Sir Francis Walsingham's anatomizing of honesty, ambition, and fortitude. (Elizabeth's notable secretary of state.)

1593, England
The Parlement of Pratlers, John Eliot. A series of Elizabethan dialogues and monologues illustrating the daily life and conduct of a gentleman touring Europe.

1594, England
The Examination of Men's Wits . . . by discovering the varietie of natures, is shewed for what profession each is apt and how far he shall profit therein. Translated by Richard Carew from Italian, but originally written in Spanish by Juan Huarte de San Juan.

1595, England
The Schoole of Good Manners; or, A New Schoole of Vertue, William Fiston.

1595, England
The Art of Riding, John Astley.

1595, England.
Nennio; or, A treatise of Nobility, wherein is discoursed what true nobilitie is, with such qualities as required in a perfect gentleman. Translated from the Italian of Giovanni Battista Nenna.

1595, England
Vincentio Saviolo his practise. In two bookes. The first intreating of the use of the rapier and dagger. The second, of honour and honourable quarrels.

1598, England
A Health to the Gentlemanly Profession of Serving Men.

1599, England
The English Secretary; or, Methode of writing epistles and letters . . . also the parts and office of a secretarie, Angel Day.

1600, France
Chemin de Bien Vivre, avec le Mirouer de Vertu, Halbert. Composed by a member of Henry IV's staff.

c. 1600, Italy
Ars Aulica; or, The Courtier's Art, Lorenzo Ducci.

1600, Italy
Nobilita di Dame, Marco Fabrizio Caroso. Rules of behavior for ladies at court.

1602, England
A discourse upon the meanes of well governing and maintaining good peace, a kingdome, or other principalities. The counsell, religion, and the policie which a prince ought to hold and follow. Against Machiavelli, the Florentine, translated into English by Simon Patericke.

1602, England
The True Knowledge of Man's Owne Selfe, translated from the French of du Plessis by Anthony Munday.

1604, England
Basilikon Doron, King James I.

1605, England
Advancement of Learning, Francis Bacon, Viscount St. Albans. Has a section on conversation and manners.

1605, England
The Schoole of Slovenrie; or, Cato Turned Wrong Side Outward, English translation of the German *Grobianus.* Another was printed in 1739.

1606, England
Foure Bookes of Offices, Barnabe Barnes. The duties of monarchs, princes and counselors, derived from Renaissance sources. Dedicated to King James I.

1607, England
Heropaidea; or the Institution of a Young Nobleman, James Cleland.

1609, England
The Gull's Hornbook, Thomas Dekker. A satirical view of the manners of the times.

1609, England
Advice to his Son, Henry Percy, 9th Earl of Northumberland.

c. 1610, France
De la Sagesse, Pierre Charron.

1610, England
The Duello, or, Single Combat: from antiquitie derived into this kingdom of England; with several kinds of ceremonious formes thereof from good authority described, John Selden.

1611, England
The Noble Art of Venerie or Hunting.

1615, England
"The arraignment of lewd, idle, froward and unconstant women; or the vanitie of them, choose you whether. With a commendation of wise, vertuous and Honest Women," Joseph Swetnam.

1615, England
Certain Precepts left by a Father to his Son and a Man of Eminent Note in this Kingdom. The letters of Lord Burleigh to his son.

1615, England
A Discourse of Marriage and Wiving, and of the greatest mystery therein contained: How to choose a good wife from a bad, Alexander Niccholes.

1616, France
Traicté de la Cour, Eustache du Refuge.

1617, England
The Smoaking Age, Richard Braithwaite.

1618, England
The Court and Country, Nicholas Breton. A discourse between courtier and countryman.

1619, England
The Booke of Demeanor, Richard Weste.

1619, England
A Happy Husband; Directions for a maid to choose her mate, Patrick Hannay.

1622, England
The Compleat Gentleman, Henry Peacham.

1623, England
The Compleat Angler, Izaak Walton.

1623, England
A Bride-bush: Or, a direction for married persons, William Whateley.

1624, England
A Care-cloth: or, A Treatise of the cumbers and troubles of marriage, William Whateley.

1625, England
A Table of Good Nurture. Manners told in doggerel, for adults and children.

1628, England.
"The Unlovelinesse of Love-locks" and "Healthes Sicknesse." Two tracts by William Prynne, the latter opposed to the drinking of toasts or "healths."

1630, England
The English Gentleman, Richard Braithwaite.

1631, England
The English Gentlewoman, Richard Braithwaite.

1631, France
Le Gentilhomme Parfait, Claude Marois.

c. 1632, England
Sir Walter Raleigh's Instructions to his Sonne.

1632, France
L'Honneste Femme, Jacques Du Bosc.

1632, England
The Crowne Conjugal, or the Spouse Royal; a discovery of the true honour and happinesse of Christian matrimony, John Wing.

1632, England
Antiduello; a treatise on lawfulnesse and unlawfulnesse of single combats, Jean d'Espagne.

1634, England
The Art of Archerie, Gervase Markham.

1634, England
The Counsellor of Estate. On the qualifications and conduct of a prince. Translated from the French of Philippe de Bethune.

1634, France
L'Honneste Homme, ou, L'Art de plaire à la Court, Nicholas Faret.

1635, England
Essay on Drapery, or the Compleate Citizen, William Scott. Lessons in courtesy for the ordinary man and tradesmen in general.

1638, England
Cupid's Messenger. Examples of love letters.

1639, England
Animadversions of Warre, Robert Ward.

1639, England
The Art of Warre, translated from the French by John Cruso.

c. 1640, England
Youth's Behaviour, or Decency in Conversation Among Men, translated by Francis Hawkins from a French Jesuit work at the Jesuit College of La Flèche, c. 1595.

1640, England
Enchyridion, Francis Quarles.

1641, England
The Country-mans Care, and the citizens feare in bringing up their children in good education.

1642, England
A Map of the Microcosme; or, A morall description of man, Humphrey Browne.

1642, England
The Holy State and the Profane State, Thomas Fuller. On matrimony.

1643, England
The Father's Counsell; especially useful for older brothers left fatherlesse in these perilous daies, William Tipping.

c. 1649, England
The Womans Glorie: a treatise, first asserting the due honour of that sexe . . . Secondly, directing wherein that honour chiefly consists, Samuel Torshell.

1650, England
The Art of Well Speaking, Sir Balthazar Gerbier.

1651, England
English Dancing Master; or, Plaine and easie rules for the dancing of country dances, with the tune to each dance, John Playford.

1654, England
The Academy of Eloquence, Sir Thomas Blount.

1654, England
Zootonia: or, Observations on the present manners of the English, Richard Whitlock.

c. 1655, England
Wits interpreter, the English parnassus; or, A sure guide to those admirable accomplishments that compleat our English gentry, in the most acceptable qualifications of discourse, or writing, John Cotgrave.

1656, England
Advice to a Son, Sir Francis Osborne.

1656, England
A fruitful and useful discourse touching the honour due from children to parents and the duty of parents towards their children, Thomas Cobbett.

1658, France
Traicté de la fortune des gens de qualitié, Jacques de Callières. Translated into English in 1675 as *The Courtier's Calling.*

1658, England
A Father's Legacy, Sir Henry Slingsby.

1659, England
The Whole Duty of Man, Richard Allestree.

c. 1660, England
The Gentleman's Calling, Richard Allestree.

1661, England
The Gentile Sinner; or, England's brave gentlemen, Clement Ellis. A satire.

1665, England
Gentleman's Monitor, Edward Waterhouse.

1665, England
Calliope's Cabinet Opened. Wherein gentlemen may be informed how to adorn themselves for funerals, feastings, and other heroick meetings, James Salter.

1669, England
Moral Gallantry, Sir George Mackenzie.

1670, France
Nouveau Traité de la Civilité, Antoine de Courtin. Translated into English in 1671.

1671, France
L'Homme de Qualité, de Chalesme.

1671, France
Le Prince Instruit en la Philosophie de France, Bessian Arroy.

1671, England
The New Academy of Compliments, erected for ladies, gentlewomen, courtiers, gentlemen, scholars, souldiers, citizens, countrey-men, and all persons of what degree soever, of both sexes. A compilation from many authors.

1671, England
Speculum Juventutis; or, A true mirror where errors in breeding noble and generous youth, with the miseries and mischiefs that usually attend it, are clearly made manifest . . . , Captain Edward Panton.

1672, England
The Gentleman's Companion: or, A character of true nobility and gentility, William Ramsay.

1673, England
The Ladies Calling, Richard Allestree.

1673, England
An Essay to Revive the Ancient Education of Gentlewomen in Religion, Manners, Arts and Tongues, attributed to Mrs. Bathsua Makin.

1673, England
Directions for the Education of a Young Prince, translated from the French of Pierre du Moulin.

1673, England
The Art of Complaisance; or, The Means to oblige in conversation. Much of this is adapted from du Refuge's *Traicté de la Cour,* 1622, translated into English at that time.

1673, England
Of Education, Obadiah Walker.

1674, England
Government of the Tongue, Richard Allestree.

1674, England
"Advice to a young man just married," Benjamin Woodroffe.

1675, England
The Gentlewoman's Companion, Hannah Wooley.

1676, France
De l'Education d'un Prince, Pierre Nicole.

1677, England
The Woman as good as the Man; or, The equality of both Sexes. Translated from the French of Poulain de la Barre.

1678, England
The Compleat Gentleman, Jean Gailhard.

1679, France
Instruction morale d'un pere à son fils, qui part pour un long voyage, Philippe Sylvestre Dufour. Translated into English, c.1690.

1680, England
Humane Prudence: or, The art by which a man may raise himself to fortune and grandeur, William DeBritaine.

1680, England
Advice to Lovers: or, Certain rules of behaviour, so as not to miscarry in the grand affair of love.

c. 1680, England
The Mysteries of Love and Eloquence; or, The arts of wooing and complementing as manag'd in the Spring Garden, Hide Park and other eminent places, Edward Phillips.

1681, England
The Character of an Ill-Court-Favourite; the mischiefs of such servants to princes.

1683, England
English Instructions for a Young Nobleman; or the Idea of a Person of Honour. Translated from a French work.

1684, England
The Schoole of Recreation.

1685, England
The Academy of Complements; or, A New Way of wooing.

1685, France
Instruction pour une jeune princesse, ou, l'idée d'une honnête femme, Cheva-

lier de la Chétardie. Translated into English, c. 1700.

1685, England
The honourable state of matrimony made comfortable; or, An antidote against discord betwixt man and wife.

1686, England
The Gentleman's Recreation, Richard Blome.

1687, France
De l'Éducation des Filles, François de Salignac de la Mothe Fénelon. Translated into English, 1707.

1688, England
A Cap of Grey Hairs for a Green Head, Caleb Trenchfield.

1688, England
The Guardian's Instruction; or, The Gentleman's romance. Written for the diversion and service of the gentry, Stephen Penton. When a young man should marry, and whom, plus other sage advice.

1688, France
L'Art de Plaire dans la Conversation, Pierre d'Ortigue de Vaumorière (?).

1689, England
Instructions to a Son, Marquis of Argyll.

c. 1690, England
Advice to a Daughter, Marquess of Halifax.

1690, France
Modeles de Conversations pour les personnes Polies, Abbé Bellegarde.

1692, France
Des Mots à la Mode, et des Nouvelles Façons de Parler, François de Callières.

1692, England
The Excellent Woman Described by her True Characters and their Opposites, Theophilus Dorrington.

1692, England
"An Account of the Societies for the Reformation of Manners in London."

1693, France
Du Bon et du Mauvais Usage, dans les Manières de s'Exprimer, François de Callières.

1694, England
The Ladies Dictionary, being a general entertainment for the fair sex: a work never attempted before in English.

1694, France
La Connoissance du Monde, Jean Baptiste de Chévremont.

1694, England
Advice to his Children, Henry Booth, 1st Earl of Warrington.

1695, England
The Whole Duty of a Woman, by A Lady.

1697, England
The Government of a Wife, translated from the Spanish of Francisco de Mello, c. 1660.

1697, England
Essay Upon Projects, Daniel Defoe. In support of educating women.

1699, England
The advice of William Penn to his children, relating to their civil and religious conduct.

c. 1700, England
"An essay for the reformation of manners."

c. 1700, England
The new help to discourse; or, Wit and mirth intermixt with more serious matters, William Winstanley.

1701, England
The Compleat Gentleman Soldier.

1701, England
"Necessity of a National Reformation of Manners." A sermon preached by John Ellis.

1701, England
The Art of Prudent Behaviour; a father's advice to his son, arriv'd to the years of manhood.

1702, England
The English Theophrastus: or, The manners of the age, Abel Boyer.

1703, England
The Town-Ladies Catechism. A satire.

1704, England
An account of the progress of the reformation of manners in England, Scotland and Ireland.

1704, England
Plain English; A sermon for the reformation of manners, William Bisset.

1704, England
The Gentleman Instructed, in the conduct of a virtuous and happy life; for the instruction of young noblemen, William Darrell.

1706, England
Reflexions Upon Ridicule; or, What it is that makes a man ridiculous; and the means to avoid it, translated from the French of Abbé Bellegarde.

1707, England
Reflexions Upon the Politeness of Manners; with maxims for civil society, translated from the French of Abbé Bellegarde.

1709, England
"A project for the advancement of religion and the reformation of manners," Jonathan Swift.

1716, England
The relative duties of parents and children, husbands and wives, masters and servants, William Fleetwood, Bishop of Ely.

1720, England
A Discourse of Duels, shewing the sinful nature and mischievous effect of them, Thomas Comber.

1720, England
The Conduct of Servants in Great Families, Thomas Seaton.

1720, England
Rules of Good Deportment, or of Good Breeding, Adam Petrie.

1721, England
Serino: or, The character of a fine gentleman, Thomas Foxton.

1722, England
Young Ladies Conduct: or, Rules for education . . . with instructions upon dress, both before and after marriage, John Essex.

1722, England
The Court-Gamester: or, Full and easy instructions for playing the games now in vogue, Richard Seymour.

1723, England
"An epistle of caution and advice to parents, recommending a godly care for the education of their children in a Christian conversation," Society of Friends.

1724, England
Art of Being Easy at all Times, translated from the French of Andre Deslandes.

1724, England
A sermon preached to the Society for the Reformation of Manners.

1725, England
Everybody's Business Is Nobody's Business, Daniel Defoe. The insolence of servants, among other matters.

1727, England
"Letter to a Very Young Lady on her Marriage," Jonathan Swift. "The Furniture of a Woman's Mind," Jonathan Swift.

1730, England
The art of knowing women, translated from the French of François Bruys.

1731, England
"Advice to a Lady." A poem by George Lyttleton.

1731, England
Chickens Feed Capon: or, A dissertation on the pertness of youth in general, especially those trained at the table.

1733, England
An Essay in Praise of Women: or, a looking-glass for ladies to see their perfections in, James Bland.

1736, England
The Man of Taste, James Bramston. A satire.

1737, England
"Essay on Conversation," Henry Fielding. In the *Miscellanies.*

1737, England
Counsells for a Young Lady of Quality, translated from the French.

1737, England
Essay on Conversation, Benjamin Stillingfleet.

1737, England
The Rudiments of Genteel Behaviour, F. Nivelon.

1738, England
Conversation of Gentlemen . . . considered in most ways that make their mutual company agreeable, or disagreeable.

1738, England
Of Politeness, an epistle to the Right Honourable William Stanhope, Lord Harrington. Satirical verse.

1738, England
A Complete Collection of Genteel and Ingenious Conversation, Jonathan Swift.

1739, England
Man Superior to Women; or, A vindication of man's natural right of sovereign authority over women.

1740, England
Man of Manners: or, Plebeian Polish'd. A satire.

1740, England
An Essay on Polite Behaviour; wherein the nature of complaisance and true gentility is consider'd. Address'd to the gentry.

c. 1740, England
The Amorous Gallant's Tongue Tipp'd with Golden Expressions: or, The art of courtship refined.

1741, England
A Present for an Apprentice: or, A sure guide to gain both esteem and estate, Sir John Barnard.

1743, England
Counsels of Prudence for the Use of Young People, Nathaniel Lardner.

1744, England
A Present for a Servant Maid, Eliza Haywood.

1744, England
"An essay towards fixing true standards of wit, humour, raillery, satire, and ridicule."

1745, England
The Lady's Preceptor; Letter to a young lady of distinction upon politeness, translated from the French of L'Abbé d'Ancourt.

1745, England
"Directions to Servants," Jonathan Swift.

1746, England
The Modern Fine Gentleman, Soame Jenyns. Satire.

1747, England
The Pretty Gentleman. Satire on effeminacy.

c. 1747, England
The Governess; or, The Little Female Academy . . . , Sarah Fielding.

1748, England
A Father's Instructions to his Son, Thomas Scott.

1749, England
The Marchioness de Lambert's Letters to her Son and Daughter on True Education. Translated from the French.

1749, England
Manners: translated from the French . . . Translated from François V. Toussaint.

1750, England
The Modern Fine Lady, Soame Jenyns. Satire.

1753, England
The Whole Duty of a Woman, William Kenrick.

1753, England
Essay on the Art of Ingeniously Tormenting: for master, wife, friend, and instructions for plaguing all acquaintances.

1754, England
A Treatise on Good Manners and Good Breeding, Jonathan Swift. Written earlier but now first published.

c. 1755, England
The Preceptor: containing a general course of education. Wherein the first principles of polite learning are laid down . . . for the instruction of youth.

1757, England
An Estimate of the Manners and Principles of the Times, Reverend Dr. John Brown.

c. 1758, England
The Art of Speaking, James Burgh.

1759, England
Female Conduct: being an essay on the art of pleasing. To be practised by the fair sex before and after marriage, Thomas Marriott.

1760, England
Advice to a Young Man of Fortune and Rank Upon Coming to the University, Edward Bentham.

1761, England
The Complete Letter-Writer; or Polite English Secretary.

1761, England
An Unfortunate Mother's Advice to Her Absent Daughters.

1761, England
An address to persons of fashion containing some particulars relating to balls: and a few occasional hints concerning playhouses, card-tables, etc. . . . , Sir Richard Hill.

c. 1765, England
The Matrimonial Preceptor.

1766, England
Sermons to Young Women, James Fordyce.

1769, England
A Plan of Education for the Young Nobility and Gentry of Great Britain, Thomas Sheridan.

1770, England
An account of the Characters and Manners of the French; with occasional observations on the English.

1772, England
The Polite Lady; or, A course of female education.

1773, England
Letters on the Improvement of the Mind, Mrs. Hester Chapone. Addressed to a young lady.

1773, England
Instruction for a Young Lady in Every Sphere and Period of Life.

1774, England
A Father's Legacy to his Daughters, John Gregory.

1774, England
Old Heads on Young Shoulders; or, Youth's pleasing guide to knowledge, wisdom and riches.

1774, England
Lord Chesterfield's Letters to his Son.

1776, England
A Father's Instructions to his Children: consisting of tales, fables and reflections; designed to promote the love of virtue, a taste for knowledge, and
an early acquaintance with the works of nature.

1776, England
The Fine Gentleman's Etiquette; or Lord Chesterfield's Advice to his Son Verified. The first book to use the word "etiquette" in its title.

1778, England
Advice from a Lady of Quality to her Children.

c. 1775, England
Principles of Politeness, Dr. John Trusler.

1780, England
An Inquiry into the Manners of the Present Age; in which it is impartially and seriously considered, whether they tend most to the happiness or misery of. man. By a Lady.

1781, England
Subjects Calculated to Improve the Heart and to Form the Manners.

1781, England
Occasional Reflections on Manners and Customs.

1790, England
"The State of the Nation with respect to Religion and Manners; a sermon."

1792, England
Grammatical, Philosophical Sketch of the Manners of the 18th Century; or, What You Please.

1793, England
Lectures on Female Education and Manners.

1794, England
Angelica Ladies Library; or, Parents and Guardians Present.

1799, England
Practical Philosophy of Social Life; or, The art of conversing with men, Baron Knigge.

1800, England
The Prevalent Customs and Manners of England.

INDEX

(Page numbers in italics denote illustrations)

Le Blond excudit auec Priuilege du Roy

Qui ne desireroit estre tout couuert dyeux
Pour bien considerer les beautez de ces Dames
Qui parent ce Balet: leurs regards et leurs flames
Peuuent vaincre les cœurs des hommes et des dieux.

Chacunes a leur tour elles entrent au Bal
Au son des violons qui donnent la cadence,
L'œil obserue attentif celle qui le mieux dance
Auecque plus de grace: ou celle qui fait mal.